ANALOGICAL POSSIBILITIES

American Academy of Religion Academy Series

edited by
Susan Thistlethwaite

Number 81
ANALOGICAL POSSIBILITIES

by
Philip A. Rolnick

Philip A. Rolnick

ANALOGICAL POSSIBILITIES
How Words Refer to God

Scholars Press
Atlanta, Georgia

ANALOGICAL POSSIBILITIES
How Words Refer to God

by
Philip A. Rolnick

Library of Congress Cataloging in Publication Data
Rolnick, Philip A.
    Analogical possibilities: how words refer to God / Philip A.
Rolnick.
        p. cm. — (American Academy of Religion academy series; no.
81)
    Includes bibliographical references.
    ISBN 1-55540-824-9 (cloth). — ISBN 1-55540-825-7 (pbk.)
    1. God—History of doctrines. 2. Analogy (Religion)—History of
doctrines. 3. Philosophical theology—History of doctrines.
4. Language and languages—Religious aspects—Christianity.
I. Title.   II. Series.
BT102.R66   1993
231—dc20   92-46630
                                                CIP

Printed in the United States of America
on acid-free paper

To Jane

CONTENTS

Introduction   1

Part One PARTICIPATION METAPHYSICS:
W. NORRIS CLARKE and NEO-THOMIST RENEWAL   11

Introduction to Part One   13

1 The Neo-Thomist Renewal: Being Action, and the Good   17
   Transcendental Thomism: The Interrogation of Being   17
   Radical Options: Judgment and Affirmation   22
   Existence, Action, and Goodness   26
      Action: The Self-Communication, Self-
      Revelation, and Self-Fulfillment of Being   29
      Actus and Epistemology   32
      The Good: Goal and Purpose of the Universe   36

2 The Metaphysics of Participation   41
   Chronological Considerations   43
   The Act/Potency Distinction   49
   The Essence/Existence Doctrine   53
   Participation   58

3 Participation and Analogous Terms   75
   Selecting and Extending Analogical Predicates   75
   'Person' as Primary Analogate   82
      Epistemological Consequences of
      Persons in Relation   84
      Metaphysical Consequences of the
      Shift to Person   87

vii

Part Two DAVID BURRELL'S GRAMMATICAL INQUIRY   95

Introduction to Part Two   97

4 Analogy, Inquiry, and Judgment   101
     Showing the Limits of Formal Schemes   102
     The Grammar of Analogy   105
         The Metaphorical Nature of Language   108
         The Reassessment of Univocation   109
     Judgment   111
     The Paradigm of the Person Inquiring   116
         Plato's Inquiry   117
         Aquinas' *Manuductio*   119
         Ontological Reticence   123

5 Exploring the Grammar of Divinity   127
     Mapping the Grammar *in Divinis*   128
         Tautologies: the Logic of Formal Features 130
         Philosophy and Religion--a Dichotomy?   135
         Performance, Proposition, and Assertion   139
     Locating the Motivating Insight: *Actus*   140
         The Intentional Activity of
             Knowing and Loving   143

6 Differentiating Aquinas through Analogy   153
     The Setting of the Inquiry   153
     The Fundamental Distinction between God
         and the World   156
     Essence/Existence: A Distinction
         to Explain the Distinction   157
     Individuality, Relations, and Creation   162
     Further Implications for Analogy   167

7 Interlocutory Remarks 171
    Grammatical Issues 171
        The Conflation of Analogy and Metaphor 171
        Extrinsic vs. Intrinsic Predication 177
        'Act of' Language 181
        Tautologies--Analytic and Synthetic
            Propositions 183
    The Neglect of Participation 184
    Summary Remarks 186

Part Three   EBERHARD JÜNGEL'S CRITIQUE AND
                 ANALOGICAL ALTERNATIVE 189

Introduction to Part Three 191

8 Jüngel's Analysis: The Aporia in Doctrinal
   and Analogical Expression 195
    The Genesis of the *Aporia* 195
    The *Aporia* Concealed by Analogy 200
    Jüngel's Doctrinal Alternative 209

9 Christological Analogy 217
    Analogia Fidei (Analogy of Faith) vs.
      Analogia Entis (Analogy of Being) 218
    Jüngel's Proposal: The Gospel as Analogy 226
        Defining God as Love 229
        The Necessity of Analogy 233
        The Analogy of Advent 235

Part Four   CONCLUSION   241

10 Critical Comparisons, Evaluations and Syntheses   243
   Analogy in Theological Context   243
   Kant and Aquinas--A Tendentious Linkage?   245
      Divergent Estimations of the Power
         of Language   254
   Event, Person, and Relationship   260
      Language and Person   260
      Creation, Structure, and Sin   262
      The Missing Category of Relationship   268
   Methodological Issues   270
      Aporia, Faith, and Reason   270
      Philosophical and Evangelical Theology   273
      Language and World: Metaphorical and
         Analogical Outlooks   277
      Analogy and Dialectic: Patterns in
         Religious Language   282

11 Concluding Conversations: Comparing
   Clarke, Burrell, and Jüngel   285
   The Common search for 'More Than'   286
   Self-Communicating Movement: Action and Event   289
   Essence vs. Existence; Defining vs. Showing;
      Correspondence vs. Participation   293
   Judgment: The Analogical Act   298
   Creation and Cross: *Analogia Entis*
      and *Analogia Fidei*   299

Selected Bibliography   301

Index of Names   309

Index of Subjects   311

ACKNOWLEDGEMENTS

There are several people whose contributions I would like to acknowledge. First, the guidance and seasoned judgment of Thomas Langford are gifts which have enriched my life as well as the concepts and design of this book. Likewise, Robert Osborn's suggestions, criticisms, and theological insight have been a continuing source of instruction, only surmounted by the joy of friendship which this respected teacher has provided.

The detailed criticisms which Jonathan Wilson of Westmont College has given me have been invaluable, and the gentleness and friendship with which he has shared such criticism are deeply appreciated. I am also indebted to Jeffrey Wattles of Kent State University, whose insightful reading of an earlier draft prompted further discoveries and whose collegial conversation is always refreshing and thought-provoking. Nancy McElveen, my colleague at Greensboro College, has carefully proofread the manuscript and taught me a great deal about stylistic matters. Jim Penny, director of computing facilities at Greensboro College has, with characteristic patience and humor, solved many a labyrinthine problem. Betty Fulk and Pamela Bennett, secretaries at Greensboro College, have provided service beyond the call of duty, especially by assisting with the indexes. Finally, my thanks go out to editors Robert Hauck and Susan Thistlethwaite for their assistance.

Having received so much from so many, I am happy to accept responsibility for any flaws which remain.

INTRODUCTION

In order to speak with any confidence in theological matters, one must have some notion of what words are doing. From the liturgical and personal question of whether God is 'Father', or perhaps also 'Mother', to the question of what we mean by 'good', the relationship between the content of thought and how thought is expressed is crucial. This work primarily examines how theologians have answered those questions by their various accounts of analogy.

When we focus our theological attention upon analogy, we implicitly engage a metacritique of theology itself; for if our way of speaking about God is invalid, then *what* we say is thereby undermined. If our methodological procedure is illicit, then the specific theological content of our proposals is invalidated. Therefore, a great deal is at stake when we consider analogy; for doctrinal commitments, metaphysical presuppositions, and anthropological determinations are embedded in analogical predication. Analogy is inherently expressive of relationships; and in doctrine, metaphysics, and anthropology, we are often in the business of expressing relationships. Our view of the world, ourselves, and our God is wrapped up in the way we use analogy. A

1

close examination of different analogical theories will unfold more basic theological and anthropological understandings.

While its origins are not entirely clear, analogy has a venerable tradition which reaches back to the early discoveries of Greek mathematicians, its first use possibly being by Pythagorus. At its root inception, the mathematical concept was that a:b :: c:d ("a is to b as c is to d"). Thus for example, 3:6 :: 5:10.[1] Two further mathematical discoveries would prove to have rich ramifications. First, analogy was able to link rational to irrational numbers; second, the middle terms or analogates were found to be interchangeable. Analogically linking the irreducible irrational to the rational would eventually stimulate philosophical thought to link the known to the unknown. Similarly, the fact that exchanging the two inner numerical analogates does not affect the overall equation suggests the possibility of some logical relationship among concepts analogically linked.

Moving beyond the merely quantitative understanding of analogy, Plato uses analogy in terms of qualitative similarities. He suggests that there is something analogical in the structure of the universe itself:

> The body of the world was created, and it was harmonized by proportion (*analogias*), and therefore has the spirit of friendship
> . . . having been reconciled to itself (*Timaeus* 32c).

Aside from theories about analogy, Plato employs analogies at key points, e.g., the analogies of the ship, the sun, and the cave in the *Republic*. Historically, Plato's analogy which compared the effects of the sun and the good is perhaps the most significant; for it is continuously reworked up to and including Aquinas:

---

[1]Our discussions below will show that Aquinas' theological appropriation of analogy does not use this direct form, something which some modern interpreters have failed to consider.

The sun is not sight, but is the cause of it, and is also seen by it?

. . .

Say then, [Socrates] said, that it is the sun which I called the offspring of the Good, which the Good begot as analogous to itself. What the Good itself is in the world of thought in relation to the intelligence and things known, the sun is in the visible world, in relation to sight and things seen (*Republic* 508b).

Hampus Lyttkens, the great historian of analogy, calls this comparison of the sun and the good "the basis of the subsequently appearing theory of the analogous knowledge of God."[2] In any case, the philosophical and theological consideration of analogy is well underway in Plato.

Notwithstanding his metaphysical differences from Plato, or perhaps even because of those differences, Aristotle further develops the analogy concept, introducing "the idea of a non-synonymous ontology."[3] In this development, Aristotle describes the various forms of being by what he calls *pros hen* (toward a one).[4] Here, being may be used in several ways, but always with reference to a common principle. The relation to the common principle unites the otherwise different uses and thereby prevents complete ambiguity. There is both a diversity and a community expressed in *pros hen* statements. As the body of this present work will show, all real analogy involves holding together the like and the unlike, the diverse and the common. Aristotle's *pros hen* statements will later be used as the basis of the analogy of attribution by Aquinas and his Christian predecessors. Later

---

[2]Hampus Lyttkens, *The Analogy between God and the World: An Investigation of its Background and Interpretation of its Use by Thomas of Aquino* (Uppsala: Almqvist and Wiksells, 1952), 27. Much of this historical synopsis is indebted to Lyttkens.

[3]Ibid., 52.

[4]Aristotle *Metaphysics* Γ2, 1003 a 33.

again, Eberhard Jüngel, one of the major subjects of this present study, will roundly criticize Aquinas' use of this analogy as part of an allegedly agnostic position. From the extensive Neoplatonic writings, two principles will play a major role in Aquinas' thought and so be germane to this present work. First is the Neoplatonic account of creation from a first cause. If creation from the first cause meant equality with that first cause, then creation and creator would be identical. Neither Christian nor Neoplatonist would countenance that kind of creation. Instead, the Neoplatonist thesis posits a declining scale of causes and effects from the highest first cause to the lowest effect which turns out to be matter, itself unable to cause any further effects. The second principle holds that "everything which by its existence bestows a character on others, itself primitively possesses that character, which it communicates to the recipient."[5]   Because Aquinas and medieval theologians in general accepted this principle, they inferred that something about the cause can be known by acquaintance with the effect. This principle, eventually developed as the *via eminentia*, provides an important component of how analogical predication about God might work.

However one assesses Aquinas, he remains a benchmark in any discussion about analogy; for Aquinas not only incorporates a great deal of the thought on analogy accomplished before his time, but his unique synthesis generates a history of its own, up to and including the debate about analogy which this present work examines. Competing interpretations of Aquinas, whether retrievals or dismissals, play a vital role in all four parts of this present work.

---

[5]Proclus, *Elements of Theology*, Par. 18, trans. E. R. Dodds (Oxford, 1933), 21, as cited in Lyttkens, *Analogy*, 67.

Part One primarily, but not exclusively, focuses on the attempt of W. Norris Clarke, S.J., to reinterpret Aquinas in dialogue with the concerns of modernity. As a background presupposition to the central theme of participation metaphysics, Chapter One examines the renewed focus on being itself, including some insights of Karl Rahner, S.J., and Bernard Lonergan, S.J. Here Aquinas' insistence that being is the most fundamental perfection (positive quality) is developed in terms of a dynamism between the finite creature who inquires about being and the infinite subsistence of God. The importance of judgment and affirmation is introduced as the necessary complement of human reason in undertaking such an inquiry. Throughout this present work, the need for judgment will not be seen as a weakness but as an exercise which fits the uncertainties of human life, located as it is between the finite and infinite, known and unknown, actual and possible. Additionally, the epistemological significance of the intrinsic link between being and action (*actus*) is explored, as is Aquinas' placement of the good within being itself, a view which distinguishes him from earlier Neoplatonic writers.

In Chapter Two, Clarke and several others show how participation metaphysics, not the analogy of proportionality, is the key to understanding Aquinas' use of analogy, even though Aquinas has been widely understood as preferring the analogy of proportionality since Cardinal Cajetan's Sixteenth Century commentary.

Chapter Three examines how analogical predicates are chosen and extended, particularly in their application to God. Additionally, this chapter considers Clarke's move to understand 'person' rather than substance as the primary analogate between God and humankind. In doing so Clarke presents points of convergence between philosophy and theology, reason and faith. As Part One will begin to show, analogy is the fitting instrument to express 'betweenness', whether of reason and faith, philosophy and theology, or finite and infinite.

Part Two will examine and evaluate the issues raised in David Burrell's three books on analogy. Burrell provides a provocative alternative to other readings of Aquinas by combining Aquinas' classic work with Ludwig Wittgenstein and the general movement of the "linguistic turn." Synthesizing Wittgenstein and Aquinas, Burrell undertakes a 'grammatical' explication of analogy with the hope of discovering something more than grammar. While Burrell, like Clarke, centers on the definition of God as *Ipsum Esse Subsistens* (Subsistent Existence Itself), Clarke's development is carried out with an overtly 'vertical' component, while Burrell's treatment remains more 'horizontal', and at times, agnostic, especially in his earlier works. This difference between Clarke and Burrell is highly significant; for Jüngel, as we will see in Part Three, strongly criticizes Aquinas for allegedly concealing agnosticism through analogy. Hence, much rests on whether Clarke's or Burrell's reading of Aquinas (and subsequent development) is more persuasive. As my analysis of Burrell's three works will show, especially in Chapters Six and Seven, Burrell ends up moving closer to Clarke's position on participation when Burrell needs to differentiate Aquinas from his medieval counterparts of other faiths, counterparts who happened to be overly agnostic in what could be said about God apart from putatively revealed texts.

Burrell creatively develops many themes first encountered in Part One, especially *actus* and judgment. Likewise, Burrell takes up the theme of inquiry, not just through substantive argumentation, which he provides in his first work (examined in Chapter Four of the present work), but also in the performative sense which his three books on analogy represent. A good inquiry should show some movement, some discovery; and I hope to show that tracing Burrell's successive works on analogy does provide such a sense of discovery and movement. Since Burrell seems to depart from some positions affirmed in Part One, Part Two concludes with "Interlocutory Remarks," a critical evaluation of aspects of Burrell's work. The clarification of some complicated positions should be helpful to the reader before moving on to Eberhard Jüngel's broad-ranging critique of the Thomist tradition.

Part Three focuses on the analogical thought of the Protestant writer Eberhard Jüngel, particularly his charge that Thomistic analogy expresses a failed metaphysics which hides an agnosticism about the nature of God. It is to be hoped that the various readings of Aquinas in Parts One and Two will have prepared the reader for the polemical engagement which Jüngel launches. Jüngel is rightly concerned that, upon closer examination, affirmations about God not turn out empty. Hence, the capacity of analogy to express positive theological content is paramount in the debate.

Unlike earlier debates between Protestant and Catholic writers on analogy, Jüngel not only agrees that analogy is useful but insists that it is indispensable in talk about God. Not whether but *how* analogy is to be used is now the central point of debate. Earlier Protestants, from Luther to Barth, had feared that Thomistic analogy would illicitly bring God and humankind too close. Jüngel criticizes those earlier fears as unfounded; quite to the contrary, he criticizes Aquinas' analogy as keeping too great a distance between God and humankind. Thus Chapter Eight displays Jüngel's analysis of Aquinas's analogy concept and how that concept has allegedly led to an aporia where the word

'God' is threatened with meaninglessness.   In the second prong of Part Three, Chapter Nine explicates Jüngel's alternative proposal that analogy and anthropology must be christologically determined. In spite of the great distinctions, even contradictions between God and humankind, Jüngel attempts to portray an even greater closeness through the divine advent in Christ.

Part Four, the concluding section, attempts to sort out Jüngel's many claims with "Critical Comparisons, Evaluations, and Syntheses." As one of the most prominent voices in the Protestant world, Jüngel's concomitant embrace of analogy and criticism of Aquinas has sparked new interest in the subject. Since Jüngel's critique of Aquinas has been countered by French, Québecois, and other writers, this chapter analyzes and evaluates the debated issues among a host of writers both past and contemporary. As indicated at the outset, using analogy raises basic anthropological, philosophical, and theological questions. Thus this chapter evaluates analogy in theological context; Aquinas' alleged linkage to Kant in their uses of analogy; estimations of the possibilities of language; event, person, and relationship, including the problem of sin; and a range of methodological questions, such as the role of reason, implications for philosophy of science, relations between philosophical and evangelical theology, and patterns in religious language.

Finally, "Concluding Conversations" specifies some perhaps unsuspected commonalities which I perceive among the main proponents as well as evaluations of continuing disagreements. In this final chapter I suggest the synthesis of creation and cross, pattern and person, through an understanding which must be culminated through living judgment--the analogical act.

In order to facilitate references and decrease the number of notes, I have adopted the following style of referring to Aquinas' *Summa Theologiae*:

ST I.11.1.1 = Part I, Question 11, Article 1, Response to Objection 1.

For purposes of articulation, I have usually adopted the translation used by the writer in question, occasionally adding the original Latin. My own English citations of the *Summa* are taken from the English Dominican Fathers' translation of 1920.

PART ONE

PARTICIPATION METAPHYSICS

W. NORRIS CLARKE AND
NEO-THOMIST RENEWAL

INTRODUCTION TO PART ONE

Thomism has a remarkable survival power, and every so often, just
when it seems that it is about to fade out, it has a way of renewing
itself, like the phoenix, usually by a double movement of deeper
return to its own sources plus the creative assimilation of some new
insight or method of later thought.[1]

From about the beginning of the Second World War to the present,
Roman Catholic scholars have been engaged in a lively re-interpretation
of Thomas Aquinas and analogy. The task of this first part is to
examine how a "deeper return" to Aquinas' thought combined with
certain creative engagements with contemporary philosophical and
theological issues has produced a new understanding of Aquinas' view
of analogy, and out of that improved historical understanding, new
approaches to contemporary use of analogy. As a way of synthesizing
the vast amount of complex literature on analogy and what turns out to

---

[1]W. Norris Clarke, S.J., *The Philosophical Approach to God: A Neo-Thomist
Perspective*, ed. William E. Ray, with an Introduction by E. M. Adams, The Fourth
James Montgomery Hester Seminar (Winston-Salem, North Carolina: Wake Forest
University, 1979), 11.

be its main support, participation metaphysics, the primary but not exclusive focus will be on the work of W. Norris Clarke, S.J.

Much of Clarke's contribution to the renewed understanding and appreciation of Aquinas has been to synthesize work done in Italy, Germany (to a lesser extent), America, and especially France. His self-understanding as a Neo-Thomist[2] has been developed in give-and-take conversation with recent philosophical developments, notably the "linguistic turn" and process philosophy. While arguing strongly for the continuing viability and even superiority of the Thomistic framework (properly understood), Clarke has conceded that some important parts of the system can be profitably dropped to enhance other aspects of Aquinas' thought. These concessions have brought harsh criticisms from some other Neo-Thomists.[3] Nonetheless, Clarke's adaptations of the medieval inheritance at least enable some dialogue with the apparently conflicting paradigm of Eberhard Jüngel.

In order to appropriate Aquinas' work on analogy for our contemporary discussion, the principles by which he supports analogical

---

[2]In introducing his James Hester Montgomery Lectures, Clarke defined Neo-Thomism as follows:

> I understand the term "Neo-Thomist" here very broadly to signify that loosely but recognizably united group of thinkers who acknowledge that the basic inspiration and structure of their thought derives from St. Thomas Aquinas, even though each one may have made various creative adaptations of his own, in both method and content, inspired by various movements of thought since the time of St. Thomas (*Philosophical Approach*, 11).

Thus defined, I have adopted the term "Neo-Thomist" as a serviceable mode of reference throughout this work.

[3]See, for example, Theodore J. Kondoleon, "The Immutability of God: Some Recent Challenges," *New Scholasticism* 58 (Summer 1984): 293-315.

speech must first be specified and explicated.   The problem is that Aquinas oftentimes just uses key principles as common assumptions as he addresses a given problem:

> The central governing principles are *used* constantly, and indeed quite explicitly, to solve these problems, but St. Thomas does not ordinarily thematize them directly in a full-fledged exposition of them in their own right as universal principles. Thus one does not find articles entitled: "Whether Act and Potency (or the Theory of Participation) Are Universal Principles for Understanding All Things." Yet one has not really understood the Thomistic system in its holistic unity and depth until one has thematized explicitly for himself these great underlying principles precisely as universal explanatory principles.[4]

Hence, one of the central tasks will be to display the metaphysical principles upon which analogy is based.   In elaborating these underlying principles, particularly causal participation, we shall thereby come to see analogy as the linguistic instrument of metaphysical inquiry, not as an abstract, independent theory.   Having first grasped the import of causal participation, the possibility of analogical predication will naturally follow.

Clarke's summary themes, outlined in *The Universe as Journey*, will be used to focus on the theoretical basis for analogical predication:

1. the *unrestricted dynamism of the inquiring mind* to understand all of being;

2. *existence* conceived as the dynamic act of presence that binds together all real things;

---

[4]W. Norris Clarke, S.J., "Action as the Self-Revelation of Being: A Central Theme in the Thought of St. Thomas," in *History of Philosophy in the Making*, ed. Linus Thro, S.J. (Washington, D.C.: University Press of America, 1982), 63. Clarke's recognition that one must pay attention to what Aquinas does as well as what he says is similar to David Burrell's Wittgensteinian emphasis upon philosophical inquiry and performance, the subject of Part Two below.

3. the *participation structure* of the universe, which allows there to be many different beings all sharing some common attribute;

4. *action*, which is the self-manifestation of each thing's inner being, and makes its presence felt to other beings in the universe, that which makes this to be an interconnected and communicating universe;

5. *the good*, which is the goal and purpose of the universe and of each thing in it, the universal magnet that lures each thing to overflow into action;

6. *the person*, or the universe as radically personalized, from and for persons as the supreme value in the universe.[5]

In order to highlight their bearing on analogy, these themes will be recombined and rearranged in the first three chapters.

---

[5]*The Universe as Journey: Conversations with W. Norris Clarke, S.J.*, ed. Gerald A. McCool, S.J. (New York: Fordham University Press, 1988), 58.

CHAPTER ONE

THE NEO-THOMIST RENEWAL: BEING
ACTION AND THE GOOD

Transcendental Thomism: The Interrogation of Being

Beginning as a response to the Kantian transcendental method, what has loosely been called "Transcendental Thomism" is generated by asking increasingly radical questions.[6] The one who asks is impelled to go on asking in the search for total intelligibility. Eventually, as Bernard Lonergan put it, one asks the "pure question, the question that questions questioning itself." And once one arrives at this level of questioning,

---

[6]Transcendental Thomism goes back to Maurice Blondel's *L'Action* of 1893, gets underway with the Belgian Jesuit, Joseph Maréchal, and continues with such well-known figures as Karl Rahner and Bernard Lonergan. Returning to Aquinas as a source, scholars from Blondel to Lonergan rediscovered the central importance of *esse* (existence or being); in turn, this rediscovery of being led to a more profound understanding of Aquinas' participation metaphysics and its role as the basis of analogical predication. For a fuller account, see Clarke, *Philosophical Approach*, 11-32; and Helen James John, *The Thomist Spectrum* (New York: Fordham University Press, 1966).

> however much religious or irreligious answers differ, however much
> there differ the questions they explicitly raise, still at their root there
> is the same transcendental tendency of the human spirit that questions,
> that questions without restriction, that questions the significance of its
> own questioning, and so comes to the question of God.[7]

The locus of the question, which appears to begin with humanity, spins itself deeper and deeper until it reaches its terminus in its infinite source, i.e., with God. At that terminus, from that source, the substance of the questioner is determined.

Transcendental Thomism, as all theologies do sooner or later, interrelates three questions:

1. the nature of God
2. the nature of humanity
3. the relationship between God and humanity.

Along these lines, Karl Rahner asserts that humanity itself, its very existence, is a question which can only make sense, only be answered by God:

> Man is the radical question about God which, as created by God, can
> also have an answer, an answer which in its historical manifestation
> and radical tangibility is the God-Man, and which is answered in all
> of us by God himself.[8]

Rahner suggests that the being of humanity cannot be meaningfully sustained as an autonomous venture; for while human being is clearly finite, the self-awareness of finitude constitutes a transcendence of finitude: "In the fact that he affirms the possibility of a merely *finite* horizon of questioning, this possibility is already surpassed, and man

---

[7]Bernard J. F. Lonergan, S.J., *Method in Theology* (New York: Herder and Herder, 1972), 103.

[8]Karl Rahner, S.J., *Foundations of Christian Faith: An Introduction to the Idea of Christianity*, trans. William V. Dych (New York: Crossroad Publishing, 1986), 225.

shows himself to be a being with an *infinite* horizon."[9] As question is predisposed to answer, human being, finite being, is peculiarly predisposed toward the infinite. In fact, human being is situated between finite and infinite. Being so constituted, humanity can never autonomously establish its freedom; instead, it must always look to its infinite source and goal in exercising freedom toward fulfillment.

In all its questioning, Transcendental Thomism takes the intelligibility of *esse* ("existence" or "being") as "the first principle of the intellectual life."[10] By contrast, when essence, definition, or form is sought as the fundamental priority, rationalist, formalized, essentialist schemata result. But in making being the primary focus, Transcendental Thomism attempts to link concept to life, essence to existence. The hope is to *enliven* the concept by starting with and keeping in view what is most significant about each thing and person--existence itself. How and why *esse* is to be understood is the first metaphysical task, a pre-structural ethos for philosophical theology and anthropology.

The presupposition of this school is that human intellect has a natural aptitude for understanding being; and reciprocally, that being is at least partially open, prepared to disclose itself, to the inquiring mind. The tension between the Infinite Reality which the inquiring agent seeks to know and the finite situation of the agent generates a dynamic relationship. In this relationship, as the mind progressively explores being, "no limits can be set to . . . this anticipated horizon of being.

---

[9]Rahner, *Foundations of Christian Faith*, 32.

[10]W. Norris Clarke, S.J., "What Is Most and Least Relevant in St. Thomas' Metaphysics Today?" *International Philosophical Quarterly* 14 (1974): 413. Some affinity will be evident between Transcendental Thomism's notion of the intelligibility of being and the long tradition of *logos* doctrine.

Any attempt to do so immediately stimulates the mind to leap beyond these limits in intentional thrust and desire."[11] Two possibilities ensue for the encounter of human intellect with being. The first would be an endless series of finite entities or structures, a problematic situation because it would condemn the intellect to a search without a final goal. So conceived, human searching

> trails off endlessly into ever-receding, always finite horizons, its inexhaustible abyss of longing and capacity ever unfilled and in principle unfillable. Once we postulate that this situation is definitive and cannot be overcome--that there is no proportion between the depths of our capacity, the reach of our mind, and what there is for it actually to grasp--the very possibility arouses a profound metaphysical restlessness and sadness within us. The dynamism of our mind turns out to be a strange existential surd, an anomaly. It is a dynamism ordered precisely toward a non-existent goal; a drive through all finites toward nothing; an innate inextinguishable summons to frustration: a living absurdity. Sartre would indeed be right.[12]

The second, more optimistic possibility is the outworking of Aquinas' presentation of God as "Infinite Plenitude," *Ipsum Esse Subsistens* (Subsistent Existence Itself). When approached as *Ipsum Esse Subsistens*, God cannot be conceived as one of a series of concrete, determinate beings; instead, God is the act of existence or "pure subsistent to-be."[13] Human existence, along with all creation, is itself caused in its limited to-be by the original and infinite act of existence. Hence, human being is not orphaned but ordered toward the Infinite Creator God, the source and goal of its existence. As a result, the

---

[11]Clarke, *Philosophical Approach*, 18.

[12]Ibid., 19.

[13]Ibid.

inherent tension of questioning and searching is made meaningful by the possibility of fulfillment.

Taking this sense of what humanity lacks but desires, and coupling this lack with what God *is*, Clarke develops the *imago dei* in terms of the tension between finite and infinite:

> For man to be truly the image of God in any strong sense, it would seem appropriate (necessary?) that there be some mark or manifestation of the divine infinity itself in man. This obviously cannot be a positive infinite plenitude; that is proper to God alone. But there can be an image of the divine infinity in silhouette--in reverse, so to speak--within man, precisely in his possession of an *infinite capacity* for God, or, more accurately, a capacity *for the Infinite*, which can be satisfied by nothing less. This negative infinity points unerringly toward the positive infinity of its original, and is intrinsically constituted by this relation of tendential capacity.[14]

The negative human infinity of "capacity and longing" is thus matched with the positive infinity of the divine *Ipsum Esse Subsistens*. By affirming this match, the striving of human intellect, will, and spirit is rendered potentially meaningful and valuable. Every possibility is not open to human striving, at least not permanently open. Human endeavor counts; success is sweet and failure costly. Being human is to inhabit the realm of responsibility, where much may be achieved, or much may be suffered and lost.

If God's infinite act of existence were only a conception, a possibility and not an actuality, then nothing could bring it into existence. But if God exists as subsistent, infinite actuality, creaturely being gains the possibility of full intelligibility through its relationship

---

[14]Clarke, *Philosophical Approach*, 27.

to this divine source.[15] Most importantly, this relationship, through which the greatest human possibility might be achieved, is not necessary.[16] The relationship can be denied, neglected, or affirmed.

RADICAL OPTIONS: JUDGMENT
AND AFFIRMATION

While thus eliminating undesirable alternatives, Clarke at least recognizes that some vital methodological questions remain:

> How does one establish *philosophically* such a radical *a priori* as the correlative aptitude of mind for being and being for mind, which is the presupposed condition for the whole quest of philosophy itself, and indeed for any meaningful use of intelligence, whether theoretical or practical?[17]

By posing the question this way, by claiming that the "whole quest of philosophy" depends upon a "presupposed condition," viz., the mutual compatibility of mind and being, the issue is highlighted, but hardly settled. After all, in the Nineteenth Century, Marx, Nietzsche, and Freud variously and powerfully denied this presupposed condition. Likewise, the unparalleled warfare, genocide, and social dislocation of the Twentieth Century seem to utter a historical denial. Other options

---

[15]Clarke dismisses a possible objection, a third possibility in which an endless series of finites would satisfy us, as collapsing because 1) it would require immortality and eternity of time, and 2) it would eventually pall, since as finite, it would consist of the same kind of experience, a kind of quantitative repetition.

[16]As we shall see below, Jüngel thematically develops the non-necessity of God.

[17]Clarke, "Most and Least Relevant," 414.

than the compatibility of mind and being appear to be available.[18] Whether we are talking about the lofty absurdity of Sartre's philosophical vision or a disgruntled postal employee who decimates former co-workers with an AK-47, modern humanity has demonstrated "an astonishing capacity for self-negation as well as self-affirmation, irrational as this may be. Man is the being who can affirm or deny his own rationality."[19]

Yet in denying the compatibility of mind and being, a "lived" contradiction takes place.[20] The lived contradiction occurs because implicit in every intellectual inquiry is the presupposition that something can be understood. It is impossible to use the mind to solve problems, argue positions, and deny the mutual relatedness of intellect and being without falling into this lived contradiction. As it is, we just find ourselves operating in a world and universe which we did not make, and this discovery presents us with two basic anthropological conceptions: whether angrily or playfully, we can see our inquiries as something like a dog chasing its tail; or, we can see ourselves as ordering a search for what is believed to be an already ordered purpose.

Since there can be no compelling logical necessity in choosing one option or the other, the affirmation or denial of rationality is the exercise of human freedom. Yet freedom seems to fit eminently with the rational option; for in the space of freedom, the possibility of value resides.

---

[18]More recently, the Deconstructionist movement in philosophy would deny the Neo-Thomist presupposition.

[19]Clarke, *Philosophical Approach*, 22.

[20]Clarke, "Most and Least Relevant," 414.

Hence, how one faces the "radical *a priori*" shapes and colors the subsequent career of reason:

> The issue lies beyond the level of rational or logical argument, because it is at the root of all rationality. Hence I would like to propose it as a radical option open to man's freedom, where he is free to assume his own rational nature as gift and follow its natural call to total fulfillment, or else to reject this call and refuse to commit himself.[21]

Accepting intelligibility as a gift, and calling for commitment to the fulfillment of that gift, Clarke contends that something more than logical imbues the logical with both meaning and value. Thus seen, the meaning of reason, its purpose and potential value, is revealed in agential acts of judgment and commitment, enactions which extend beyond reason, but are in no sense unreasonable.

Acts of judgment give life to particular connections between mind and being. In acts of judgment, what reason recognizes and the mind affirms is realized on deeper, existential levels. Earlier in this century, the French Neo-Thomist André Marc contended that being could be captured alive in the act of judgment. In the act of affirmation, the meaning of *esse* (being) is discovered, realized as act both in things and in the mind:

> The very form of the affirmation reproduces the structure of finite being. The act of affirmation, the act at once of the object affirmed and of the affirming mind, is the point of contact between the logical and the real.[22]

If this "point of contact" is only reached through particular judgments, then tremendous responsibility rests upon the agent who judges. In this

---

[21]Clarke, "Most and Least Relevant," 414.

[22]André Marc, *L'Idée de l'être chez saint Thomas et dans la scolastique postérieure* in *Archives de Philosophie* 10 (1933): 101-103, as paraphrased in Helen James John, *Thomist Spectrum*, 67.

sense human being is responsible being; for the realization of reality, or its failure to be realized, depends upon human judgment. In what might be called realized understanding, our concepts are enlivened, made real, by being affirmed through judgment. Such realized understanding is as firm or as fragile as the contact made or missed. In undertaking and culminating the inquiry (at least in part), the act of judgment affirms the gift of reason, thus exercising a kind of philosophical faith. Hence, an act of judgment synthesizes faith and reason.

From its inception, the Thomist tradition has presupposed the complementarity of reason and faith. For Aquinas, the joint project of philosophy and theology, reason and faith, is the development of analogies from the created realm of nature and the revealed realm of grace:

> The gifts of grace are added to us in order to enhance the gifts of nature, not to take them away. The native light of reason is not obliterated by the light of faith gratuitously shed on us. Hence Christian theology enlists the help of philosophy and the sciences. Mere reasoning can never discover the truths which faith perceives; on the other hand, it cannot discover any disagreement between its own intrinsically natural truths and those divinely revealed. Were there any contradiction, one set or the other would be fallacious, and, since both are from God, he would be the author of our deception, which is out of the question. In fact the imperfect reflects the perfect; our enterprise should be to draw out the analogies between the discoveries of reason and the commands of faith.[23]

The enterprise of analogical development will be largely accomplished through judgment. Neither faith alone, nor reason alone, will suffice. Analogy will involve more than faith and more than reason; yet analogy

---

[23]*De Trinitate*, II.3, as cited in *Theological Texts*, selected and translated with notes and introduction by Thomas Gilby (Durham, NC: Labyrinth Press, 1983), 7.

will incorporate as much faith and reason as possible in its unique synthesis.

In its interrogation of being, Transcendental Thomism expresses a doctrine of creation, where God is the source and may become the goal and fulfillment of all created being. Possibility, which may appear to be infinite, is predetermined, fated, by the prior creative activity of God and the particularities of human history. However, a great responsibility lies with humankind: the enactment of our particular possibilities for good. Martin Buber could rightly say: "Freedom and fate embrace each other to form meaning; and given meaning, fate--with its eyes, hitherto severe, suddenly full of light--looks like grace itself."[24] Affirming the particular possibilities of our own lives, with all their predeterminations, does not have to do with limits so much as with completion and fulfillment. Expressing those affirmations and judgments will be accomplished through analogy.

EXISTENCE, ACTION, AND GOODNESS

The interrelated themes of existence, action, and goodness serve as a kind of prolegomena to the metaphysics of participation and its more direct link to analogy. Synthesizing and developing the work of Etienne Gilson, Joseph de Finance, André Marc, L. B. Geiger, Cornelio Fabro, and Louis De Raeymaeker, Clarke has brought the rediscovery of the act

---

[24]Martin Buber, *I and Thou*, trans. Walter Kaufmann (New York: Charles Scribner's Sons, 1970), 102.

of existence (*actus essendi*) to English readers.[25] In this renewal Aquinas is read with a new alertness to how *esse* functions as the central and unifying perfection of all that is:

> This philosophical awakening to the primacy of the act of existence as the deepest level in every being and the ultimate bond of unity between all things, with all its systematic implications for God, the theory of knowledge, etc., is the great central pillar of St. Thomas' and of my own metaphysical vision of the universe.[26]

Clarke's discussion of *esse* attempts to point the reader to a contemplation of being per se, and finally, to a penetrating involvement in being itself. As such, being cannot be entirely specified as content, and should not be limited to *concept*, but should be contemplated as that which enlivens content and concept. As Clarke puts it:

> It is the most fundamental common attribute that all real things share, deeper even than form or essence, that which makes them stand out sharply and distinctly from the surrounding darkness and emptiness of non-being and become a member of this most ultimate of all communities, the community of all real existents.[27]

So one must "awaken" to the central import of existence and try to grasp something of what it means as the common bond of all things and the possibility of community. While many in the history of philosophy have

---

[25]Some works commonly cited by Clarke include: Etienne Gilson, *The Christian Philosophy of St. Thomas Aquinas* (New York: Random House, 1956); Joseph de Finance, *Etre et agir* (Paris: Beauchesne, 1945); L. B. Geiger, *La Participation dans la philosophie de S. Thomas d'Aquin* (Paris: J. Vrin, 1942); C. Fabro, *La Nozione metafisica di partecipazione secondo s. Tommaso d'Aquino* (Turin: Società Editrice Internazionale, 1945). Two early articles of Clarke's which helped introduce some of the concepts to English readers are: "The Limitation of Act by Potency: Aristotelianism or Neoplatonism?" *New Scholasticism* 26 (1952): 167-94; "The Meaning of Participation in St. Thomas," *Proceedings of the American Catholic Philosophical Association* 26 (1952): 147-57.

[26]Clarke, *Journey*, 64.

[27]Ibid, 62.

considered existence an "intellectually opaque fact impervious to any further intrinsic analysis,"[28] Aquinas' thirteenth century focus on actual existence is distinctive and original.

Without ignoring the 'what' or essence of a thing, Clarke, *après* Aquinas, is trying to shed light on "an inner dynamic *act* of presence that makes all forms or structures actually present as diverse modes of the radical 'energy' of existence."[29] Existence does not really sit still; it has its own energy, its own power, what Aquinas called *virtus essendi*, the power of being. Hence *esse*, to be, does not just mean to be present,

> but to be a *presence-with-power*, a power-filled presence in the world. Thus active power is inseparable from existence; it is impossible to be at all without some proportionate power. It is precisely this notion of existence as active, power-filled presence that renders *degrees of being* possible.[30]

Clarke attributes the bafflement of many analytic philosophers regarding "degrees of being" to their reduction of "to be" to the "bare, minimum brute fact of existence."[31]

Were existence not amplified by its own energy or power, it would indeed be opaque to us. However, if existence is inextricably linked to action through its own "power-filled presence," then we can shift from the fact of existence to the inner act of existence. The resultant amplification enables a positive account of the unity and differentiation of all things:

---

[28]Clarke, "Most and Least Relevant," 415.

[29]Ibid.

[30]Clarke, *Journey*, 62-63.

[31]Ibid., 63.

In focusing on the supra-formal, supra-essential factor of the act of existence as the root of all perfection and the all-pervasive bond of unity in all beings, St. Thomas has also made it possible to include the entire range of reality--from the most evanescent subatomic particle, that burns out its being in a micro-second flash, to the infinite and eternal plenitude of God himself--under one completely positive viewpoint, yet without being forced to constrict the mystery of the divine Infinity into our own limited categorical concepts.[32]

The *positive* account of the *actus essendi* (the act of being) of both God and creatures will be the basis of participation metaphysics and the closely related use of analogy. Clarke is quite critical of overly negative theologies in which God is said to be "Wholly Other." Instead, by positively portraying God as *Ipsum Esse Subsistens* (Subsistent Existence Itself), the divine transcendence is maintained, but the relatedness of all things to God (the Creator of all other being) and to one another may be metaphysically explicated.

ACTION: THE SELF-COMMUNICATION
SELF-REVELATION AND SELF-
FULFILLMENT OF BEING

While continuing to delineate the justifications of analogy, we have now arrived at a crucial juncture; for in Aquinas' view of *actus* (action), epistemology and metaphysics are melded together. How we know and what we know are joined as action reveals what we may know of being.

By considering the implications of its rejection, we may more readily perceive the "openness" of being. That is, were being in

---

[32]Clarke, "Most and Least Relevant," 417.

principle self-enclosed, and completely opaque to our inquiries, then we could know very little, either about our world, ourselves, or God. On the other hand, if the world, and we as agents operating within it, can be known in some significant way through the effect we have on others and vice versa, then action becomes the medium in which knowledge and reality are joined. Summarizing "the whole of Thomistic epistemology," Clarke contends: "All human knowledge of the real is an interpretation of action."[33]

If inner being were not revealed in action, or at least potentially revealable to some degree, then the being itself could make no difference to any other thing or being. As a totally unmanifest existence, it might as well not be at all. Of the existence within things themselves, Aquinas says that it has "a kind of light," which illuminates itself to other things. Even though all existent things are lit up or shining to a degree, (*ipsa actualitas rei est quasi lumen ipsius*), existent things possess only a derived light, not the light itself which would belong to the being of God (*ipsa lux*).[34]   Hence, we get another glimpse of the interlocking relationship of being and action, as well as the minimal degree to which we can discuss them separately:

> If the act of existence is the basic static bond of the unity of the universe, making all things intrinsically similar to each other, action is the basic dynamic bond, bringing them together, connecting them to each other so that they can make a difference to each other, thus

---

[33]Clarke, "Action as the Self-Revelation of Being: A Central Theme in the Thought of St. Thomas," in *History of Philosophy in the Making*, ed. Linus Thro, S.J. (Washington: University Press of America, 1982), 64.

[34]*Journey*, 64, as cited from Aquinas' commentary on Pseudo-Dionysius, *Super librum De causis expositio*, ed. Saffrey (Fribourg, 1954), Cap. 1, lect. 6.

truly making a universe to them (*universum* = turned toward unity).[35]

Action is the "natural overflow" of being, its self-revelation. Thus Aquinas repeatedly declares: "*Agere sequitur esse*" (Action follows upon being).[36] The immanent act of existence itself is closely related to its outgoing aspect, its dynamism.

> The act of existence of any being (its "to be" or *esse*) is its "first act," its abiding inner act, which tends naturally, by the very innate dynamism of the act of existence itself, to overflow into a "second act," which is called action or activity. Every second act of a being points back toward its first act as to its ground and source, and every first act, in turn, points forward to its natural self-expression in a second act.[37]

If being were not intrinsically dynamic, if it did not overflow into this second act of self-communication, then there would be no possible link between any two beings. There would be no possible ground for knowledge of others; therefore, there could be no community. At best, we would be limited to a solipsistic Cartesian *cogito*.

The very notion of community and communication hangs on the capacity of being, the *virtus essendi*, to present itself to others as "*active presence.*" For Clarke, community is not just a historical phenomenon; community is itself rooted in the metaphysics of action. While he gives a limited affirmation to Wittgenstein's "form of life," he also criticizes this notion as not going far enough.[38] For as one who unabashedly

---

[35]Clarke, "To Be Is To Be Self-Communicative: St. Thomas' View of Personal Being," *Theology Digest* 33 (1986): 442.

[36]*De Potentia* Q.2, a.1; *SCG* I.43 and II.7, as cited and commented upon by Clarke, "Action as the Self-Revelation of Being," 64.

[37]Clarke, "Action as the Self-Revelation of Being," 64.

[38]Clarke, *Philosophical Approach*, 56.

advocates explanatory metaphysics, Clarke is suggesting that community to any degree, including "form of life," can make sense only on the condition that action is revelatory of being. As Aquinas variously stated the position:

> The operation of a thing shows forth both its existence and its nature (*SCG* II.94 and II.79).
>
> The nature of each and every thing is shown forth by its operation (*ST* I.76.1).
>
> It is in the nature of every actuality to communicate itself insofar as it is possible. Hence every agent acts according as it exists in act (*De Pot.* II.1).

Action is the dynamism of being, "the primary communication system of the universe,"[39] and the ground and possibility of all community.

ACTUS AND EPISTEMOLOGY

From the implications of *actus*, Clarke develops a realist but moderate epistemology. Augustine, Descartes, and Kant present very different views about a wide range of topics; yet epistemologically, all three manifest a strong sense of interiority. By contrast, for Aquinas the primary mode of knowledge is through contact with the sensory world, where things and beings reveal themselves through the essential character of their action upon us. Because action is revelatory of the being of the agent, it is the "mediating bridge" by which things and

---

[39]Clarke, "Most and Least Relevant," 418.

beings gain *trustworthy* access "into the interiority of our consciousness."[40]

If the action that flowed out from being were entirely indeterminate, or just raw energy, then only randomness could be expected in our relation to sensory objects. However, the manifest regularity of what we do perceive suggests that action is characteristically *"essence-structured action"* ("Action," 71). That is, action reveals the existence and essence of its source. Thus Aquinas says: "The operation of a thing shows forth its power, which in turn points to [or points out: *indicat*] its essence" (*SCG* II.94). A key aspect of action is the conscious reception of intelligible messages which the receiver does not initiate: "Action, by the very fact that we do not originate or control it, but receive it to some degree passively, "suffer" its influence, . . . is the natural sign of the real presence of another-than-self" ("Action," 72).

Since so much of Neo-Thomist metaphysics and epistemology depends upon the validity of action, Clarke's writings maintain a running polemic against "Kantian agnosticism."[41] As Clarke emphatically reiterates:

> All knowledge of the real is an interpretation of action--period! There is simply no way a real being can make itself known except through its self-expression, its self-revelation, through its characteristic actions. I know myself as real because I am aware of *myself acting*

---

[40]Clarke, "Action as the Self-Revelation of Being," 71. In the remainder of this section, references to this article will be cited parenthetically as "Action." Translations of Aquinas are likewise taken from this article.

[41]See for example, "Action as the Self-Revelation of Being," 75-77; *Journey*, 73-75; and especially, "Interpersonal Dialogue as Key to Realism," in *Person and Community*, ed. Robert J. Roth, S.J. (New York: Fordham University Press, 1975), 141-54.

> (thinking, desiring, willing, creating, etc.); I know other things than myself by knowing them as *acting on me.*[42]

The contradiction which Clarke sees in Kant is that he uses something like a notion of action, the raw material of sensory data which impinges upon our minds, in his attempt to reject a pure idealism. However, Kant simultaneously holds that our minds are imposing their a priori forms on the raw sensory data.

> What this comes down to is that Kant on the one hand admits the necessity of the action of the thing-in-itself on us, but on the other hand denies that such action is in any way *revelatory* of the being from which it proceeds. Action is not in any way a self-communication, an information-bearing message from its source, but merely the delivery of amorphous material with no intelligible structure of its own, waiting to be intelligently structured by us. The intelligible message is ours, not the thing's itself ("Action," 75).

Clarke concludes that Kant either needed to embrace idealism (which he did not want to do), or he needed to admit at least some realism to the role of action:

> He cannot hold *both* that the things in themselves truly act upon us, penetrate our consciousness, and at the same time that this action is non-informative, non-communicative of anything in the nature of these agents, in a word, that action is completely non-revelatory of nature. For such a notion of non-communicative action cannot be thought through coherently ("Action," 75).

Even the human self is known, both to others and to itself, by the mediating bridge of action. Action reveals something about essence, but no single action can reveal the entirety of the essence: "Every action of a finite being (or even the action of an Infinite Being as received in a finite being) is always at once revealing and concealing, to use Heidegger's marvelously apt language ("Action," 76). If nothing of the inner nature were revealed, it would not be action at all; yet there

---

[42]Clarke, *Journey*, 71.

remains a "reservoir of active potency," the presently concealed aspect of being.

So while Aquinas provides a framework for a realist epistemology, he carefully limits what is claimed, stipulating that there is no unmediated grasp of essence, of thing-in-itself. What Clarke calls the modesty of St. Thomas's epistemology, can be seen in the following limitations of our knowledge:

> The substantial forms of things, which according as they are in themselves, are unknown to us, shine forth to us (*innotescunt*) through their accidental properties (*ST* I.77.1.7).

> Our knowledge is so weak that no philosopher was ever able to investigate perfectly the nature of a single fly. Hence we read that one philosopher passed thirty years in solitude in order that he might know the nature of the bee (*In Symbolum Apostolorum Expositio*).

There is a twofold qualification of knowledge involved in this epistemology. First, the entire essence is not revealed in action. Secondly, there are limitations within the receiver which further qualify what is known: "Whatever is received is received according to the mode of the receiver" (*SCG* II.74). The consideration of this oft-repeated text of Aquinas permits the "contemporary insistence on the perspectival character of all human knowing" to be harmonized with this doctrine of knowledge through action ("Action," 73). Hence, in view of the fact that something but not everything is communicated and received in action, a middle ground is sought:

> It is precisely this ground of moderate "relational realism" that St. Thomas occupies--the only kind of epistemological realism, it seems to me, that fits our human condition. And after all, what is it that is most significant and crucial for us to know about the real world around us: the static inner essences of things as they abide in themselves alone in splendid isolation, or as they actually relate to us existentially and *make a difference* to us by their self-communicative action? The notion of a real being totally prescinding from all self-

communication is probably not intelligible at all. If to be self-communicative belongs to the very inner nature of being in act, as St. Thomas invites us to recognize, then to form a notion of real being that abstracts from this is to leave behind the living core and abstract only an empty formal shell ("Action," 76).

An existent substance, a being, is a being in act, communicating itself to others and receiving the communication of the being of other selves through action. So conceived, the finite universe is an interlocking network of dynamic, ontological communications. In contrast to Descartes and Locke, the picture of substance which emerges is not static. As Heidegger once chided philosophy for its "forgetfulness of being," so Clarke plays upon that celebrated remonstration, in turn chiding contemporary philosophy for "the forgetfulness of being as active" ("Action," 78).

THE GOOD: GOAL AND PURPOSE
OF THE UNIVERSE

For Clarke the good is the "goal and purpose of the universe" and "the universal magnet that lures each being to overflow into action."[43] Were the universe not good, the intelligible linkage between being and action would be severed. As the magnet which draws being out of itself into dynamic interactions, as the constitutive pull of being toward its action, the good is virtually the inner cause of intelligibility in an interacting universe.

Being, action, and the good are inseparably intertwined in the same dynamic metaphysical vision: "Just as action is woven into the

---

[43]Clarke, *Journey*, 58.

very fabric of being itself, so too is the good woven into the very fabric of action and thereby of being."[44] This vision implies that being and value are similarly inseparable, because every action, consciously or unconsciously, is ordered to a goal or end. Action is thus never entirely indeterminate: "The intelligibility of any action comes half from behind, from the agent that is its source, and half from ahead, from the goal the action is tending toward."[45] The good is ingredient in both the final causality present in all creation ("from behind") and the will-directed, purposive behavior of agents ("from ahead").

Considered historically, the treatment of the good is a pivotal issue; for on this issue Aquinas parts ways with Plato and the Neoplatonic tradition. Aquinas does not really think less of the good than Plato, but he does reposition it, thoroughly integrating its value within being.

In Plato's *Republic*, Socrates declares that the good is so high and lofty that he cannot deliver an account of it. Instead he offers to describe what appears to be "the offspring of the Good and most like it" (506e).[46] Socrates proclaims that the good is both cause of knowledge and truth and the proper object of knowledge (508e). In Socrates' account the good is above truth and knowledge; even more, "the Good is not being but superior to and beyond being in dignity and power" (509b). Later, the Neoplatonic tradition continued to differentiate the good from being, for being was still understood as a limiting essence. Since something had to do the work which *actus* (action) accomplishes

---

[44]Clarke, *Journey*, 75.

[45]Ibid.

[46]*The Republic*, trans. G. M. A. Grube (Indianapolis: Hackett Publishing, 1974).

in the Neo-Thomist epistemology, the Neoplatonists held that *bonum est diffusivum sui* (the good is self-diffusive) as well as self-communicating.

By contrast, Aquinas fuses the good with being, in what may have been one of his most powerful and original contributions:

> Goodness is no longer something other than or higher than being. Rather, existential being itself, of its very nature, is good, and thus has this self-diffusive character to it, from the highest to the lowest. Thus God for St. Thomas is at once the supreme Act of Existence and by that very fact supreme Goodness also.[47]

The Thomistic fusion of being-in-action with the self-diffusing good is the ground of all ontological and logical communication. It is also the philosophical affirmation of the refrain of Gen.1: "And God saw that it was good." Because the self-diffusion of being in action is inherently good, "To be is *to make a difference to others*."[48] On the other hand, where the Neoplatonic tradition separates the good and being, it exhibits its greatest weakness: ideas cannot of themselves act. However, they could "become ingredient in the real by becoming active forms, the intelligible structure of action."[49] In short, Aquinas' linking being to action through the good capitalizes on this problem, turning a former weakness into a strength.

The primacy of being is thus the first and greatest perfection. God, as the supreme Act of Existence, as the Good who is by nature self-diffusing, shares this basic perfection and all other possible ones with a contingent, created world. The "fecundity" or "generosity" of

---

[47]Clarke, *Journey*, 70.

[48]Ibid., 71.

[49]Ibid.

being[50] provides the natural juncture of Aquinas' philosophical expositions and his theological commitments:

> For natural things have a natural inclination not only toward their own proper good, to acquire it, if not possessed, and, if possessed, to rest therein; but also to diffuse their own goodness among others as far as possible. Hence we see that every agent, insofar as it exists in act and possesses some perfection, produces something similar to itself. It pertains, therefore, to the nature of the will to communicate to others as far as possible the good possessed; and especially does this pertain to the divine will, from which all perfection is derived in some kind of likeness. Hence if natural things, insofar as they are perfect, communicate their goodness to others, much more does it pertain to the divine will to communicate by likeness its own goodness to others as far as possible (*ST* I.19.2).

From the innate generosity and fecundity of being, the good which inheres in being itself, Clarke concludes that since

> the highest instance of both being and the good is God as spiritual and personal being, it follows that the ultimate explanation of the fecundity of being, of the self-diffusiveness of being as good, must be that Infinite Being is also by its very nature Infinite Love. "God is love," as St. John tells us; and here St. Thomas' metaphysics of natural reason comes by its own path to join hands with Christian revelation.[51]

Methodologically, "by its own path" is highly significant; for it is the way of Neo-Thomism to work reason until it delivers us back to some point of convergence with revelation.[52]

---

[50]Clarke, "Action as the Self-Revelation of Being," 66.

[51]Clarke, "To Be Is To Be Self-Communicative," 443.

[52]Clarke adopts this point of convergence in order to appropriate specifically Christian doctrines. For example, see *Philosophical Approach*, 99; *Journey*, 77-78; "To Be Is To Be Self-Communicative," 443; and "Action as the Self-Revelation of Being," 67.

CHAPTER TWO

THE METAPHYSICS OF PARTICIPATION

Analogy is the expression, the semantic counterpart, of Aquinas'
metaphysics. According to Clarke, one cannot begin to understand
analogy without first understanding

> the capital importance of the ontological bond of similitude deriving
> from causal participation as the indispensable metaphysical
> underpinning for giving meaning to language about God in Thomistic
> (and, I do not hesitate to say, I think *any* viable) philosophical
> theology. It is a source of constant amazement to me how critics of
> Thomistic analogy . . . consistently and habitually omit any mention
> of the metaphysical foundation for analogy when they bring up and
> discard analogy as an inefficacious tool.[1]

The "metaphysical underpinning" of religious language, whether explicit,
implied, or ignored, is a prior ontological communication:

> Even the language of Revelation, to be meaningful for us who receive
> it, must presuppose and implicitly build upon the community in being
> and intelligibility established by the causal bond contained in the

---

[1]Clarke, *Philosophical Approach*, 55-56.

notion of creation, even though this may never have been worked out in an explicit technical metaphysics.[2]

Thus for Clarke, and for the Neo-Thomists in general, ontological communication precedes linguistic expression. Because the world is a *created* world, the possibility of language rests upon the prior communication of God in creation.

Somewhat atypically of those in the Neo-Thomist tradition, Clarke delivers an unblushing criticism of Aquinas' "Five Ways," his proofs for the existence of God.[3] This criticism sets the stage for several of the main themes of this section. First, by allowing that the Five Ways are no more than "quick, condensed sketches of philosophical approaches to God . . . intended for 'beginners,'" and that all the arguments are either insufficient or flawed, especially the first three taken over from Aristotle, Clarke begins to distinguish Aquinas from Aristotle. Second, by conceding the inadequacy of the Five Ways, he can then shift the focus to Aquinas' much stronger argument of participation metaphysics. Where the Five ways may be subject to Paul Tillich's criticism of arguing to an absent God,[4] one of the key aspects of causal participation is that because intrinsic perfections are shared between God and creatures, God is neither absent from creation nor unknown to creatures. More or less dismissing the Five Ways accords a certain flexibility, if following Clarke, we know that we need not adhere to everything in the thirteenth-century corpus.

---

[2]Clarke, *Philosophical Approach*, 55.

[3]Ibid., 35-37. The Five Ways are in *ST* I.2.3.

[4]Paul Tillich, "Two Types of Philosophy of Religion," in *Theology of Culture*, ed. Robert C. Kimball (New York: Oxford University Press, 1959), 10-29.

CHRONOLOGICAL CONSIDERATIONS

Even more importantly, recent chronological studies of the Thomistic corpus have demonstrated a doctrinal development in Aquinas' use of analogy over the course of his career. Building upon Hampus Lyttkens' major study of Aquinas on analogy, which considered historical sources leading to Aquinas and the commentaries which followed him, George Klubertanz, S.J., attempted to systematically arrange all of Aquinas' comments upon, and uses of, analogy in chronological order.[5] Klubertanz produced an Appendix to his study of Aquinas in which he extensively (if not exhaustively) arranged Aquinas' uses of analogy in the chronological order of his forty-four published works. Klubertanz's effort was also indebted to the work of Ignatius Eschmann, O.P., who in 1956, between the publication of Lyttkens' work (1952) and Klubertanz's work (1960), published a chronological catalogue of the Thomistic corpus.[6]

By the chronological alignment of Aquinas' writings on analogy, Klubertanz presents a different picture than most earlier commentators. Where previous commentators on analogy in Aquinas had argued from allegedly "key texts," Klubertanz places the hundreds of references in the corpus into categories according to terminology used in the texts themselves. He presents a chart of his findings, showing "Frequency of

---

[5]George P. Klubertanz, S.J., *St. Thomas Aquinas on Analogy: A Textual Analysis and Systematic Synthesis* (Chicago: Loyola University Press, 1960). Also see Hampus Lyttkens, *The Analogy between God and the World: An Investigation of its Background and Interpretation of its Use by Thomas of Aquino* (Uppsala: Almqvist and Wiksells, 1952).

[6]I. T. Eschmann, O.P., "A Catalogue of St. Thomas' Works: Bibliographical Notes," in Etienne Gilson, *The Christian Philosophy of St. Thomas Aquinas* (New York: Random House, 1956), 381-439.

Use of Thirteen Terms in Six Works."[7] Since the six chosen works cover the span of Aquinas' career, the picture of doctrinal developments that emerges is all the more convincing.

While Klubertanz delineates five of these doctrinal developments, the most vital for our present purposes are the discussions of proportionality and participation. In the relatively early work *De Veritate*, Aquinas does seems to consider proportionality as the most important form of analogy:

> Knowledge is predicated neither entirely univocally nor yet purely equivocally of God's knowledge and ours. Instead, it is predicated analogously . . . according to a proportion. Now, an agreement according to a proportion can be of two kinds. According to this, two kinds of community can be noted in an analogy. There is a certain agreement between two things having a proportion to each other because they have a determinate distance between them or some other relation to each other, as two is related to one because it is its double. Sometimes an agreement is also noted between two things between which there is no proportion but rather a likeness of two proportions to each other, as six agrees with four because six is two times three, just as four is two times two. The first kind of agreement is one of proportion; the second of proportionality.
>
> . . . .
>
> Because in those terms predicated in the first kind of analogy there must be some determinate relation between the things to which something is common by analogy, nothing can be predicated analogously of God and creature according to this type of analogy; for no creature has such a relation to God by which the divine perfection could be determined. But in the second kind of analogy no determinate relation is noted between the things to which something is common by analogy; so according to this kind, nothing prevents us from predicating some name analogously of God and creatures (*De Ver.* II, 11, c., Klubertanz's trans.).

Here Aquinas rejects the interdetermining analogy of proportion (*proportionis*), but he accepts the analogy of proportionality

---

[7]Klubertanz, *Aquinas on Analogy*, 21.

(*proportionalitatis*) where something in God's being is to God's nature as something in creaturely being is to creaturely nature. In this application, when six acts as a double to three, and four acts as a double to two, six and four are not interdetermining; but they do possess similar relationships. So Aquinas says of proportionality:

> As the infinite is to the infinite, so the finite is . . . to the finite. In this way there is a likeness between the creature and God, because as He is related to the things which belong to Him, so the creature is related to what is proper to it (*De Ver.* XXIII, 7, ad. 9).

However, this proposed way of relating God and creatures is deeply problematic; for although it avoids diminishing the transcendence and the "infinite distance" of God (*De Ver.* II, 11, ad. 4), it fails to relate God and creatures in anything but a trivial manner:

> Proportionality predication involves either agnosticism about one set of the terms of the proportions involved (as in figurative predication not based on an independent knowledge of both things referred to), or is merely an extrinsic comparison of beings which are known independently from other sources.[8]

Following Klubertanz we may conclude:

1. If Aquinas were to base analogous knowledge of God on proportionality, he would eventually have to admit agnosticism about God, something he clearly does not want to do.

2. In order to retain proportionality, it would have to be used as a derivative or secondary form of analogy in combination with an analogy which expressed a more direct relationship.

3. Not enough is learned if we may only say something like "God's essence is to God's being as the creature's essence is to the creature's being."

---

[8]Klubertanz, *Aquinas on Analogy*, 98.

4. Evidently seeing all of the above, Aquinas drops proportionality completely after the *De Veritate* text of 1256 and develops other forms of analogy.[9]

Klubertanz's analysis is helpful in several ways. First, it helps us understand how Cardinal Cajetan, whose insistence that the analogy of proportionality was central in Aquinas, could dominate the discussion for four hundred years. Second, it shows us that analogy must express more than extrinsic attributions (as proportionality does) but must actually express some degree of intrinsic commonality (as the analogy based on causal participation does). Third, Klubertanz's chronological alignment of the texts in fact does show that Aquinas turns to the analogy based on participation in order to express a more profound relation between God and creatures.

The analogy of participation turns out to be used more abundantly (126 times) than any other kind of analogy in the Thomistic corpus. Furthermore, it is employed over the entire span of Aquinas' writings, with increasing emphasis in the later works. Participation analogies are closely linked to exemplarity analogies and analogies of causal proportion; indeed, in Aquinas' later works, exemplarity and causal proportion seem to be subsumed in participation analogies. Klubertanz, in turn summarizing the thought of Robert J. Henle, concludes:

> St. Thomas (1) rejects purely formal, noncausal Platonic exemplarism, especially if it is also merely extrinsicist; (2) rejects Aristotle's assertion that the *natural* goal directedness of finite agents sufficiently handles the problems which Platonic exemplarity was intended to solve; (3) accepts an exemplarity doctrine which describes a similarity between created effects and (ultimately) a created

---

[9]Klubertanz, *Aquinas on Analogy*, 98-99.

intelligence which is operating *through efficient and telic causality*; (4) transforms the Platonic forms (and the Augustinian divine ideas) into a *single entity*, the divine essence, which knows itself as imitable in various ways.[10]

Implied in the above is the familiar Neoplatonic principle that an effect receives something of the essence of its cause, a reception limited by the potential of the effect.

If the effect receives the entire actuality of the cause, then the cause is said to be univocal. For example, within a species causation is univocal, as when an oak tree generates other oak trees, or as Aquinas often put it, as man is the cause of a man.[11] But the generation of a whole species itself (or the creation of all that is) requires a higher cause which is only partially realized in the created effect. Such a higher cause, which is only partially realized by its effects, is said to be an analogous cause.[12]

Because God is understood as being the infinite actuality of the perfections present in creation, the cause of those perfections, and that

---

[10]Klubertanz, *Aquinas on Analogy*, 53, n. 30.

[11]While Aquinas' understanding of biology and physics is unquestionably erroneous in places, his overall conception of causality may still bear some fruit.

[12]See Klubertanz, *Aquinas on Analogy*, 24-26, where he shows another of Aquinas' doctrinal developments. In this case, Aquinas shifts from a notion of univocal cause in his early texts, to a transitional position of equivocal cause, and ends up with his notion of analogous cause:

> St. Thomas first bowed to the logical demand for clarity and definability but later rejected this claim in favor of the irreducible diversity of the real order, which cannot be enclosed by man within the limits of a clear concept (ibid., 26).

Here again a central theme is touched; for while analogy expresses likeness, it does not do so by violating "the irreducible diversity" of the way we discover our existence to be.

which may draw the creature to increasing participation, several of Aquinas' terminologies overlap. Thus "the analogy of causality becomes the analogy of causal eminence and ultimately the analogy of causal participation."[13]   One earmark of analogy is that it relates different levels and intensities while referring to a common property or perfection.   The crucial issue is always whether God and creatures possess a given perfection *intrinsically*. Where metaphorical predication remains entirely extrinsic to one of the analogates (*ST* I.13.6), analogical predication claims more by virtue of some ontological commonality between the analogates.   This commonality is warranted by the doctrine of God's causal eminence and its corollary, creaturely participation:

> God alone is being by His very essence; all other things participate in being (*CG* II, 53).

> A perfection common to both cause and effect exists in a higher way in the cause than in the effect, for it flows from the cause to the effect. Whatever exists in the lower causes, therefore, and is attributed to the first cause of all, belongs to it in a most excellent way (*De Substantiis separatis*, 13, 14).

> A perfection which is predicated of both God and creatures is predicated of God essentially and of the creature by participation. . . . The participated form in the creature falls short of the intelligibility of that which is God (*De Pot.* VII, 7, ad. 2).

These passages all link the creature and the Creator, and they likewise maintain the transcendence and the priority of God.   God *is* the given perfection (once it has been purged of all imperfections known in the creaturely realm), and the creature *has* the perfection to a relative degree.

---

[13]Klubertanz, *Aquinas on Analogy*, 153.

Participation thus functions as the framework within which a host of metaphysical problems are addressed and synthesized. Cornelio Fabro neatly frames the issues of participation metaphysics:

> In an attempt to solve crucial issues of the constitutive relation between God and creatures, between the Infinite and the finite--such as those concerning total dependence (creation and divine motion), radical structure (composition of *essentia* and *esse*) and fundamental semantics (analogy)--St. Thomas had placed the Platonic notion of participation at the very foundation of the Aristotelian couplet of act and potency. The theory was then advanced, which both text and context have supported and clarified, that the very notion of *ens* and that of *esse* as intensive emergent act, sprang in Thomism from within that same notion of participation and marked the definitive overthrow of both classic and scholastic essentialism (formalism).[14]

Let us separately consider the components of participation en route to bringing them back together as the mature Aquinas' warrant for analogical predication.

THE ACT/POTENCY DISTINCTION

In his 1952 article, "The Limitation of Act by Potency," Clarke demonstrates that Aquinas is, metaphysically considered, not simply an Aristotelian, but a creative synthesis of Aristotle and Plato.[15] Critically, Aquinas distinguishes himself from his Hellenistic

---

[14]Cornelio Fabro, "The Intensive Hermeneutics of Thomistic Philosophy: The Notion of Participation," trans. B. M. Bonansea, *Review of Metaphysics* 27 (1973-4): 450.

[15]Clarke, "The Limitation of Act by Potency: Aristotelianism or Neoplatonism" *New Scholasticism* 26 (1952): 167-94. This article, itself a synthesis and development of much of the previous research, has had a broad influence in Neo-Thomist circles.

predecessors with a fundamentally different view of infinity. Where the Greeks had seen infinity as chaotic and negative, Clarke documents the change begun in earnest in Plotinus, which revalued infinity as an ultimately positive property, and so one attributable to God.

The notion of an eternal world, against which Aquinas crusaded for years in his work at the University of Paris, is closely related to this ancient Greek idea of infinity as a negative property.[16] In the *Timaeus*, Plato's Demiurge Creator God had to struggle to impose as much order as possible upon *anankē*, the necessity already existent in pre-matter. In fact, Platonic dualism in large part results from this notion of creation alongside an eternal world. By contrast, the *creatio ex nihilo* doctrine of the Christian tradition, with its assertion that the world created is good, allows Aquinas to develop his much more integrated conception of participation in the patterns of the created world.

In the Platonic (and Aristotelian) cosmology, the imposition of order, finite order, holds the highest rank. In fact, Clarke considers this valuation of finite and infinite one of the greatest weaknesses of Greek philosophy:

> According to this conception the infinite is identified with the formless, the indeterminate, the unintelligible--in a word, with matter and multiplicity, the principles of imperfection--whereas the finite or limited is identified with the fully formed, the determinate, and therefore the intelligible--in a word, with number, form, and idea, the principles of perfection.[17]

---

[16]For an account of Aquinas' struggle against the Averroist doctrine of the eternal world and other issues, see, James A. Weisheipl, O.P., *Friar Thomas D'Aquino: His Life, Thought, and Works* (Washington, D.C.: The Catholic University of America Press, 1974), 272-285.

[17]Clarke, "Limitation," 175.

The radical reversal of this valuation, given impetus by sundry sources such as Philo, Syrian astronomy, and an influx of Eastern mystery religions, attained a firm footing with Plotinus, and, through Proclus and Pseudo-Dionysius, continued to shape Christian thinking up to and including the times of Aquinas. As Léon Brunschvicg observed: *"Le divin change de camp; il passe du fini à l'infinie"* (Divinity changes sides: it crosses from finite to infinite).[18]

As Clarke portrays it, Aquinas took both the "central piece of Aristotelian metaphysics, the doctrine of act and potency," as well as "the central piece of the Neoplatonic metaphysical tradition, the participation-limitation framework."[19] In each case, Aquinas was able to capitalize on the respective strengths while bypassing their respective weaknesses. For instance, where the doctrine of act and potency was wholly used by Aristotle to express change and composition within a being, and where the Neoplatonist understanding of participation left the relationship of participant and participated vague and ambiguous,

> the achievement of St. Thomas was to recognize that the strength of each doctrine remedied precisely the weakness of the other and to fuse them into a single highly original synthesis, condensed in the apparently simple yet extremely rich and complex formula: Act is not limited except by reception in a distinct potency.[20]

Clarke further differentiates Aquinas from the following defects of the received Neoplatonic participation framework:

> 1) its lack of clear distinctions between genuine ontological participations and mere logical subordination of abstract concepts;

---

[18]*Le rôle du Pythagorisme dans l'évolution des idées* (Paris, 1937), 23, as cited by Clarke, "Limitation," 184, n. 33, my translation.

[19]Clarke, "Limitation," 190.

[20]Ibid.

2) its tendency to superimpose layer after layer of participated forms upon the receiving subject with no intrinsic unifying principle to knit together the composite into a genuine per se unit;

3) the tendency in its non-Christian forms to make the entity of the participating subject as recipient independent of the higher source of the perfection participated.[21]

Aquinas' paradigmatic insight into the infinity of God as "the supra-formal act of existence"[22] brought about a quantum leap in the evolution of the notion of infinity. For his part, Clarke's development of this theme over many years and in many publications is one of his greatest contributions to understanding Aquinas and his sources.[23] The identification of God as Infinite, as *actus essendi* (the act of existence), "the fundamental ontological perfection of the universe,"[24] would lead to Aquinas' well-known dictum that God is not in any genus, but it would also allow that all created beings, whether angelic or human, could then participate in the most fundamental perfection--existence-- while being limited in act by creaturely form. What had been a 'horizontal' concept in Aristotle, i.e., limited to a context of change within a being, becomes a 'vertical' principle of participation in Aquinas, one in which finite and infinite can be meaningfully related.

Looking at the evolution of thought in Aquinas, Clarke adds that the originality of Aquinas' synthesis is attested by the fact that his early works do not exhibit this principle. It is only from the *Contra Gentiles*

---

[21]Clarke, "The Meaning of Participation in St. Thomas," *Proceedings of the American Catholic Philosophical Association* 26 (1952): 150.

[22]Clarke, "Limitation," 191.

[23]In addition to works already cited, see Clarke, "Infinity in Plotinus," *Gregorianum* 40 (1959): 75-98.

[24]Clarke, "Limitation," 191.

onward that he unites his limitation principle with the originally Aristotelian principle of act and potency as a centerpiece of his metaphysics. Identifying the divine *actus essendi* with substantive infinity lets Aquinas take the great but in some ways limited insights of both Plato and Aristotle and combine them in his own original vision. By explicating this vision of causal participation within the framework of Christian creation, Aquinas uncovers new fields of meaning in the relations of finite and infinite. In evidence here again is the impact of chronological studies for interpreting Aquinas, studies which consistently point to an evolution of thought in the medieval master.

THE ESSENCE/EXISTENCE DOCTRINE

The essence/existence distinction is one of the key aspects of Aquinas' metaphysics and closely linked to the metaphysics of participation:

> It is common knowledge that the essence-existence doctrine of St. Thomas is the central piece in his whole metaphysical system. It is a doctrine both of creatures and of God in their mutual relations, the central vantage point from which he views all creatures as participating in limited fashion through their respective essences in the unlimited plenitude of God's own perfection as Subsistent Act of Existence (*Ipsum Esse Subsistens*).[25]

---

[25]Clarke, "What Cannot Be Said in St. Thomas' Essence-Existence Doctrine," *New Scholasticism* 48 (1974): 19. (In the remainder of this section, this article will be cited parenthetically within the text as "Essence-Existence.")

In working towards a deeper understanding of participation metaphysics, Clarke's claim about the essence-existence doctrine needs to be clarified vis-à-vis his similar claim about the act-potency doctrine. In "The Limitation of Act by Potency," written some twenty-two years earlier, Clarke tells us that the act-potency doctrine "is generally conceded to be the keystone of the Thomistic metaphysical system"

Before looking at what the essence/existence doctrine and its linguistic limits might mean, let us sketch Clarke's outline of it.

In addressing the ancient problem of the many and one, diversity and unity, a common bond is sought for what intelligibility may exist:

> For St. Thomas, in this general tradition, the central perfection of the universe is the very act of existence itself (*esse*). This exists in pure, unlimited plenitude in God alone, who thereby contains all perfections in a supereminent way in His simple concentrated unity. All other beings, created by God, participate this basic all-inclusive perfection of existence according to the limiting modes of their respective essences. Every being aside from God is thus a limited participation in the perfection of existence, and hence a real metaphysical composition of its particular act of existence and its respective limiting essence, in a relation of act to potency ("Essence-Existence," 20).

The essence/existence doctrine, understood as part of a participation framework, accounts for the similarity and dissimilarity of God and creatures in their respectively infinite and finite modes of existence. All created being is similar to its Creator to the degree that it participates in the basic perfection of the act, power, and energy of existence. The difference is that the divine infinite essence is identical to the divine act of existence. Within this identification of essence/existence, there is absolutely no limit to the divine infinity. In contrast, the creature's act of existence is limited and specified by its essence. In technical Thomistic terms, God is 'simple', and creatures are 'composed'.

---

(168). The interesting point about these competing claims is that both can be taken as central only in that they both end up pointing to the more inclusive and broader doctrine of participation. Though not identical, the notions of act-potency and essence-existence are inherently interrelated and overlapping in the framework of participation. As such, both doctrines play key roles in understanding the basis of analogy, i.e., participation metaphysics.

Commenting on the inevitable difficulties of essentialist schemes, but particularly as they surfaced in Plotinus, Clarke points out that whatever ultimate perfection an essentialist scheme might choose, e.g., goodness, unity, etc.,

> the nagging question always arises in these systems--whether faced explicitly or not--as to just what to do with the embarrassing little "is" (or its equivalent) which always somehow seems to be left over, to resist complete reduction to anything else but itself. Thus the question intrudes itself: are we not forced to say that goodness (or whatever the ultimate perfection is called) *is*, is *real*, actually is present and is not just an ideal or hope or abstraction? It seems that somehow such an affirmation must be made, implicitly or explicitly ("Essence-Existence," 21).

Clarke's emphasis on the "is" and the "nagging" problem it presents if left untreated brings out the force of Aquinas' central perfection of the *actus essendi* (the act of existence):

> If the "is" refuses to be reduced to anything else, then, since duality cannot be the last word, the only alternative is to reverse the picture and reduce all else to the "is." This is just what his doctrine of essence-existence carries out systematically ("Essence-Existence," 23).

This metaphysical vision of existence, of the "is," does not see perfections as something added to existence, "but as diverse modes of participation, through interior *limitation* (i.e., partial *negation*) in this one all-inclusive positive 'attribute' of existence" (ibid.).

Regarding God, Clarke concludes:

> What St. Thomas is inviting us to do in describing the essence of God as the Subsistent Act of Existence itself is to transcend the most radical and irreducible distinction of linguistic forms in our language, that between subject (noun) and verb ("Essence-Existence," 24).

The simpleness of God, the identity of essence and existence, subject and verb, cannot be properly expressed in any form or expression of any

language; however, something can and must be said, but never with the
directness that a purely essentialist account would claim. Instead,

> it can be evocatively suggested by a special use of language and
> shown forth as something that must be affirmed if reality is to make
> ultimate sense. . . . This does not prevent language from being used
> in a way that summons the living thrust of the mind to transcend in
> a leap of insight the limitations of its own linguistic product, and in
> that very act somehow to know what it is doing and why, though it
> cannot further express what it knowingly intends. The last "word" of
> the doctrine, we might say, is therefore a dimension of eloquent
> silence ("Essence-Existence," 25).

A mere surrender to silence and mystical apophaticism is not being
advocated; for, as we have seen, the act of existence is not entirely
opaque. Nonetheless, language about God cannot exhaust the divine
reality because essence cannot exhaust (or limit) the divine existence.
From this point of view, language about God does not exhaust what is
known; in fact, if properly communicated it may stimulate further
discovery. This process of stimulation Aquinas calls *manuductio*[26]
(leading by the hand).

Pushing the essence/existence question further, Clarke asks: Can
one term of the fusion of subject and verb, essence and existence in
Aquinas be said to "win out"? While the strict answer is no, Clarke
muses:

> That in some significant sense the verb finally wins out. The "is" is
> deeper than the "what." And a sign of this is that St. Thomas himself
> chooses a verb form, *esse* (to be) to express the subject in God, and
> not vice versa ("Essence-Existence," 26).

---

[26]The term is cited by Clarke in *Philosophical Approach*, 29. Aquinas uses it in
ST I.12.12 and I.84.7. Below, Burrell will develop his exegesis of Plato's Socratic
dialogues along this same thematic line, as well as his reading of Aquinas in *Analogy
and Philosophical Language*.

In so strongly emphasizing the act of existence, the reality of the essence can become problematic.[27] Clarke describes two alternative understandings as "thick-essence" and "thin-essence." In the former

> essence is still looked on as possessing a certain positivity of its own, received indeed from existence as ultimate act, but giving it a distinct positive role of its own, precisely *as distinct* from the act of existence, so that the essence becomes the positive *subject which* exists, distinct as positive subject from the act of existence which it exercises ("Essence-Existence," 36).

The thin view, which Clarke prefers, sees existence

> not so much as the actualizer of anything positive other than itself, but rather as the whole inner core of all the perfection the being contains. Essence, in its turn, becomes nothing but the interior limiting principle, the inner limit or partial negation (*omnis determinatio est negatio*, as Spinoza put it in his classic phrase) of the perfection which resides properly within the act of existence itself. The act of existence, accordingly, *as thus limited*, becomes the very subject which exists (ibid.).

Having stated his own preference, Clarke is quick to add that the textual evidence is inconclusive and that the thin-essence view raises difficulties in how to talk about it. The problem is not in recognizing that beings other than God are limited; the problem is in specifying what the reality of the limit itself might be. Returning to more central questions:

> One must indeed tone down rather drastically the "reality" and solidity of the so-called "real distinction"--a strong expression which . . . is only rarely used by Thomas himself. He prefers "other and other" (*aliud et aliud*). To my mind, the essential point truly worth holding on to in the doctrine of St. Thomas is the notion of *limited participation* in the central perfection of existence, not the technical solution of how to express this, whether by "real distinction," or some other way.

---

[27]This question has in fact been the source of controversy among leading figures of understanding participation in Aquinas. See, for example, Cornelio Fabro, *Participation et Causalité selon S. Thomas D'Aquin* (Paris: Nauwelaerts, 1961), 63-73, where Fabro criticizes the position of L. B. Geiger.

But let us face squarely the main question: what is the reality of limit as such? Here, I think, is another case where we have reached the limits of language ("Essence-Existence," 37).

Having run us up against the limit of what may be grasped in this essence/existence doctrine, Clarke points back again to our central concern of participation as both the "essential point" and as something which though still mysterious itself, might afford us a better grasp of its workings by being rooted "in a more luminous and accessible mystery" ("Essence-Existence," 32).

PARTICIPATION

Clarke cites three common criticisms of analogy: 1) analogy is too formal--it is actually empty of content; 2) it is essentially agnostic; 3) it is based on a dubious metaphysics.[28] As we have seen, traditional understandings of analogy based on proportionality are indeed vulnerable to these criticisms; but analogical talk about God based upon participation is not vulnerable to them. The central import of participation and how Aquinas employs it differently than his predecessors can be seen in Fabro's historical summary:

> Whereas Platonic vertical participation is actualized merely as imitation of the Idea and hence as a fall, as it were, into non-being and the phenomenon, the Aristotelian horizontal causality is like an endless repetition of universal essence in the singulars. The result is that both theories tend to emphasize formal univocity. In contrast, the Thomistic notion of participation, founded in *esse* as supreme intensive act, makes it possible to pass from finite to Infinite Being

---

[28]Clarke, *Philosophical Approach*, 50. Below, Jüngel will adopt all three of these criticisms of Aquinas and the metaphysical tradition.

through analogical discourse, which has in participation its beginning, middle, and conclusion.[29]

Definitions and Clarifications. While Aquinas refers to participation in his early works, he does not really begin to work the doctrine out for himself until the *Commentary on the Hebdomadibus of Boethius*, probably his tenth published work, circa 1256-1261. Here Aquinas faces the problem of participation more explicitly:

> To participate is to receive as it were a part; and therefore when anything receives in a particular manner that which belongs to another in a universal [or total] manner, it is said to participate it; as man is said to participate animal, because he does not possess the intelligible notes (*ratio*) of animal according to the latter's total "community" [i.e., universality]; and for the same reason Socrates participates man; in like manner also a subject participates an accident, and matter form. . . . Similarly, an effect is said to participate its cause, and especially when it does not equal the power of its cause (*In Boeth. de Hebd.*, 1.2).[30]

An excellent commentary on this passage by John F. Wippel, itself indebted to the work of Fabro and Montagnes, shows how the three cases illustrated in the above passage form two basic kinds of participation: predicamental and transcendental.[31]

The first two cases above involve predicamental participation. In the first case, the intelligibility of animal includes man but is broader than that of man, so man is said to participate in the intelligibility of animal. However, this type of participation is strictly within the logical

---

[29]Fabro, "Intensive Hermeneutics," 481.

[30]Translation is taken from Clarke, "The Meaning of Participation in St. Thomas," 151.

[31]"Thomas Aquinas and Participation," *Studies in Medieval Philosophy*, ed. John F. Wippel (Washington, D.C.: Catholic University of America Press, 1987), 117-58.

order.   In *SCG* I.32, Aquinas further distinguishes this kind of participation because it allows univocal predication:

> Everything which is predicated of many things univocally pertains to each of those things of which it is predicated only by participation. For a species is said to participate in a genus, and an individual in a species.[32]

The second case from the *De Hebdomadibus* text, which deals with subjects participating in accidents or matter in form, is likewise capable of univocal predication, with the difference that this case is also ontological, not merely logical, as in the first case. Here matter or the substantial subject, receives what is more general, constituting an ontological composition of a receiving principle (matter or the subject) and the perfection or form received. In this manner, Socrates is said to participate humanity. While this second case goes beyond a less extended concept sharing in a more extended concept, as the first case has done, both cases of predicamental participation are restricted to finite relations.

The third case, transcendental participation, bears directly upon analogous talk about God. Here again is the principle that an effect can participate in its cause but not be equal to the power of that cause. While transcendental participation is only given a general description in the *De Hebdomadibus* commentary, Aquinas eventually develops it as the basis of relating God and creatures through the divine *actus essendi*, which, for Aquinas, is also the divine causality.

What Aquinas has begun to do in the *De Hebdomadibus*, he further specifies in *SCG* I.32: "Nothing Is Predicated Univocally of God and Creatures." The metaphysical justification of this inability to speak

---

[32]Wippel's translation, taken from "Aquinas and Participation," 130.

univocally of God and creatures lies in the two doctrines considered above: the limitation of act by potency and the essence-existence distinction. Univocal predication of God and creatures is impossible because divine simplicity and infinity stand in sharp contrast to the creature's limited act.

In spite of the contrast between God and creatures, the self-communication of being in action renders the created universe potentially intelligible to the finite inquiring mind. Although in a limited, partial, and incomplete manner, we participate in the effects of the divine being which causes itself to be known. Our common participation in creation, in the effects of the divine act of being, permits the moderated realism of analogous talk about God. Nonetheless,

> nothing is predicated in the same order of God and other things, but according to priority and posteriority: since all predicates of God are essential, for He is called being because He is very essence, and good because He is goodness itself: whereas predicates are applied to others by participation; thus Socrates is said to be a man, not as though he were humanity itself, but as a subject of humanity. Therefore it is impossible for anything to be predicated univocally of God and other things (*SCG* I.32).

Because the divine being fuses subject (noun) and verb, essence and existence, we are not prevented from speaking realistically about God; however, we are forced to consider the way our predicates, always conceived through the creaturely mode of composition, may apply to God's different mode of being.

Aquinas directly confronts the epistemological problem which his act/potency and essence/existence doctrines raise for how creatures may know (and thus speak of) God. In addressing the question, "Whether Affirmative Propositions Can Be Formed About God?" he illustrates how "true affirmative propositions may be formed about God" (*ST*

I.13.12). The claim of Objection 3 says that the human mind cannot make positive affirmations about God, since the human intellect has a composite mode of understanding, and yet the existence of God is without composition. Aquinas counters:

> Any intellect which understands that the thing is otherwise than it is, is false. But this does not hold in the present case; because our intellect, when forming a proposition about God, does not affirm that He is composite, but that He is simple. . . . For the mode of the intellect in its understanding is different than the mode of the thing in its essence. Since it is clear that our intellect understands material things below itself in an immaterial manner; not that it understands them to be immaterial things; but its manner of understanding is immaterial. Likewise, when it understands simple things above itself, it understands them according to its own mode, which is in a composite manner; yet not so as to understand them to be composite things. And thus our intellect is not false in forming composition in its ideas concerning God (*ST* I.13.12.3).

I consider this passage to be of critical importance in understanding Aquinas; for all too often, one of his isolated statements is raised to a level of generality which does not stand in the light of the overall corpus. For example, the statement that we cannot know God as God is in this life (*ST* I.13.1.2) can be dangerously misleading unless tempered by the above statement of how it is that we do know both God above us and things below us. Human intellect can understand something about a stone without needing to exist on the same level as the stone which it understands. Similarly, human intellect can understand some things about God without existing on God's level.

Klubertanz has shed light on this methodological problem of forming generalities too quickly from a given text. By citing eight different statements of Aquinas on analogy which seem to be individually generalizable, but in fact would generate contradictions with the other texts, Klubertanz concludes:

First, not every discussion that appears to be a general description applicable to all analogies is such in actual fact. This is true even when the description is couched in categorical language and no qualifications at all are explicitly made. Such categorical language is used in all of the texts just cited, and yet each of them describes a specific type of analogy. . . . Moreover, types of analogy like participation or imitation, so prominent throughout St. Thomas' writings, are nowhere mentioned in these "general" descriptions of analogy. Yet even without adverting to this fact, if we read these texts in context, we see that their categorical language is deceiving. The description they give of analogy *tout court* invariably turns out to be tailored to the exact dimensions of some particular problem. The "general" descriptions are not general.[33]

Having seen how the human intellect can at least comprehend something of the divine being, noted the danger of too quickly generalizing a given text of Aquinas', and remembering Clarke's earlier warning that certain principles which indeed are general are not always made explicit in Aquinas, we can now consider the main problem of transcendental participation: How does the human *actus essendi* relate to the divine act of being?

The Relation of the Human and Divine Actus Essendi. There are strong connections among the self-subsistent but also self-communicating nature of the divine being, the derivative self-communication of being in action, and participation. However, it must not be assumed that both God and the creature share being in the participation structure, or, that the creature participates directly in the divine *esse*. There is a link between God and creatures, but if it were the link of creatures participating

---

[33]Klubertanz, *Aquinas on Analogy*, 37-38. Klubertanz does cite two seeming exceptions, where the texts strongly insist upon "a prime analogate in *every* analogy" (ibid., 38, n. 3).

directly in the being of God, then nothing would prohibit a univocal predication of God and creatures, just as nothing prohibits univocal attribution when a species participates a genus or matter participates its form. If being is construed with creatures directly participating in the divine being itself, then Duns Scotus would be correct in asserting a univocal core to every so-called analogy--participation would fall into a kind of essentialism with being as a kind of superform shared by both God and creatures. True to form, the linkage that Aquinas does provide is a kind of *via media*--the participation in being *caused* by God.

Among the Three Persons of the Trinity, the divine essence is shared fully and infinitely. On the other hand, finite essence is the limit of finite existence. If finite essence did not limit finite existence, then creatures would be infinite. Yet if creatures were to possess infinite existence, then logically, they would be no more than duplicates of the infinite existence which God already possesses. Such a hypothetical notion of *creation* is a contradiction in terms. For were God to bring us into existence as infinite beings, such an act would be more akin to repetition than creation. The freshness of creation requires creaturely limits. The development of the act/potency and essence/existence distinctions are metaphysical counterparts to the uniqueness and originality of creation. Creation of a finite realm implies the act/potency and essence/existence distinctions.

Hence, creaturely participation is not in the divine *esse*, but in the *esse* received *from* God, an affirmation which is consistent with *creatio ex nihilo*. Allowing a direct participation in the divine *Ipsum Esse Subsistens* might generate a pantheistic account of creation, essentialism, or something like Scotus' assessment of being as a univocal core common to God and humankind. Instead, Aquinas keeps the Infinite

God and finite creature distinct while providing an account of their similarity through the divine being as cause of all other being. Wippel's paraphrase taken from the *Commentary on the Divine Names* will clarify the point:

> The divine essence itself remains uncommunicated, . . . remains unparticipated; but its likeness, through those things which it communicates to creatures, is propagated and multiplied in creatures. In this way, therefore, divinity may be said to proceed into creatures and to be multiplied in them, that is, by likeness, but not by its very essence.[34]

Thus creature and Creator share a certain "likeness" but not the same essence.

Where Aquinas denies that creatures participate directly in the divine being, he contends that all that exists participates in *esse commune* ("universal being," or "being in general"). Aquinas goes to some length to distinguish *esse commune* from the divine *Ipsum Esse Subsistens*, which is asserted to exist independently (separately) of created being:

> God's being which is his essence is not universal being, but being distinct from all other being: so that by his very being God is distinct from every other being (*De Pot.* III.7.2 ad. 4).

Aquinas thus distinguishes the being of God from created, participated being and thereby avoids the problems caused by Plato's separated forms (as in the *Parmenides*). Through the synthesis of his participation scheme with the Christian doctrine of *creatio ex nihilo*, Aquinas develops a methodological teamwork between faith and reason, theology and metaphysics: "Thus reason proves and faith holds that all things are created by God" (*De Pot.* 3.5).

---

[34]Wippel, "Aquinas and Participation," 146-47, paraphrasing Aquinas' Commentary on the *Divine Names*, II. 3.

The Problematic Status of Esse Commune. By granting independent
ontological status to God as *Ipsum Esse Subsistens*, and by seeming to
deny independent ontological status to *esse commune*, we are left with
the perennial problem of what status, if any, universal predicates might
possess. With participated *existence*, the difficulty is exacerbated
because we cannot even utilize the notion of an intelligible form. What
reality remains to participated existence in creatures? Is this just a
logical commonality?

Clarke outlines two solutions which he deems less than satisfactory
before detailing his own attempt at a deeper grounding of participation.
First, he characterizes Wittgenstein's solution as "a simple and drastic
one. You simply should not ask this kind of question."[35] This is the
notorious "language on holiday," language which has been diverted from
its normal functioning which it accomplishes rather well, but has now
been asked to attempt a job that it cannot perform acceptably. As
Clarke summarizes the Wittgensteinian critique,

> You can properly ask, "Is this or that real? Are dogs or cats real?"
> But you can't properly ask, "Is humanity or redness real?" Predicates
> just can't function as subjects in this way.[36]

Clarke concedes that his metaphysical question about the reality
of participated existence is not using language in its ordinary function.
He further admits that if one does go ahead and ask the meta-linguistic
question about "ontological underpinnings of thought and language,"
then

> one must be very careful about how one asks such questions and what
> kind of answers he expects or will accept. But it still seems to me that
> our radical drive toward total intelligibility, which involves bringing

---

[35]Clarke, "Essence-Existence," 28.

[36]Ibid., 29.

all of our taken-for-granted presuppositions out into the light of critical consciousness as far as possible, cannot remain satisfied with merely taking the successful working of language as a brute fact, and not reflecting in depth on the very roots of its possibility.[37]

Not satisfied with the "brute fact" of language that is functioning fairly well, Clarke just makes a different decision than Wittgenstein about when to "stop doing philosophy."

Perhaps even more unsatisfactory to Clarke is the nominalist-empiricist type of response as in William of Ockham. For Ockham, the fact that Plato and Socrates are similar does not suggest that they are similar *in* something else. Once again there is just a "brute fact" of an objective similarity which is alleged not to require further grounding. But for those who do not want to "stop doing philosophy" when Wittgenstein and Ockham do, then the alternative is some form of an ontological participation doctrine which, following Aquinas, Clarke attempts to give.

With regard to universals, Aquinas, as is his wont, takes a median position between strong realism and nominalism. In rejecting the strong realism position, Aquinas argues:

> That which is common to many is not something besides those many except only logically: thus *animal* is not something besides Socrates and Plato and other animals except as considered by the mind, which apprehends the form of animal as divested of all that specifies, and individualizes it: for man is that which is truly an animal, else it would follow that in Socrates and Plato there are several animals, namely animal in general, man in general, and Plato himself. Much less therefore being itself in general is something apart from all things that have being; except only as apprehended by the mind (*SCG* I.26).

Once again, God's being, which really does exist outside the mind, is not to be identified with being in general (*esse commune*). Other than

---

[37]Clarke, "Essence-Existence," 29.

rejecting strong realism, Aquinas remains reticent on specifying the existence and unity in participated, created things. While Clarke offers a more direct response to the problem, he does not do so without carefully suggesting that some mystery remains

> in a quite real and objective participation-situation (real and objective as an indivisible whole) which eludes being pinned down any further in language or concept. It cannot be directly said, but can only be understood, or, perhaps better, recognized, in the course of reflecting on the whole dynamic process of participation at once: namely, a real source, sharing actively its own real perfection, which is truly one in its source, with many different participants, so that because of this real communication all the participants are objectively similar to each other and to their source.[38]

So the commonality is not so much on the side of creatures as on the divine source from which perfections are communicated to creatures through the act of being.

Drawing upon the innovative work of André Hayen, Clarke further asserts that the unity of a participated perfection "lies in the creative *intentional act* of its source."[39] This "creative intentional act" is a kind of willingness to share, a self-communication of the source which gives rise to an "ontological complement." Thus the ultimate ground of the one-many problem lies in the source's intentional act which has the power to communicate being to diverse recipients:

> The only kind of reality in the universe--and of course it is not properly a thing but a unique kind of act--which has the peculiar property of joining together in the unity of a single act both one and many, singular and universal, is an intentional act, which either

---

[38]Clarke, "Essence-Existence," 31.

[39]Ibid., 33. Also, see André Hayen, *L'Intentionnel dans la philosophie de S. Thomas*, 2e. ed. (Brussels, 1946); and Hayen, L'Intentionnalité de l'être et métaphysique de la participation," *Revue néoscolastique* 42 (1939): 385-410.

intends actively to share a one with many, or *post factum* recognizes such a sharing when executed.[40]

This intentional act brings together all three components of the participation framework:

> 1) The one source with its perfection as model or exemplar, 2) the many as recipients or participants, and 3) the actual sharing of the one perfection of the source with the many, diversely in each.[41]

The moderated realism of this argument lies in its placement of the fully actualized commonality outside the many in the common source. Yet Clarke goes a bit further, claiming that the unity of the source's intention,

> precisely as *intention* to-share-a-one-with-many, somehow carries over into each of the participants and is incarnated there under the sign of ontological similarity, waiting to be picked up and formally reconstituted in its original unity by a mind capable of recognizing the sign for what it points to. . . . The power of intentional consciousness, the conscious and efficacious act of willing to share one's own riches with others, is thus the ultimate reason and ground, of both intelligibility and being, for the universe precisely as *uni*verse, as one world, as a unified order of reality.[42]

While admitting that this solution simply grounds the mystery by pushing it back a step further into the divine intentional act, Clarke claims some satisfaction in having traced the mystery to its ultimate root, thus making it "considerably more luminous." Furthermore, basing the entire endeavor on an intentional act renders the Many completely dependent upon the One for their very existence; and it radically personalizes and theologizes the metaphysics involved. So Clarke concludes:

---

[40]Clarke, "Essence-Existence," 33.

[41]Ibid.

[42]Ibid., 34.

And is it not as it should be that the truly ultimate mystery of the universe, that which illumines all else, should turn out to be the mystery of self-communicating love? There *is* no further explanation possible for anything, if "God is Love," as St. John says.[43]

TWO BASIC ARGUMENTS FOR PARTICIPATION

From Many to the One. Before considering the implications for analogy of Clarke's arrival at the personal, let us examine his two basic arguments for participation metaphysics.[44] Above, as we distinguished the divine act of existence (*Ipsum Esse Subsistens*) from being in general (*esse commune*), we have in large part anticipated the first basic argument which proceeds from the Many to the One. The heart of this originally Platonic argument is that unity or even similarity cannot proceed from diverse causes. As Aquinas appropriates it, he shows that there is not only a like source but a single source:

> If in a number of things we find something that is common to all, we must conclude that this something was the effect of some one cause: for it is not possible that to each one by reason of itself this common something belongs, since each one by itself is different from the others: and diversity of causes produces a diversity of effects. Seeing then that being is found to be common to all things, which are by themselves distinct from one another, it follows of necessity that they must come into being not by themselves, but by the action of some cause. Seemingly this is Plato's argument, since he required every multitude to be preceded by unity not only as regards number but also in reality (*De Pot.* 3.5).

Yet a decisive difference between Plato and Aquinas is that Aquinas' notion of the *actus essendi* as the fundamental perfection allows him to develop a more unified argument, one which

---

[43]Clarke, "Essence-Existence," 35.

[44]Clarke develops these two arguments in *Philosophical Approach*, 38-49.

is applied by him not merely to participation in a world of ideas or forms but to participation in the most radically concrete and existential of all perfections, the power or energy of existence itself as the ultimate inner act of each real being.[45]

After all, what gift or quality could be more fundamental than life itself? What could any other positive quality mean without existence?

From Finite to Infinite. The second basic argument comprises two steps: first, it moves from the finite to the Infinite; and second, it shows that the Infinite must be one. As defined by Clarke, the specific sense of finite

> has nothing to do with a beginning or end in space and time, with a *quantitative* finite. It is a strictly *qualitative* notion, signifying a limited degree of an intensive perfection in the qualitative order, capable of higher and lower degrees of intensity. So too, "infinite" does not mean having no end in space or time (although not a few ancient, medieval, and modern thinkers have been quite fuzzy on this, confusing metaphysical infinity of perfection with eternity or omnipresence). It means rather the unrestricted qualitative plenitude of a perfection as it is in its unparticipated state, contrasted with any limited mode of participation, which possesses the perfection in question imperfectly and incompletely.[46]

The first part of the argument begins by displaying the contradiction in the finite's being the ultimate source of its own perfection.[47] Since many degrees of a given perfection are possible, there must be some explanation why a particular being has a perfection to one limited degree rather than another. But if the possessor of this

---

[45]Clarke, *Philosophical Approach*, 40.

[46]Ibid., 42.

[47]Clarke extracts the steps of the argument from: *De Pot.* 3.5; *SCG* II.15; *ST* I.93.6.

given perfection were the ultimate source of its own perfection, then it should possess the perfection in plenitude rather than partially and by degree. Also, it would have to determine its own nature, in order to possess the perfection even to a limited degree. However, this is self-contradictory, since in order to determine its own nature, it would have to pre-exist itself. Now something cannot pre-exist itself in an indeterminate nature and then actively cast itself into a particular and determined nature. So Clarke dismisses the possibility that the finite can be its own ultimate source; instead, the finite points beyond itself to what must be an Infinite Source possessing the perfection in unlimited degree:

> Now if we apply this general participation schema to the basic transcendental perfections which contain no imperfection or limit in their meaning and hence can be applied to God--such as existence, goodness, love, power, intelligence, etc.--of which the most fundamental for St.Thomas is existence itself, we find that every finite possessor of these perfections points beyond itself to an Infinite Plenitude-Source of the same, from which all finite possessors receive these perfections--primarily existence itself--according to the limited nature and capacity of each. There must, therefore, be an Infinite Source of existence itself, as the ground of all other perfections.[48]

The second part of the argument simply points out the impossibility of two actually existing infinites in the same order of perfection. Were there two such infinites, one would have to possess something which the other did not; but this lack would disqualify the one(s) lacking something from the status of infinity. Hence, the positive, qualitative infinity, especially as regards existence as the ultimate perfection of all perfections, must be one.

---

[48]Clarke, *Philosophical Approach*, 43.

While these "proofs" will be not be convincing to all, their value rests in the term Aquinas uses, *reductio*, a leading back of the mind. If considered as *reductio*, as a heuristic device, either proof or their cumulative effect may shed some light on the meaning of finite participation in creation.

As Clarke portrays it, participation is really a manner of *creaturely belonging*. It specifies the source and the goal of existence and so assists us in appreciating the giftedness of creation. Being related to the same source and at least potentially moving toward the same divine goal, we are meaningfully related to one another. Just as divine intention freely shares a one with the many, causing the one perfection to be "incarnated under the sign of ontological similarity," human mind is free to reconstitute the original unity through its own conative expressions and actions. The discovery of such implied unity energizes the explorations of the creature and confirms the sense of belonging to what is ultimately a friendly and good creation.

CHAPTER THREE

PARTICIPATION AND ANALOGOUS TERMS

SELECTING AND EXTENDING ANALOGICAL PREDICATES

Having explored the metaphysical underpinnings of analogy, we are now prepared to focus more directly on analogous usage itself. Clarke suggests that we need "activity terms" such as existence, goodness, knowledge, power, love, etc., in order to express the real similarities which "range over many different forms and essences." These activity terms are distinguished from form terms because "the same kind of activity can be performed in quite different ways by different agents on different levels of being." Thus even 'unity' and 'presence' are best understood as activity terms, as "the act of cohering" or "the act of presence-ing."[1]

Analogous terms are "systematically vague." They defy rigid definition. As Clarke felicitously puts it, an analogous term signifies a

---

[1]Clarke, *Philosophical Approach*, 51. For the remainder of this and the following section, this work will be cited parenthetically within the text.

"stretch-concept" (*Philosophical Approach*, 52). A stretch-term is known "by running up and down the scale of its known examples and seeing the point, catching the point," of the similarity which it alone can express. The elasticity of the term permits us to express commonalities which we see up and down the scale of being. But just because an analogous term cannot be rigorously defined, it does not follow that it is empty of meaning. Analogous terms are useful, even indispensable, precisely due to their flexibility; for they are markers of one of the most important exercises of our humanity: acts of judgment. The elasticity of the term must be combined with the commitment of the one who uses the term. In other words, an analogous term is incomplete without an act of judgment which its particular assertion embodies:

> We cannot properly understand the analogous range of a concept and the partial shift in meaning it undergoes in a particular usage simply by examining the concept itself. The analogous shift occurs only as the concept (and term) is actually used in the living act of judgment when the mind actually applies it to a given subject and knows what it is doing (*Philosophical Approach*, 52).

The necessary ingredient of judgment leads Clarke to reject all formal, logical attempts at depicting analogy, such as that of James Ross. Yet analogy is not opaque mystery, for we use it frequently in any given day at the juncture of the theoretical and practical intellect. Clarke rightly claims: "Analogy is found and understood only in the *lived use* of concepts and language which takes place in the act of judgment" (ibid.). Such lived use joins the concept (essence) to existence in the agent's attempt to actualize a greater participation.

While analogy is unarguably used as "stretch-terms" running up and the down the field of human experience, some account must still be given of how or if such terms can represent anything beyond human experience, a far more problematic endeavor. Clarke's arguments for the semantic validity of analogy are very similar to his arguments for the supporting metaphysics, i.e., a combination of the intelligibility and compatibility of the inquiring mind and being, and, an inference from created effects to some resemblance in the cause.

He begins by citing the historical example of Freud, who extended awareness of the operations of mind beyond conscious levels. Of course in doing so, Freud never *consciously* experienced unconscious levels of mind. That would be self-contradictory. However, he was able to draw some inferences from consciously experienced effects back to a hidden source. Thus Clarke postulates this general rule:

> Whenever the mind finds it rationally necessary or fruitful, either under the anticipation of a possible new dimension of experience or under the pressure of finding necessary conditions of intelligibility outside our experience for what we encounter within our experience, it simply expands its conscious horizon of being as intelligible to open up some new determinate beachhead in the already unlimited, indeterminate horizon of being in which the mind lives implicitly all the time. This is the very nature of the inexhaustible dynamism of the human mind, the root whence all its particular activities flow (*Philosophical Approach*, 53).

Clarke claims that in its continuous exploration of the intelligibility of being, the mind first discovers something new and only then seeks a linguistic description of that "new determinate beachhead." The language used must be flexible enough to cross over to the new beachhead; hence the need for analogous stretch-terms. If the first term chosen does not function well in the performance of this flexible duty, then we seek another term which will perform the envisioned task better. This gives rise to something like a dialectic between experience and description: "This progressive stretching of concepts is going on ceaselessly in our intellectual life, as our experience and our explanatory hypotheses expand" (*Philosophical Approach*, 54). Nonetheless, following its inherent "dynamism of intentionality," it is the mind, not language which allegedly first "leaps ahead":

> Analogy comes along only afterwards to *organize* the newly conquered territory and work out the *conceptual* and *linguistical* expression of the bonds of community with the already known (*Philosophical Approach*, 54).[2]

While maintaining this controversial claim about priority of occurrence, Clarke does recognize the interwovenness of the discovered intelligibility and its analogical expression: "From the very beginning of our intellectual life there is a necessary mutual co-involvement of being, intelligibility, and analogy" (*Philosophical Approach*, 53).

The task of analogy is not to create a connection between God and humanity but to express one that has already been discovered, realized, or revealed.   Explicating creation in terms of essence/existence, act/potency, and especially, causal participation, carries analogical use along in tandem:

> There is only one bridge that enables us to pass over the cognitive abyss between ourselves and God and talk meaningfully about Him in our terms: the bridge of causal participation, or more simply of efficient causality, taken with all its implications. If God were not the

---

[2]Clarke's position that there is more to mind than language is strongly supported by the work of Michael Polanyi, particularly in his phenomenological account of new discoveries, which Polanyi calls "crossing a logical gap." Briefly put, Polanyi's position is that if there were already an articulated language and logic, no problem would have been solved. To the contrary, great discoveries result from intellectual movement to positions which have not yet been held, as in historic moments of scientific breakthroughs. Crossing the gap between what was previously known and what is about to be known involves what Polanyi calls tacit knowledge as well as the passionate participation of the discoverer. See *Personal Knowledge: Towards a Post-Critical Philosophy* (Chicago: The University of Chicago Press, 1962), 123-130; 143.

The position that human mind first discovers things which are only later articulated linguistically has important ramifications for analogy. Below, Jüngel will present a quite different claim.

ultimate causal Source of all the perfections we find in our world, we would have no way of talking meaningfully about Him at all. It is the causal bond which grounds all analogous predication about God (*Philosophical Approach*, 54).

According to Clarke, not just philosophical theology, but even the language of revelation, cannot be meaningful unless the causal bond of creation is presupposed. Whatever the methodological approach, the possibility of the meaningfulness of language must "build upon the community in being and intelligibility established by the causal bond contained in the notion of creation" (*Philosophical Approach*, 55). If one denies or cuts this bond of causal participation between creation and Creator, the only remaining alternative for speaking of God is "poetic, metaphorical, symbolic language." Four deleterious results are common to such attempts. They inevitably tend to be:

1) empty;
2) excessively anthropomorphic;
3) without a clear principle of conceptual control; or,
4) contain a hidden presupposition of the causal bond of similitude (ibid.).

Once he has assumed the causal link between God and creatures, from which it follows that some analogous predicates may properly be applied to God, Clarke addresses the vital question of which attributes those may be and its methodological corollary: how can we select those attributes? The selection process follows Aquinas in seeking "simple and pure perfections," i.e., "purely positive qualitative terms that do not contain as part of their *meaning* any implication of limit or imperfection" (*Philosophical Approach*, 56). Having located such a term through creaturely experience or thought (as in *ST* I.13.5), we purify it of any limitations by taking it through Clarke's "stretch" procedure:

Any attribute that cannot survive this process of purification or negation of all imperfection and limitation in its meaning without

> some part of its very *meaning* being cancelled out does not possess
> enough analogical "stretch" to allow its predication of God
> (*Philosophical Approach*, 56).

Rather than losing meaning during the stretch procedure, successful candidates for analogical predication of God will actually intensify their meaning when applied to God. Their positive meaning is neither as rigid as univocation nor as arbitrary as equivocation. Analogous terms are partly determinate in meaning, so as to avoid being empty, and partly indeterminate in application, so as to be capable of some stretch and transcendence of context. In fact, they must be flexible enough to transcend all particular modes of their finite expression, even enabling us to predicate them of God in the mode of infinite plenitude. The higher the level of being under discussion, the more intensive the meaning of the analogical predicate.

Aquinas, appropriating an argument from Alexander of Hales, addresses this issue by distinguishing between the way of signifying (*modus significandi*) and the thing signified (*res significata*). The way of signifying, which is based on the order of knowing, is differentiated from the order of being and yet related to the order of being through divine causality. The end result is something like a conceptual bidirectionality:

> From the point of view of what the word means it is used primarily
> of God and derivatively of creatures, for what the word means--the
> perfection it signifies--flows from God to the creature. But from the
> point of view of our use of the word we apply it first to creatures
> because we know them first. That . . . is why it has a way of
> signifying that is appropriate to creatures (*ST* I.13.6).

In one sense, Aquinas is combining his preference for an Aristotelian epistemology 'from below' with a Platonic epistemology 'from above'. The *modus significandi/res significata* distinction recognizes the human location and terminology drawn from the world of sense, but it leverages such human meanings because it is a *created* world of sense. So while human beings first encounter such qualities as goodness and wisdom in the manifold interactions of human life, upon theological reflection, we know that God the Creator does not just cause these perfections to exist in us, but that God also possesses (Aquinas would say that God *is* the given perfection) them without blemish to an infinite degree. As the mind moves from its human encounter with say, goodness, it is led to contemplate the divine source and fulfillment of goodness, and in so doing, to intensify the human realization of goodness. Hence, the *modus/res* distinction is another way of explicating the analogy of causal participation.

While the final selection of analogical predicates comes down to a "delicate judgment" meeting the existential demands of "a particular historical culture" (*Philosophical Approach*, 56-57), there are two basic kinds of analogical terms and attributes--those with "absolutely transcendental properties" and those with "relatively transcendental properties":

> 1) those attributes whose meaning is so closely linked with the meaning and intelligibility of being itself that no real being is conceivable which could lack them and still remain intelligible--i.e., the so-called *absolutely transcendental properties* of being, such as unity, activity, goodness, and power--and

> 2) the *relatively transcendental properties* of being, which are so purely positive in meaning and so demanding of our unqualified value-approval that, even though they are not co-extensive with all being, any being higher than the level at which they first appear must be judged to possess them--hence *a fortiori* the highest being--under pain of being less perfect than the being we already know, particularly ourselves: such are knowledge . . . love, joy, freedom, and personality, at least as understood in Western cultures (*Philosophical Approach*, 57).

Specific judgments must still be made about whether *this* is good, *this* is true, *this* is love.   But in contrast to "inhumanly narrow" epistemologies, the analogy of causal participation is developed as a "positive signpost" on the human journey (*Philosophical Approach*, 60).[3] Once analogy has expressed the likenesses between Creator and creature and perhaps pointed us along our way, it has performed the most that one can ask of a philosophical knowledge of God. Judgment must still bridge between the known and the unknown, the certain and the probable, the actual and the hoped for realization of greater actuality.

'PERSON' AS PRIMARY ANALOGATE

In his reappropriation of Aquinas, Clarke engages Kant, the "linguistic turn," process thought, and even his own tradition with the vision of God and humankind as persons. The meaning and purpose of there being a world at all is tied into the giftedness of created being and its appreciation by persons. The most fundamental perfection of the universe is existence, and the most positive existence is personal existence. Thus Clarke asks:

> What could possibly be the point of a created universe entirely plunged in the darkness of unconsciousness, unable to know or appreciate that it is there at all?

---

[3]Clarke's protest against "inhumanly narrow" epistemologies bears another strong similarity to themes of Michael Polanyi in *Personal Knowledge*.

. . . Mind and love are at the root of all being. The person is
ultimately the key to why there is anything at all and not rather
nothing.[4]

Drawing from a variety of sources, both medieval and modern, Clarke

moves from the notion of person to the *interpersonal*: "There is no 'I'

without a 'Thou,' and hence a 'We.'"[5]

The refusal of certain traditions of thought to take into account a

vision of the personal "stems partly from a failure to pursue far enough

the analysis of analogy."[6] Clarke's exploration of the personal and

relational, and his linkage of the personal to analogy, allows him to

respond to the process challenge and show Neo-Thomist thought to be

something other than a "metaphysical iceberg."[7] His response to

process thought calls for a new "framework-decision," which would

address the problems of our time by emphasizing the relatedness of God

to creatures through the metaphysics of the person. The primary

framework thus shifts

from the physical and biological world, which was the prime
analogate of metaphysical concepts for Aristotle and St. Thomas
following him (although significant expansion has already begun in
the latter), to the order of the person and interpersonal relations as the
prime analogates.[8]

This proposed shift has important epistemological and metaphysical

consequences for analogy.

---

[4]Clarke, *Journey*, 80-81.

[5]Ibid., 81.

[6]Ibid., 79.

[7]Clarke, "A New Look at the Immutability of God," 45.

[8]Clarke, *Philosophical Approach*, 91.

EPISTEMOLOGICAL CONSEQUENCES
OF PERSONS IN RELATION

In "Interpersonal Dialogue: Key to Realism," Clarke ties together the
Neo-Thomist emphasis on action as the self-communication of being
with the phenomenology of interpersonal dialogue. This undertaking is
an extended polemic against Kant and a justification of the Thomistic
epistemology of action. Due to his shift to the person in relationship,
Clarke is forced to relinquish some standard terminology of traditional
Thomism; but he does strengthen the notion of *actus* (action) by
connecting it with interpersonal dialogue.

Over against the Kantian view that the mind imposes form on
incoming data, Clarke's thesis is that successful interpersonal dialogue
proves the *reception* of patterns or forms in the mind. From the
prepackaged patterns of intelligibility coming to the mind, Clarke
extends the argument to relations with the material world. By contrast,
in the Kantian system's interaction of world and human, "man alone in
such a 'dialogue' does all the talking--if only the inner talking of
thinking. The world cannot answer back directly if man interprets to
himself incorrectly."[9]   Now while Clarke does not think that Kant's
view holds even in the case of interaction between the human agent and
the non-personal world, he believes the Kantian view to be untenable in
the light of personal dialogue:

> When I listen to someone else speaking to me, answering my
> question, I am not imposing my own *a priori* formal patterns on the
> raw material of sound coming from him, structuring it any way I wish
> (or any way my immanent nature demands). His message comes to
> me precisely *as a message*, already prestructured by the sender into

---

[9]Clarke, "Interpersonal Dialogue: Key to Realism," in *Person and Community*,
ed. Robert J. Roth, S.J. (New York: Fordham University Press, 1975), 145.

an intelligible, meaningful pattern incarnated in the material medium of sound--a message which I must receive and understand substantially as it already is in the minds and words of the *other real person* if I am to carry on a successful dialogue at all. The whole point here is that to receive a meaningful message in human language is to receive an already structured, formal, and intelligible pattern from a real source outside of me, and already pre-existing in this other. This means that my cognitive faculties are in principle and in fact capable--given the appropriate conditions--of *receiving* already constituted formal structures from the outside basically as they pre-exist independently of my own cognitive activity, and not merely capable of imposing my own forms on amorphous raw data. A similar conclusion could be drawn from an analysis of the even more basic phenomenon of learning an already constituted language from an already established community into which I come. The essence of any communication situation is that two or more real participants share-- communicate and receive--substantially the *same* formal message (despite the always present but more or less minor, non-essential, distortion of "noise" in the system).[10]

Clarke limits his claim to a "'moderate' realism and not an exaggerated or pure picture-copy type." He realizes that "noise" in the system, such things as presuppositions, prejudices, fears, etc., always attaches a certain amount of personal interpretation to what is received. His point is the limited but important one that "*substantially the same message*" must be received in spite of mitigating factors, or "there is simply no meaningful *communication* at all; hence no genuine dialogue."[11] Clarke illustrates this contention by saying that regardless of the emotional and other accompaniments, when someone tells you "There is a fire in your garage," you hear something like, "fire-in-garage," and not "flood-in-kitchen." Furthermore, if you did incorrectly

---

[10]Clarke, "Interpersonal Dialogue," 146.

[11]Ibid., 147.

hear "flood-in-kitchen," interpersonal dialogue could correct such a faulty reception.

Once we determine that we do in fact receive formed messages from other persons, there is nothing to stop us from receiving some sort of pre-existent formal structure from non-personal sources. In any case, we must at least have the equipment to do so. Remembering our above understanding of being-as-action, Clarke's reiterated definition now has renewed force: "All action, as structured and determinate, must to some significant degree be a communication system, conveying something of the active agent to the at least partially passive recipient."[12] The case for moderate realism does not need a one-to-one correspondence, only a "fixed determinate correlation" between what is sent and what is received.[13]

How does all this work to strengthen arguments for analogy? First and foremost, it supports the fundamental thesis of causal participation by strengthening the account of action-as-communication which acts as a metaphysical support for analogical predication. Hence Clarke's repeated claim: "All knowledge of the real is an interpretation of action, either of myself as acting or of myself as being acted on, plus the implications thereof.[14] Upon this moderate surety rests the confidence to undertake any valid communication. And this moderate realism is something like the moderate realism of analogy, which claims to be more than equivocation but less than univocity.

---

[12]Clarke, "Interpersonal Dialogue," 150.

[13]Ibid., 151.

[14]Ibid., 153, n. 2.

METAPHYSICAL CONSEQUENCES
OF THE SHIFT TO PERSON

Some consequences of Clarke's framework shift to the person in relations do not have a direct bearing on analogy and so fall outside the scope of this present study; however, other consequences of the person as the basic analogate create an overlapping space with the otherwise very different account of Eberhard Jüngel. As we shall see in our concluding chapter, whatever compatibility may exist between them will be in terms of arrival and not in the method of getting there. Still, as Michael Polanyi has pointed out, making a move in the right direction often opens up unexpected positive effects; and this is what I believe Clarke's move to the person as the best paradigm for analogy to have accomplished.[15]

In his engagement with process philosophy and existential religious thought, Clarke set himself the task of exploring Thomism's metaphysical resources, asking: "How far it is capable of making a place for a God who can enter into truly personal relations with His creatures?"[16] The problem stems from the traditional insistence upon divine immutability, as a result of which God can have no "real relations," i.e., necessary relations, in the technical, Aristotelian sense which Aquinas adopts. Even though he shows a way to defend the traditional Thomistic terminology and thinking, Clarke eventually declares:

> The price of doing so has become so high, and the returns so diminishing, that I think it is wiser strategy for the Thomistic

---

[15]See Polanyi, *Personal Knowledge*, 310-11.

[16]Clarke, "A New Look at the Immutability of God," 45.

metaphysician today to shift frameworks and simply drop this doctrine.[17]

In applying the received Aristotelian doctrine to God, any change in God would imply that God's being before the change could be brought to a higher level, hence the traditional insistence upon immutability. However, neither the Aristotelian Prime Mover nor the Neoplatonic One adequately suits the job description of the Judeo-Christian God. Most notably, problems are generated because "the model of being as object rather than subject" leads to

> the self-absorbed, unrelated self-contemplation of the Aristotelian Prime Mover or the Neoplatonic One (the latter above all otherness even in its knowledge, since this would imply real duality). Such a notion of immutability simply does not fit our new sensitivity of the meaning of being as interpersonal, with its exigency of mutual relatedness and reciprocity--a notion which is itself perhaps largely the result of the "good news" of the revelation of the Judaeo-Christian God of love.[18]

Recognizing the foreign nature of these historical sources, Clarke can more easily jettison that aspect of traditional Thomism en route to higher metaphysical ground.

The engagement with process and existentialist thought does not just remove parts of traditional Thomism in Clarke's account of analogy; for by primarily focusing on person, several gains of clarification are accomplished, the most important of which is the emphasis that God is love. Clarke considers the person a prime example of a crucial tenet of Aquinas' thought which is not explicitly declared to be a central doctrine. He contends:

---

[17]Clarke, *Philosophical Approach,* 90.

[18]Clarke, "Immutability," 66.

The human person can be taken as the primary model or analogue for us of all the basic metaphysical concepts, such as unity, activity, efficient causality, act and potency, etc.--the privileged vantage point from which we know *from within* what each concept stands for and from which we extend it by analogy both below and above us.[19]

Clarke's move to the person is hardly just a modern sensibility. As Aquinas stated: "Person signifies that which is most perfect in all nature" (*ST* I.29.3). The rationale for the analogous understanding of God as person had been worked out earlier in the development of analogy in *ST* I.13.6:

Names [of perfections] are applied to God not as the cause only, but also essentially. For the words, *God is good,* or *wise,* signify not only that He is the cause of wisdom or goodness, but that these exist in Him in a more excellent way. Hence as regards what the name signifies, these names are applied primarily to God rather than to creatures, because these perfections flow from God to creatures; but as regards the imposition of the names, they are primarily applied by us to creatures which we know first.

Aquinas applies this same analogical argument regarding the human and the divine persons: what humans possess as "most perfect in all nature," God possesses also, "but in a more excellent way" (*ST* I.29.4). This application of person to God again demonstrates how Aquinas uses analogy; for once one sees the metaphysical basis of a given perfection found in finite creatures, one can carefully, moderately, *analogically*, predicate that perfection of its divine Source.

Additional gains derive from reconsidering the immutability of God (an attribute which Jüngel, in agreement with process thinkers on this point, will strongly attack below). Facing the question of immutability, Clarke first places the issue in context. For it is the divine perfection which is paramount; immutability is a corollary of perfection,

---

[19]Clarke, "Most and Least Relevant," 425.

not vice versa. Hence he can nuance the notion of divine immutability in order to protect the more important claim of Infinite Plenitude of Perfection. The issue only arises because God's ability to experience real joy, love, and perhaps even sorrow in relations of real mutuality with creatures is called into question by some understandings of immutability. The traditional, technical Thomist positions of divine immutability and "real relations," i.e., creatures are related to God but not God to creatures, seem to block the affirmation of mutuality.

To these substantive criticisms Clarke responds that once we accept the importance of the personal, then the positive infinity of God would require that "the field of His loving consciousness should be contingently other because of His personal relations to us."[20] In other words, perfection demands a certain kind of change as the created finite changes. The "metaphysical iceberg" God would not be perfection at all. The change in God which Clarke conceives is in the divine consciousness and intentionality (*esse intentionale*), not in the intrinsic being of God. An important distinction is thus made in modes of being: first, the natural being of a person or object (*esse in re, esse naturale*); second, the being which exists as a cognitive object in the consciousness of the other, whether it be intended, known, or willed (*esse intentionale, esse cognitum, esse volitum*).[21]

If these two orders of being are not distinguished, then two absurdities result. First, in order to know something like a real fire outside of me, there would also have to be a real fire inside my consciousness. Second, if the knowledge within my consciousness were

---

[20]Clarke, "Immutability," 48.

[21]Ibid., 53.

the *esse in re* of the object, then my knowledge would no longer be of the real object outside of me, but would constitute a second real object within me. This state of affairs would destroy the whole point of knowledge, "which is precisely not to create a second real world in duplication of the first, but to know one and the same identical real world already existing."[22]

All this amounts to something of a pretty good defense of the traditional Thomist position; however, once he has shown how the system could answer the objections, Clarke criticizes the Thomist tradition's handling of the problem for its insensitivity to contemporary needs of religious belief and practice. It is not that the Thomist position on this point is wrong, just that it is now "aesthetically inadequate." Reiterating his affirmation that God is truly related to us, Clarke adds, "What is important should be termed 'real,' and what is most important, 'most real.'"[23] This crucial realm of the divine-creature relation should not go unsaid in order to maintain the technical correctness of Thomism:

> Metaphysical discourse is not a timeless essence but an on-going, historically rooted process; and when the metaphysician realizes he has reached a certain threshold of diminishing returns in the rhetorical effectiveness of his discourse, he should be ready to cut his losses and shift to a new, more effective conceptual-linguistic framework.[24]

Another clarification is gained by questioning the personal relationship in the light of God's infinity. Can the Infinite be enriched by receiving finite joy, love, praise, etc.? Clarke's response is twofold, again being determined by the newness of creation and the divine response to the creature as person:

---

[22]Clarke, "Immutability," 53.

[23]Ibid., 58.

[24]Clarke, *Philosophical Approach*, 91.

> To add the finite to the infinite can only be in the mode of a sharing,
> an overflow, an expression of the plenitude which is already infinite.
> There is genuine novelty, to be sure, both in the real being God
> communicates to creatures and in the intentional content of His
> consciousness determinately knowing and willing them. But this is not
> change in His own intrinsic being or perfection.[25]

Clarke's metaphysical hunch that the finite can be added to the
infinite, but that this never brings about a state higher than the original
Source, squares quite well with Georg Cantor's now widely accepted
mathematical investigations of infinity. Working in the late nineteenth
century, Cantor proved that an infinite set is not enlarged by the addition
of any finite; nor is the infinite lessened by the subtraction of a finite.[26]
While apparently unaware of Cantor's findings, Clarke evinces some
similarity to the mathematical while pursuing qualitative, metaphysical
investigations: "The old correlation, *infinite = no enrichment whatsoever*,
is too simplistic and not suited to the unique characteristics of personal
being as truly loving."[27]   Through the maintenance of infinity
regardless of addition or subtraction, Cantor's mathematical argument
obviates the either/or question for metaphysics: either infinite, or truly
related to the finite, but not both.   What Clarke has defended by
drawing from the well of "intentional consciousness," mathematics
likewise confirms.   The infinite can relate to the finite without
imperiling intrinsic infinity. The *Ipsum Esse Subsistens*, as an Infinite
Plenitude, can create a contingent finite universe, care for, love and be

---

[25]Clarke, "Immutability," 49.

[26]See Georg Cantor, *Contributions to the Founding of the Theory of Transfinite Numbers*, trans., Philip E. B. Jourdain (New York: Dover Publications, 1915).

[27]Clarke, *Philosophical Approach*, 97.

mutually related to creatures, and still be an Infinite Plenitude. Thus Clarke stresses the inner qualitative intensity of the divine infinity:

> The infinite, contrary to an all too common misunderstanding, does not exclude all other being than itself, as though it were a single motionless block already including in itself actually all possible real being. It excludes not other beings, but only a *higher level* of being, of intensive qualitative perfection, than itself.[28]

Thus the character of God can be personally immutable while enjoying relational mutability.

The possibility of analogical predication about God is wrapped up in this relation of finite to Infinite Plenitude. Without a participation metaphysics, God's infinity is in danger of becoming an empty, abstract concept which only serves to make such a God infinitely distant from the creature. However, if the finite is a participant in *created* being, then this mediated relation to the divine being, *Ipsum Esse Subsistens*, allows a moderate epistemology of the real and a moderated speech about divine perfections encountered through creation--i.e., analogy. In this relationship, God does not become finite because God loves a finite being; nor do we become infinite because we love an Infinite God.

The finite may speak of God through the mode of analogy because in our created being derived from the divine Source, we reflect the nature of the Creator. The "law of the innate generosity of being" is differentially but consistently manifested in both the trinitarian being of God and the derived being of the creature:

> It is the very nature of the Divine Being, in the person of the Father, to generate within himself a perfect image or expression of himself which we call the Son (as generated according to the same nature) and the Word (as a self-knowing of the Father). The Son possesses the identical nature of the Father, the only difference being that the Father possesses the divine nature as origin, as giver, where the Son

---

[28]Clarke, *Philosophical Approach*, 98.

possesses it as receiver, as gift. Then the Father and the Son together "spirate" or "breathe forth" the Holy Spirit as the self-expression of their mutual love, subsistent love possessing the identical divine nature of Father and Son. Thus it is the very nature of Infinite Being, the supreme perfection and fullness of being itself, to pour over into two immensely rich, *real*, personal self-communications within the unity of its one nature. Therefore, the fullness of being demands of its very nature as being that it be self-communicative. It is contrary to the very nature of being to remain alone, isolated, unshared.[29]

Human beings, understood as the image of God, as participants within created being, are created to imitate the divine way. The law of being, derived from its trinitarian Source, is to pour over to others in self-communication, in sharing of the self. If this innate communitarian drive of being is resisted, the "hold on being itself becomes precarious. Strangely, the more we give ourselves away to others, the more we can hold on to ourselves, and vice versa. Such is the law of the innate generosity of being."[30]

In sum, what Clarke and the general sweep of Neo-Thomist thought have done through philosophical investigation is to elicit knowledge of the character of the Creator through investigating the character of being derived from this divine Source. And this most recent trend in Neo-Thomist studies is in keeping with Aquinas' view that since "nature is the prelude to grace," one of the tasks of philosophy, in the service of Christian theology, is "to declare analogies common to nature and grace."[31]

---

[29]Clarke, "To Be Is To Be Self-Communicative: St. Thomas' View of Personal Being," 448-49.

[30]Ibid. Cf. Mk. 8:35: "For whoever would save his life will lose it; and whoever loses his life for my sake and the gospel's will save it."

[31]Exposition *de Trinitate*, II.3, as cited in *Theological Texts*, 7-8.

PART TWO

DAVID BURRELL'S GRAMMATICAL INQUIRY

INTRODUCTION TO PART TWO

David Burrell's three books dealing with Aquinas and analogy span a period of thirteen years and instantiate one of his own guiding principles: the philosophical demand upon the inquirer of on-going commitment and judgment. While drawing freely from many sources, Burrell's greatest philosophical debt is to Ludwig Wittgenstein:

> For the guide throughout will be Wittgenstein, whose manner requires us to become more and more aware of what it is we are after, of how we are undertaking it, and of how little we can say of what it accomplishes for us and in us.[1]

Yet Burrell would still fit Clarke's definition of a Neo-Thomist:

> That loosely but recognizably united group of thinkers who acknowledge that the basic inspiration and structure of their thought derives from St. Thomas Aquinas, even though each one may have made various creative adaptations of his own, in both method and content, inspired by various movements of thought since the times of St. Thomas.[2]

Approaching Aquinas through the "linguistic turn,"[3] Burrell couples the

---

[1]David Burrell, C.S.C., *Analogy and Philosophical Language* (New Haven and London: Yale University Press, 1973), 5.

[2]Clarke, *Philosophical Approach*, 11.

[3]The term is originally from Richard Rorty, "The Subjectivist Principle and the Linguistic Turn," ed. George Kline in *Alfred North Whitehead: Essays on His*

medieval and the modern in the hope of generating new insights. In this manner his work exemplifies the pattern of Neo-Thomist renewal--it takes a seminal thinker or movement of thought from the contemporary period and examines whether relating it to Aquinas can bear additional fruit. In the first three chapters of this part, I shall try to display the considerable élan with which Burrell adapts Aquinas and his historical sources en route to elucidating analogy. Most of my criticism will be reserved for Chapter Seven, the last chapter of Part Two.

Burrell's three books address different aspects of Aquinas and analogy, but they share the common project of attempting a *manuductio*, a progressive "leading by the hand," which Clarke likewise found thematic in Aquinas. In the hope of recreating Burrell's *manuductio*, I shall take a chronological approach to the three works; for the first study is more general while the following ones are more specific applications and continuations of the originally announced project.[4] While the general direction of his inquiry remains constant, Burrell makes some important adjustments as he proceeds, particularly in clarifying Aquinas' position (and his own) through a reconstructed, ecumenical dialogue with Ibn-Sina and Maimonides in his third study.

Where Clarke has attempted explanatory metaphysics in reappropriating Aquinas, Burrell will follow Wittgenstein and attempt to let close attention to grammar say what can be said, more or less limiting himself to descriptive metaphysics. *Analogy and Philosophical Language* asks about how we normally use language, especially

---

Philosophy (Englewood Cliffs, N.J., 1963), 134-57.

[4]Burrell's second book is *Aquinas: God and Action* (Notre Dame, IN: University of Notre Dame Press, 1979); the third is *Knowing the Unknowable God: Ibn-Sina, Maimonides, Aquinas* (Notre Dame, IN: University of Notre Dame Press, 1986).

analogous terms, with the hope of shedding some light upon the more extended theological use of analogical terms. Burrell's exposition of how analogical terms are chosen and used will share some of Clarke's views and complement others; however, in his first work, Burrell's allegiance to Wittgenstein will restrain him from talk of 'being' and lead him to quite different conclusions about the nature of language.

Aquinas: God and Action elucidates the grammar of Questions 3-11 in the *Summa Theologiae* and then tests its conclusions against some modern objections, notably, process thought's claims about God's relation to the world.[5] *Knowing the Unknowable God* is undertaken in the dialogical spirit of Vatican II and respectfully differentiates Aquinas' position from his medieval "conversation partners," Ibn-Sina (Avicenna) and Maimonides. In this work, Burrell is forced to show where Aquinas went beyond his Muslim and Jewish counterparts in specifying *positive* attributes of God. Because Burrell's earlier accounts of Aquinas are so strongly apophatic, this dialogical clarification will play a key role, particularly in looking ahead to Jüngel's polemic against negative theology.

---

[5]Both Clarke and Burrell engage process thought's challenge to Neo-Thomism. My interest is not to compare Neo-Thomist and process thought. The importance for this study is that Jüngel, while not a process theologian, will address some of the same questions raised in the Neo-Thomist/process debate. Lacking a direct engagement of Clarke and Burrell with Jüngel himself, the engagement with process thought provides at least some field of comparison.

CHAPTER FOUR

ANALOGY, INQUIRY, AND JUDGMENT

In his first major work on analogy, *Analogy and Philosophical Language*, Burrell tries to distance himself from "the excessively intramural cast" and the "endless intramural discussions" that he attributes to traditional Thomism.[1] His hope is "to liberate the entire discussion from the confinement of a particular school and articulate a more catholic interest" (*APL*, 9). The strategic plan is twofold: first, to expose the inadequacy of traditional, formal accounts of analogy, especially those based on the analogy of proportionality; then, in lieu of a *theory* about analogy, establish his own thesis that paying close grammatical attention to the way analogous terms are actually *used* will demonstrate the freedom, fluidity, responsibility, and judgment actually involved in such usage. Using analogous terms reveals something about the human situation:

---

[1]Burrell, *Analogy and Philosophical Language*, 9,171. Within the rest of this chapter, further references to this work will be cited parenthetically as *APL*.

> If language is bound up with consciousness, and consciousness with
> some self-correcting feature, expressions of this sort will prove
> indispensable, for they reflect into language itself the reflective
> awareness which a responsible use of language demands (*APL*, 168).

As he engages a host of writers, ancient and modern, philosophical and
theological, "the self-correcting feature" winds through his
conversational engagements and is set against the woodenness of
foundational theories. In historical exegeses of Plato, Aristotle,
Aquinas, Scotus, and Ockham, Burrell discovers the same two-edged
sword: these classical writers were at their greatest when explicating
"the self-correcting feature" of engaged dialogue; and conversely, the
least helpful and even illusory work was produced, most notably in
Scotus and the Cajetanian interpretation of Aquinas, in the attempt to
reach closure by theory-building.

SHOWING THE LIMITS OF FORMAL SCHEMES

Burrell, like Clarke and Klubertanz, finds the analogy of
proportionality (a:b :: c:d) to be inadequate; but Burrell's dissatisfaction
arises from his unique concerns and is pursuant to a different purpose.
According to Burrell, not just proportionality, but any formal scheme
promises more than it can deliver and then covers its shortcomings with
various sleight-of-hand arguments such as "insight" or "intuition."
Chasing down the logic of such arguments, Burrell contends:

> There can be no "content" common to the various uses because any
> phrase that might substitute for 'good' contains analogous terms itself.
> What is common then can only be the *schema*, and schemata are

designedly "empty of content," reflecting only what can remain invariant from one context to another, the formal properties of logic.[2] Thus Burrell dismisses formal, logical schemes because they just do not tell us very much. Believing that such formal approaches do not uncover what is really going on in analogical usage, Burrell hopes that his Wittgensteinian focus on *use* will reveal something that formal accounts inevitably miss.

Burrell employs John Duns Scotus as another type of "antiwitness" (*APL*, x) because Scotus takes the common-sense position that analogy essentially reduces to a univocal core of common meaning.[3] Burrell's

---

[2]Burrell is specifically commenting upon I. M. Bochenski, "On Analogy," *Thomist* 11 (1948): 424-47. Bochenski was additionally the translator of Cajetan's *De Analogia Nominum*.

[3]This position has continued to attract prominent thinkers over the centuries. In our own century, Wolfhart Pannenberg has taken a position similar to Scotus'. See Wolfhart Pannenberg, "Analogy and Doxology," in *Basic Questions in Theology*, Collected Essays, vol.1, trans. George H. Kehm (Philadelphia: Fortress Press, 1970), 212-238. For an analysis of Pannenberg's views on analogy, see Elizabeth Johnson, C.S.J., "The Right Way to Speak about God?: Pannenberg on Analogy," *Theological Studies* 43 (December, 1982): 673-92.

Of particular interest is the fact that Pannenberg has not published his *Habilitationsschrift* (inaugural dissertation), because he apparently feels some dissatisfaction with his "solution to the question of how the relation between the problem of history (and thereby of revelation) and the problem of analogy may or may not be resolved" (Johnson, "The Right Way To Speak about God?" 688). By contrast, Burrell contends: "Those who can dispense with history must demand a clear, univocal sense for each expression, while those sensitive to historical shifts in meaning can appreciate the need for analogical uses" (*Knowing the Unknowable God*, 113). Given Pannenberg's focus on history, I find his hesitation on this point revealing.

Richard Swinburne has also advocated a position more in line with Duns Scotus than Aquinas in *The Coherence of Theism* (Oxford: Clarendon Press, 1977), 50-84. While the differences between what is claimed for analogy and what is claimed for univocity are subtle, I think that Swinburne has failed to see that by allowing that analogical use "results from loosening up the syntactic and semantic

basic historical analysis is that Aristotle translated "as much of Plato as he could into common-sense parlance," and Scotus did much the same for (or, more unkindly, "to"), Aristotle (*APL*, 98). Evidently reacting to what he thought was a latent agnosticism in Aquinas, Scotus developed his doctrine of the univocity of being:

> If the same word names (or signifies) different things, then it must do so by a feature they hold in common. Analogical usage, then, must ultimately reduce to a solid univocal core of meaning as its justification.[4]

Burrell sees Scotus' reading of Aristotle as dubious (*APL*, 99-100), sees his understanding of analogy as more informed by Henry of Ghent and Avicenna than by Aquinas (*APL*, 96-97), and implies that Scotus' introduction of "intrinsic modes" to explicate the difference in being between God and creatures inadequately resolves the problem that being does not designate a genus (*APL*, 101).

The emptiness of the formal proportionality schema on the one hand and the problematic nature of Scotus' common "core of meaning" on the other are used to set up Burrell's thesis. These two foils for his argument function a great deal like the two problems which Aquinas wanted to avoid--equivocation and univocation. Certainly, one of the central points of *ST* I.13.5 is that nothing can be said univocally of God and creatures; but neither are we merely equivocating when we speak of God. Aquinas' solution, analogy, takes a median location, avoiding the two extremes. So in an important sense, the task of explicating analogy amounts to elucidating this median position of predication, one that is fitting to the median position of the human situation, a situation in which

---

rules" (ibid., 84), he has arrived at the same realization which originally led Aquinas to deny that univocal speech about God is possible (*ST* I.13.5).

[4]Oxon, d8, q3, n27; IX 626b, as cited in Burrell, *APL*, 109.

we evidently know something, but one in which we also find ourselves epistemologically and morally limited. While we must reject the equivocation extreme in order to have our thoughts and words retain any significance at all, the question is greatly sharpened when we reject Scotus' univocal core of meaning. What does it mean to reject Scotus' univocal position and affirm *analogous* usage? If there is no common core of meaning in analogy, then how might we go about explaining analogy at all? Perhaps Burrell's most important contribution is that he shows a way to do so.

THE GRAMMAR OF ANALOGY

In many respects, Burrell's first treatise on analogy is a development of the median position of humanity. Thus he sees analogy as "the project of putting ambiguities to work," and not as

> a doctrine or a canonized set of procedures. Harnessing ambiguities to systematic service requires a skill and a know-how that can be acquired only within a particular domain of discourse. Yet the very fruitfulness of the enterprise invites an investigation sensitive to the myriad ways we shape and use our language, while on the lookout for enough similarity to warrant the common name (*APL*, 11).

Burrell's thesis is that analogy and the purposive use of language are closely interrelated. As such, his investigation of analogy becomes a meta-investigation of human language, and through language, of human life. As for the problem of how analogical terms may be extended to God, Burrell adopts a working hypothesis:

> Should a certain class of terms prove indispensable to language, the characteristics they exhibit would be considered indigenous to the linguistic enterprise. Metaphysical or theological discourse would then show itself to be a quite natural development of ordinary usage. Whatever peculiarities might be exhibited in these remote areas would

already have been adumbrated in the "ordinary" behavior of the terms
employed there. We would then be asked not so much to justify the
move to a metaphysical order as to show, by a collation of ordinary
uses embodying the same expressions, that there is hardly a "move"
at all. If much of our ordinary usage is already quite "extended," it
becomes superfluous to seek a justification of extended usage
generally (*APL*, 21-22).

Keeping this strategy in mind, we can proceed to Burrell's analysis of
how analogy actually functions.

Burrell focuses upon the venerable class of analogous terms
known as transcendentals, among which he includes: 'one', 'same',
'good', and 'true'.[5] Just as Clarke pointed out above, Burrell also
observes that these terms are resistant to definition and exhibit a
"propensity to employment in diverse contexts" (*APL*, 23). In contrast,
merely 'general' terms may share a certain vagueness and "open
texture," but they do not possess the contextual flexibility which
analogous terms have. Forcing general terms to work outside their
native context gives rise to metaphor, not analogy (ibid.). The shared
vagueness of general and analogous terms helps to undermine the quest
for a common definition, since a rigid core of meaning would prove
Scotus' contention that analogy is at root univocal.

Unlike Scotus, who accepts a univocal core of meaning in
transcendentals, Clarke and Aquinas nuance the problem of universals
by reference to divine intention to share a one with a many. Burrell
takes another approach and addresses the issue through *human* intent:

What *is* common to these diverse yet not unrelated uses seems to lie
more on the side of intent. And this is related to the essential
difference between generic and analogous usage: the *need* to use

---

[5]Significantly, Burrell's lists of transcendentals usually omit 'being', where
Clarke and most other Neo-Thomists would list it as the primary instance of a
transcendental.

certain expressions in widely diverse contexts, coupled with the fact
that we do so use them and use them freely (ibid.).

In terms of his material argument, the exploration of 'intent', both human and divine, is central to all three of Burrell's books. But the question that seems to be driving this first study is: Why do we insist upon using these terms which we cannot define? And, if we cannot define them, what can we discover about ourselves from looking at how we use them? Once again, the question about analogy has become a question about anthropology.

In addition to the transcendentals, Burrell identifies another set of terms with similar usage--appraisal or evaluation terms. These include such words as 'just', 'fruitful', and 'genuine'. While he declares that "it would be misleading to say that I am seeking to explain analogous usage on the model of evaluative terms" (*APL*, 209), Burrell comes very close to doing so:

> The leading edge of my historical analysis of key figures, as well as
> many other attempts to elucidate analogous discourse, keeps turning
> up affinities with evaluative language. It seems quite clear that all
> terms of evaluation are analogous; it is not certain whether every term
> we should want to use analogously would be playing an evaluative
> role as well (ibid.).

He then notes that no one has yet succeeded in finding "nonevaluative" examples. What he wants us to see is that both analogous and appraisal terms "display important structural similarities, and the discovery that language is freighted with evaluative expressions seems not unrelated to recognizing the ubiquity of analogous terms in our discourse" (ibid.). True to his methodological promise, he follows Wittgenstein and *looks* at what we say and how we say it when language is doing the everyday job which it does rather well. And Burrell's close look at what is going on in language leads him to reconsider the nature of language and some of its most important categories.

THE METAPHORICAL NATURE OF LANGUAGE

While Burrell allows that the natural manner in which analogy is employed transcontextually differentiates it from metaphor, he believes that analogy and metaphor share a great deal in common; and he contends that analogous terms, like all language, include a metaphorical component. An important part of Burrell's account of metaphor could virtually be exchanged for his account of analogy:

> Metaphorical language . . . is a sign of the capacity for reflective discrimination which is bodied forth so explicitly in our use of analogous terms. Learning how to use metaphor with ever greater precision exercises that capacity (*APL*, 262).

Since there are few canons for the correct use of either metaphor or analogy, Burrell's insistence that both rely upon judgment creates the impression of even greater similarity (*APL*, 208).

Burrell claims that language is not an innocent description of the way the world really is, but instead, incorporates the Weltanschauung of the language user:

> The more we are led to recognize the ubiquity of metaphor in ordinary speech, the less plausible is the Renaissance account of its role as decorating a skeleton of expository prose or rational argument. In fact, the contrary seems to be the case: metaphor plays a unique and irreplaceable part in human discourse, from poetry to ordinary conversation to scientific models. Nor is this merely a thesis about language. For as the decorative theory reflected a world view--that of the Age of Reason--so does the contrary inherent theory.
>
> And the implications of the contrasting world views are extraordinarily far-reaching. The nub of the Renaissance theory about

metaphor was an assumption about the nature of the universe, and one shared in many ways by later-day positivism. Counting metaphor as a replaceable rhetorical device presumes that we must always be able, sooner or later, to hit upon a proper and unambiguous description. But this presumption reaches to the very structure of the world (*APL*, 257-258).

Burrell asserts that language is inherently metaphorical because of its inescapable uncertainty, an uncertainty which reflects the more original uncertainties, including the ethical and theological uncertainty, of the human situation.

THE REASSESSMENT OF UNIVOCATION

Developing Wittgenstein's insights from the *Investigations*, Burrell reassesses one of the fundamental categories which has historically framed the discussion of analogy--univocation. In fact, the very possibility of univocal usage is called into question because "evaluative terms function irreducibly at the heart of our language" (*APL*, 209). For what was previously assumed to have been univocation was shown by Wittgenstein and others to be context-dependent, subject to counterexamples, and vulnerable to "gray areas of application" (*APL*, 218). Without a fixed definition, allegedly univocal terms do not quite live up to the name. Hence Burrell wants us to become "sensitized to the latent metaphor" in the most generic expressions and presumedly univocal usage (*APL*, 23).[10] One impact of this observation is to

---

[10]Burrell does admit that the border between univocation and metaphor is crossed in both directions. Metaphorical usage, which normally begins by "crossing over" the meaning of a term to another term or context, often ends up settling down in ordinary usage to what amounts to virtual univocation. See *APL*, 221. This

dislocate and blur the univocal boundary line often cited to locate analogy, as in *ST* I.13.5. Given the ubiquity of "latent metaphor," Burrell concludes: "We dare not continue to claim a perfectly adequate division between univocal and analogous usage" (*APL*, 220). Instead, he proposes that "ordinary usage" replace the Aristotelian classification of univocal (*APL*, 220).

Burrell asserts that the overlapping relationships of language in actual use weaken the more imperious claims of analogy while strengthening his own thesis: "Analogous usage may not prove so privileged a feature of language as some have thought, but it remains a provoking one, especially in the way it intimates the capacity of men to judge and discriminate" (*APL*, 29). Again we see him carrying out the joint project of undermining formal analyses while exploring the "provoking" fact that analogy is used at all.

Community and evaluation. Preceding any individual's choice of expression, the community has already made many determinative decisions about evaluative terms. Within the community, meaning, use, evaluation and analogy are interrelated:

> Meaning may be described as use provided we recognize the interposition, indeed the prior presence of the community. Use, then cannot simply amount to the way *I* want to use an expression but represents the weight of community sanction. . . . For the kind of language we invoke in justifying different courses of action is evaluative in intent and analogous in structure.[11]

---

concession of Burrell's will be important for my later criticism of his conflation of metaphor and analogy.

[11]Burrell refers to two of Wilfred Sellars works: "Substance and Form in Aristotle," *Journal of Philosophy* 54 (1957): 694, n. 11; *Science, Perception,and*

Thus there is an unavoidable ethical implication in the way we use analogous and appraisal expressions, for invoking one of these terms positions the one who does so with regard to their context. Developing increasing linguistic skill in *using* these expressions partially depends upon the prior and generally recognized values of a community in a complex interaction with the individual's ethical intentions and judgments, an interaction displayed in analogous usage. For example, in order to say that a given policy of my church or nation is good (or perhaps not good), I must take a stand, enact a judgment, about what constitutes the good, as well as what constitutes the good for us--the good in our situation. Such judgments shape both the self and the community, the very community from which the first notions of what counts as good are learned.

JUDGMENT

The import of Burrell's particular objection to the analogy of proportionality should now be clear: the necessity of the agent's judgment[12] renders impossible a "mere schematic rule or pseudodefinition of an analogous term" (*APL*, 207). Given the absence of strict definitions, a great deal is at stake in the very use of an analogous term, both for the individual who uses it and for the community in which it is used. While judgment need not be illogical

---

Reality (London: Routledge and Kegan Paul, 1963), 38-40, 316; as cited in *APL*, 211.

[12]Burrell acknowledges (*APL*, 245, 251) that his thematic development of judgment is indebted to the various works of Bernard Lonergan and Etienne Gilson, *Christian Philosophy of St. Thomas* (New York, 1956).

or irrational, it possesses qualitative, evaluative factors which are not reducible to logic. Thus Burrell cites Gottlob Frege with favor: "A judgment is not merely the apprehension of a thought or proposition but the acknowledgement of its truth.[13] As the truth or falsity of a given position is acknowledged, analogy expresses commitment:

> Framing an assessment . . . requires that we take a stand. And if stands are taken *on* a spot, they must also be taken *in* terms which try to exhibit the quality of judgment shaping the assessment.
> More simply, we must appreciate that the taking of a stand itself will be an indispensable ingredient in any assessment (*APL*, 244).

The reasons we can offer for taking a given stand resemble elucidation more than syllogism and "will be framed in analogous terms" themselves (ibid.). Judgment appears to be the resilient factor which at one and the same time defies a formal, propositional account of analogy and gives us some little purchase, some "ability to monitor our use of analogous terms" (*APL*, 251). For we can track our judgments through their analogical expression; and we begin to see that the analogical expression of judgment functions at the deepest levels of our lives.

As an activity, judgment engages both intellect and will. New vistas are perceived when "reflection opens the category of the cognitive out beyond concept formation to judgment" (*APL*, 134). Through judgment, the cognitive is connected to the more than cognitive. Yet unlike Clarke and other Neo-Thomists, Burrell is unwilling to let the question expand to existence itself. Characteristically, he prefers to explore existence through its footprints in language:

> Closer attention to *willing* was implicit in [Aquinas'] decision to entertain seriously the question of the intelligibility of existence. For

---

[13]"On Sense and Nominatim," in *Readings in Philosophical Analysis*, ed. H. Feigle and W. Sellars (New York: 1949), n. 7, 91, as cited in *APL*, 204, n. 8.

once the issues are existential, something more than argument is involved. In fact, we can trace more precisely the manner in which inquiry is extended to existence itself by noting how the will makes its presence felt (*APL*, 141).

Analogous expression lets reason and will work in tandem, combining thought and aspirations which "invite (or compel) us to carry inquiry beyond its reasonable limits" (*APL*, 146). Recognizing that normal human language has already moved beyond reason

> suffices to open the way for a move to God. . . . The procedure itself intimates that whatever such a move may be, it will not be a proof. This is so not merely because no unobjectionable one has been proposed, but specifically because the language here is inextricably intertwined with that of willing--'fulfillment', 'aspiration', etc.--which renders the very notion of proof obscure. It follows, then, that an adequate description of the "move to God" will exhibit not only logical and analogical components but also involve dimensions of the person not patient of logical or semantic analysis (*APL*, 146).

Burrell's great insight is that the self-involving nature of this "move to God" is really no different than a great deal of what goes on in human life and language; and if such a move is licit in ordinary discourse, then at least methodologically, the move is licit in extending discourse to God. Otherwise, one would have to deny much of what we take human language and life to be.

Burrell is attempting to show how our actual use of language, especially the use of transcendentals and appraisal terms, points to rarefied regions which cannot be accessed by straight argumentation. On the other hand, he does not advocate a naked emotivism in which anyone might use analogous terms as they please. To avoid this latter danger, he invokes the notions of 'awareness' and 'responsibility' as part of the activity of judgment:

> We can . . . speak of someone's knowing how to dance a reel without being able to tell us how he does it. What is at issue . . . is a certain

level of awareness that cannot and need not be rendered explicit. In
a similar way, we can know what we want to explain, yet admit to
not having found the explanation as yet (*APL*, 156).

According to Burrell, we can test a judgment by our ability to recognize
inadequacies, whether they be of particular instances or of entire
frameworks of thought. Additionally, he sees some important but
admittedly imperfect monitoring of judgment obtained through the
presence of a community and through subjection to criticism within that
community:

> Only in responding to comment and criticism, in our ability to discern
> what is relevant, to refute or to incorporate, will we be able to show
> (and to know) *how* responsible a statement it was. This capacity to
> respond to criticism (our own or others) is the only measure we have
> of our awareness in making the original assertion (*APL*, 161).

Analogy incorporates an irreducible interplay of thought, freedom, and
responsibility. Therefore, we cannot render a strict account of analogy
without doing it conceptual violence. Because agential judgment is
expressed in analogous use, and because judgment is only exercised in
the face of competing possibilities, analogical use signals the arbitration
of "essentially contested concepts." Something so basic is being
exercised in invoking analogical terms that "no general method is
available for monitoring their proper use, yet ongoing inquiry can
discriminate among uses by helping us recognize one as more
appropriate than another."[14]

Here I think that Burrell has not adequately demonstrated how the
judgment involved in using analogous terms avoids becoming emotivism.
Where Burrell names judgment as "the ability to recognize one account

---

[14]W. B. Gallie, "Essentially Contested Concepts," *Pro. Aris. Soc.* 56, (1955-56,
reprinted in *Importance of Language*, ed. Max Black, Englewood Cliffs, NJ, 1962,
121-46), as cited in *APL*, 265, n. 2.

as preferable to another" (*APL*, 160), and where he convinces us that all strictly formal accounts will be inadequate, he does not say enough about the reality about which we seek to make judgments. As Burrell points out, responding to criticism is helpful, as is the presence of community. However, these suggestions do not go far enough. For why should we prefer one judgment over another? Why should we prefer one community's viewpoint over another? After all, judgments are sometimes made which call into question a community's basic presuppositions.

I think that Burrell's position can be clarified by Michael Polanyi's notion of "universal intent." In this notion the judgment of the individual agent is submitted to the universal status of that which the agent seeks to know:

> In those who exercise . . . judgment competently it is completely determined by their responsibility in respect to the situation confronting them. In so far as they are acting responsibly, their personal participation in drawing their own conclusions is completely compensated for by the fact that they are submitting to the universal status of the hidden reality which they are trying to approach. . . . Responsible action excludes randomness, even as it suppresses egocentric arbitrariness.[15]

Yet to be fair, Burrell has given us many of the components of Polanyi's argument: the taking of a stand; the demand for responsibility "above all" (*APL*, 244); and the requirement that a given thought be acknowledged as true. What Burrell has not done is to connect these components of judgment to the *universal*. Yet as I see it, judgment

---

[15]Polanyi, *Personal Knowledge*, 310. While Burrell does cites this work in support of another issue (*APL*, 156, n. 68), he does not make use of "universal intent" nor is he inclined to speak of a "hidden reality" towards which inquiry is directed and judgments are culminated. Here the restraining influence of Wittgenstein is at work.

enacts the universal in its particular affirmations. Each act of judgment is the cutting edge of self-involvement, participation in the reality of the universal which aspires toward ever greater participation. Judgment carries the human response to the possibilities of creation.

THE PARADIGM OF THE PERSON INQUIRING

One gets the sense of a certain restlessness in Burrell's understanding of analogy, as though confronting what is going on in analogous usage reflects the question back upon the one who asks it, and so tests the inquirer's courage to stay with the question.[16] Burrell's purpose is to inject greater flexibility into the discussion, to move beyond the doctrinal stiffness of a theory of analogy and into an exploration of analogical use. His anti-theory hopes to involve writer and reader themselves in ongoing inquiry, as in Wittgenstein's dictum: "Philosophy is not a body of doctrine but an activity."[17] Ironically, any good philosophical account must find a way to expose its own inadequacy. It can never be a question of just getting it right once and for all; rather, it is a question of continuing to move in the right direction, although one can certainly build upon one's gains. In this light Burrell cites Wittgenstein's remarks on selecting an appropriate metaphor:

> Often I might only say: "It simply isn't right yet." I am dissatisfied,
> I go on looking. At last a word comes: "That's it." *Sometimes* I can

---

[16]The influence of Lonergan can be seen in this 'turn to the subject'.

[17]Ludwig Wittgenstein, *Tractatus Logico-Philosophicus*, trans. D.F. Pears & B.F. McGuinness with an Introduction by Bertrand Russell (London: Routledge and Kegan Paul, 1961), 4.112, 25.

say why. This is simply what searching, this is what finding, is like here.[18]

Whatever truth can be known is more akin to a performance than to a theory. As such, truth, inquirer, and inquiry are bound together. Truth comes alive in its interrelationship with the inquirer, but this new life must be personally appropriated *in* the inquiry. The event of truth takes place as its meaning and value are discovered or revealed to the inquirer.[19] In this sense one could memorize theory but never truth.

PLATO'S INQUIRY

Burrell's readings of Plato and Aquinas adduce support for his notion that something happens in the process of inquiry itself which is not available elsewhere. He sees Plato's central contribution as showing that "a search for the ultimate goal of all inquiry is in reality a laying bare of the rational principles we find pervading inquiry itself" (*APL*, 65). This "laying bare" is not offered as a propositional truth claim. Its availability is *in* the inquiry itself, which Plato significantly leaves us in the form of *dialogues*, i.e., conversations. Furthermore, many of these dialogues end inconclusively (*Laches, Cratylus*, etc.), and they often express the virtual impossibility of a straightforward account. Perhaps the most significant of these is Socrates' insistence in the *Republic* that he cannot give an account of the good itself, only an account of the offspring of the good (506e). And Burrell reminds us

---

[18]Wittgenstein, *Philosophical Investigations* (Oxford, 1953), 218, as cited in *APL*, 28.

[19]In Part Three Jüngel will develop the event nature of truth christologically, 'from above'. Burrell develops the event nature of truth anthropologically, 'from below'.

that the offspring of the good is demonstrated by *analogies*. Especially
within the early dialogues, Socrates persistently demands of himself and
his conversation partner that they manifest complete fidelity to the
pursuit of the question, regardless of where that pursuit might lead them.
The method involves using all the logic and rationality at one's disposal
in the attempt "to break through to a new kind of account (*logos*)"
(*APL*, 46). Because this breakthrough cannot occur without the total
commitment of the inquirers, the Socratic indignation is most commonly
unleashed against those who refuse to accept responsibility for a position
which they have taken when once its flaws have been exposed. For one
cannot pursue the truth if his primary motivation is to protect a position.
Hence Socrates' words to Callicles: "And if you refute me, I shall not
be vexed with you as you are with me, but you shall be enrolled as the
greatest of my benefactors" (Gorgias 506c).

Once a dialogue or inquiry has begun, all those who enter into it,
author, characters, and readers, can participate in the possibilities which
inquiry alone may unfold. There is a vivacity within the committed time
and space of an inquiry which is not present to a cold consideration of
propositional truth claims. Above we saw Clarke's notion of being as
"being present to." In the inquiry which pursues truth, an event is
happening--it is *being made present to* the person(s) who inquires.
During this happening enhanced possibilities of discovery are present.
And this is why "philosophy cannot be content, as mathematics is, with
an account in words alone. Authentic philosophy entails a pursuit in
deed as well" (*APL*, 47). More is possible to the person engaged in
philosophical pursuit, but the account of that pursuit must honestly face
its own inadequacy in order to increase its chances of adequacy. Thus
Burrell speaks of Plato's awareness "of the limits of language as well as

the need to exploit those very limits" (*APL*, 48).[20] Plato typically exploits those limits by expanding the question "from 'What Is X' to 'the Good'" (*APL*, 51-58).

As we saw above in Chapter One, human aspiration naturally (but not necessarily) expands its questions, making them more and more radical. For Burrell, aspiration is a norm and guarantor of our humanity; it energizes the inquiry which is expressed and developed in analogical terms:

> Either there is a radical affinity for order in man as inquirer or there is no sense to inquiring. But if inquiry is senseless, then many if not all human aspirations are void or absurd, for each presupposes the power of discrimination native to inquiry.[21]

Every energetic inquiry presupposes that there is something to be discovered. In committing oneself, in searching, one hopes to reach "the point where subject and object meet in the very ground structure of inquiry" (*APL*, 59).

AQUINAS' *MANUDUCTIO*

Taking Aquinas' *manuductio*[22] as "the key to his treatment of naming God" (*APL*, 115), Burrell sees a similarity among Wittgenstein's *Investigations* (##59-67, 96-109), Plato's engaged inquiry,

---

[20]The "limits of language" remains a crucial consideration throughout this study of analogy. Above, we saw Clarke's conscious attempts to press those limits to our advantage. Below, we shall see Jüngel's very different account of language limits and expansions.

[21]*APL*, 57, in turn citing as support: *Republic* 611e; *Phaedrus* 242e; *Philebus* 58d; *Sophist* 253, 259; *Gorgias* 487e, 495e.

[22]Burrell's development of *manuductio* is from the following texts: *De Ver.* 10.6 ad. 2, 11.1; *In 1 Eth.* 4, 53; *In 9 Meta.* 5, 1826-27; *De Pot.* 7.5. ad. 3-4; *ST* I.117, I.51.3. ad. 1.

and Aquinas' use of examples "to take us by the hand and lead us on" (*APL*, 123). According to Burrell, Aquinas fits his anti-theoretical thesis:

> The twin testimonies of recent textual research and centuries of confusing commentaries assure us that Aquinas had no clear-cut theory of analogical predication. The omission is all the more exasperating as he seemed to depend upon one, invoking it in the transcendent region of theological discourse.[23]

Consistently eschewing the search for a theory, Burrell explores "the host of semantic issues released by [Aquinas'] assertion" that God is principle of all and so beyond any genus (*APL*, 125). Much of Burrell's work on Aquinas and analogy centers on these "semantic issues" and their attempted clarification. While a certain apophatic tendency pervades Burrell's reading of Plato, this apophaticism grows in strength in his treatment of Aquinas:

> In more contemporary terms, such an assertion means that God is outside any of the universes of discourse that provide the contextual meanings for the terms we use. . . . Aristotle's use of analogous to call attention to similarities among the biological genera themselves would suggest its use beyond any genus. But the situation is still more radical when we are speaking of the principle of all.
>
> . If God must remain outside of any genus, he is properly unknowable. Such an assertion would seem to end in pure agnosticism. Yet Aquinas refuses to settle for that and goes on to drive a wedge: then God must be improperly knowable, namely by analogy (*APL*, 125-126).

---

[23]*APL*, 124. Let me only say at this point that "recent textual criticism" is not unanimous in support of Burrell. Klubertanz and Montagnes argue cogently in other directions. Furthermore, Burrell has seriously misread Klubertanz's major work, accusing him of advocating the analogy of proportionality when, in fact, much of Klubertanz's careful textual analysis is devoted to showing the opposite. For Burrell's misreading, see *APL*, 203, n. 6. For Klubertanz's exposition of how Aquinas began with the analogy of proportionality and later dropped it, see, Klubertanz, *Aquinas on Analogy*, 80-100, which I have commented on in Chapter Two above.

This passage raises ultimately determinative issues for theology--issues whose proffered solutions will have to do with how one handles the problem of analogical predication. That is, a broad spectrum of confidence in thinking and speaking about God is displayed in various analogical expressions.[24] Once Burrell raises the question of whether Aquinas' insistence that God remains outside any genus commits him to a "pure agnosticism," Burrell quickly moves away from this abyss, but not too far away. For he tells us that Aquinas has gone on "to drive a wedge," and that "God must be improperly knowable." Now a great deal of our final conclusions about analogical talk about God will depend upon whether we emphasize the "improperly" or the "knowable." While I think that Burrell's first study generally tends to emphasize the "improperly," he does soften his above remarks:

> The implication is, of course, that God is at all costs knowable; or rather, Aquinas implies that something must be able to be said about him. Why?
> For a believer, or his theologian, the answer should be plain: there must be sufficient cognitive linkage so that he knows to what he is assenting (*APL*, 126).

However, Burrell soon reverses this positive direction of thought (and so, I think, heads back toward the abyss) by "incorporating Kant."[25] Within the inquiry, the *manuductio*, one might discover

---

[24]Burrell's apophatic tilt here has been influenced by Victor Preller, *Divine Science and the Science of God: A Reformulation of Thomas Aquinas* (Princeton, NJ: Princeton University Press, 1967). Preller reads Aquinas as strongly separating philosophy, where Aquinas tends toward agnosticism, and revelation, where Aquinas claims certainty through assent. If Preller's reading of Aquinas is comprehensively correct, then Jüngel's criticism of Aquinas and analogy (which would also apply to Burrell) would be virtually victorious.

[25]*APL*, 132ff. Burrell's claim plays into Jüngel's linkage of Kant and Aquinas, leaving either Aquinas vulnerable to Jüngel's criticism, or else Burrell vulnerable to the criticism Jüngel will receive (Chapter 10 below) for linking Kant and Aquinas.

something more than *that* God exists, but precise, determinative concepts will remain elusive:

> The God to whom we are led by demanding a ground for existence bears the imprint of the style of reflection which leads us on: if we can (indeed must) affirm *that* he is, yet cannot say *what* he is, it is because God is proposed as first cause or principle of all. So Aquinas' denial that we cannot know what he is had a purpose--to anticipate the critique of Kant and others of the first cause formulation. For this expression too must be analogous: "'to make'," Aquinas says, "is used equivocally of the universal production of all things and of other productions" (*In 8 Phy.* 2974). Hence the meaning of the term God remains an undetermined one.[26]

Since subsequent predication of God "will be justified by reference to causality," there are "serious implications" in this indeterminate notion of causality (*APL*, 132). Thus when analogous transcendentals like 'good' or 'just' are applied to God, this analogous application is itself dependent on an analogous use of 'cause'. So Aquinas goes beyond the "merely symbolic" theories of Maimonides or Tillich but systematically resists reducing analogy to a core of meaning, a univocal base. To the contrary,

> Aquinas' views seem to threaten any move to God, for he is apparently acknowledging that any justification for using analogical predicates will be circular, since the meaning of these predicates is secured only through an analogical use of cause (*APL*, 133).

Drawing again from Wittgenstein, Burrell sees circularity as a problem only if we try to *justify* such usage. Any such justification would amount to a theory or canon of use such as he has been emphatically opposing. His alternative proposal is that "use yields

---

[26]The complexity of Aquinas' treatment of 'cause' is not done justice by this one reference. For a discussion based on selections from the entire Thomistic corpus, and one that shows some important relation to analogy, see Klubertanz, *Aquinas on Analogy*, 24-26, 46-48, 70-73, passim.

meaning" (*APL*, 162). Furthermore, the way we use these terms suggests a progressive, on-going process:

> But the extent of our knowledge of justice-in-itself lies in our ability to recognize a better form of justice when we come upon it. No formula can capture the core of justice; any which tries will inevitably be schematic (*APL*, 162-163).

Any and all moves to justify what we are doing revolve in circularity. Judgment breaks that circularity, but its presence signals the loss of complete logical control. Burrell's idea is to get off this merry-go-round of justification and plunge into the inquiry. But inquiry cannot succeed without the total commitment of the inquirers. Hence he concludes: "The paradigm is the person inquiring" (*APL*, 139); for while logic can set parameters, only a person can feel the need to make and assert judgments. So just as Clarke argued above that 'person' should be the prime analogate, 'person' likewise underlies Burrell's work on analogy. Burrell's analysis implies that at the heart of language, and at the heart of the person using analogical language, we encounter the presence of progressive judgments about what is real, good, and true. Thus Aquinas aptly characterizes the inquiry about God in the idiom of *manuductio*: "As the mind is led on from what the senses apprehend to [what the thing is], so things understood lead it on to some knowledge of the divine" (*APL*, 134).

ONTOLOGICAL RETICENCE

The very presence of an analogous term shifts what is going on in a statement or discussion to something beyond straight logical discourse; hence, "the affinity between this privileged set of terms . . .

and metaphysical inquiry" (*APL*, 226). So what began as a grammatical inquiry, a close look at how analogous words are being used, ends by involving the inquirer in the most radical anthropological and theological questions:

> My proposal is that the move is not necessary but reflective. Just as the recognition of similarities leads to the formation of a common term and functional similarities lead to analogous predication, so reflection on the need to look for similarities, together with the ability to recognize them, points to an inner demand for intelligibility. Defining God as what fulfills this demand, we can also say of him that he would fulfill the cognate demands for justice, magnanimity, and the rest (*APL*, 134).

Once Burrell adopts the language of "inner demand for intelligibility" and contends that we possess an inherent "ability to recognize" something like intelligible patterns, his argument converges with the more overtly metaphysical themes of Transcendental Thomism.   So while Burrell has taken much from the guidance of Wittgenstein, he goes beyond Wittgenstein in affirming the "twin requirements of intelligibility--order and fulfillment" (*APL*, 153).

Nonetheless, Burrell's early work on analogy retains much of Wittgenstein's ontological reticence, preferring not to venture into the metaphysical implications of pre-existent order and potential fulfillment. What consistently strikes Burrell as most unusual and most important about analogy is that we insist on using such language in spite of our inability to specify strict standards for its use:

> And all these facts of language: the grammar of words like recognition, the peculiar role of analogies in shaping general usage, the deliberate and dramatic crossing of kinds, the unabashed employ of transcendentals, as well as our facility with appraisal terms--all of these point from language to the language user. Or rather they speak of language as emanating from a person with aims and purposes.
>
> And of course this *is* the context of language--human life and life's concerns (*APL*, 243).

Burrell shares with other Neo-Thomists the self-involving inquiry which tends to generate more and more radical questions, but he sharply differs from the kind of Neo-Thomism we saw above in Part One by his focus on *language* and avoidance of *being*:

> Closer scrutiny of the facts of language ought to discourage any direct reference to being, for the same appreciation of language corroborates that *being* is not a characteristic nor marked off by any set of characteristics. Hence being presents no normal subject of discourse (*APL*, 196).

Thus this early work of Burrell's avoids talk of participating in being, preferring to focus on the ubiquitous use of analogous language: "The ways in which we find ourselves employing analogous expressions exhibit something of the manner in which we participate in our language and in the world which that language lays open to us" (*APL*, 267). In methodological contrast to Clarke, who explored the ontological underpinnings of analogy, Burrell's more minimalistic focus is on the grammar of analogy, its lived use in language. Concerned by the elusiveness of the underlying ontology, Burrell's strategy is that more will be discovered through an examination of language than through language that directly focuses on being. Thus he contends: "It is left ambiguous whether, in talking about being, we *say* important things about it, or *show* them" (*APL*, 199).

Whether more can legitimately be said, as Clarke and others have tried to do, or more can legitimately be shown, as Burrell has done, I think that both types of account succeed, when they succeed, by provoking the reader/hearer to greater awareness of language and participation in the life upon which that language reflects. In both views, judgment is necessary to enact analogy within the context of human life. Judgment does not threaten the validity of analogical use;

it guarantees it. In all its constitutive uncertainty and risk, judgment is the human response to the possibilities of creation. Hence it is the intelligible arena of anthropological responsibility.

CHAPTER FIVE

EXPLORING THE GRAMMAR OF DIVINITY

Although focusing more explicitly on Aquinas' theological language, Burrell's second major work, *Aquinas: God and Action*, still shows strong continuities with his first. The Wittgensteinian influence shifts back to the *Tractatus*, where Wittgenstein's close attention to tautologies helps Burrell elucidate the logic in Aquinas' "Grammar of Divinity," the subtitle of Part I.[1] Remaining an enthusiast of the "linguistic turn," Burrell does not see the distance of seven intervening centuries as a disadvantage in interpreting Aquinas. He contends to the contrary: "Our experience with philosophical analysis in this century gives us a better working grasp of Aquinas' working premises than even his most sympathetic commentators from the centuries intervening."[2]

---

[1]Burrell even adopts the numbering scheme of the *Tractatus* and will continue to use the *Tractatus'* numbering scheme in *Knowing the Unknowable God*.

[2]*Aquinas: God and Action* (Notre Dame, IN: University of Notre Dame Press, 1979), 36-37. In the rest of this chapter, further references to this work will be cited parenthetically as *AGA*.

A second continuing influence is Bernard Lonergan, particularly in Part II. Crediting Lonergan for the inspiration, Burrell reiterates that his account of analogy can only succeed when it becomes a performance (*AGA*, 118), a familiar theme from Burrell's first work. *Manuductio*, which had been the center of his reading of Aquinas in the first work, remains important, but is now more often referred to in terms of "intellectual therapy" as one pursues religious questions. The therapy largely consists of letting go of the need for theories and doctrines of God. On the continuing issue of how to interpret Aquinas, Burrell argues that Aquinas was not presenting a doctrine of God but was doing something like this therapy or *manuductio* in Qq.3-11 of the *Summa*.

The theological focus of this second book is a response to Burrell's own question from *Analogy and Philosophical Language*: What might a move to God be like? The two parts of *Aquinas: God and Action* present his twofold thesis of how Aquinas (with a little help from Wittgenstein) can still show us a way forward. First, let the contours of the question be determined by an analysis of the grammar *in divinis* (in matters divine). Second, show how Aquinas used his "master metaphor" or basic analogy of *actus* to speak about divinity without ever resorting to a univocal core of meaning.

MAPPING THE GRAMMAR *IN DIVINIS*

The Purposes of grammatical exploration. This first part of Burrell's work offers a focal study of Aquinas' grammatical way of structuring the formal features of divinity. As Burrell characterizes his own work:

"The thesis of this book is that Aquinas deserves to be placed among the 'critical' philosophers if we scrutinize how he employs philosophical grammar to circumscribe discourse about God" (*AGA*, 79). As Burrell represents the *Summa*, particularly I.3-11, but also the well-known I.13 which addresses analogy under the rubric of *"de nominibus Dei"* (The Names of God), the strategy is:

> Determine what must be stated grammatically, so that we can recognize what sort of things cannot be asserted of God. Such prescriptions offer a grammatical base for learning how to interpret the things that are in fact asserted (*AGA*, 84).

Because they warn us of logical errors and provide a base from which we might venture interpretations, "grammatical statements turn out to be indispensable instruments of conceptual clarity" (*AGA*, 104).

Nonetheless, Burrell recognizes that while such grammatical exercises may yield a certain nourishment and even point us in the right direction, "grammar remains a thin gruel indeed" (*AGA*, 115). Burrell assigns a propaedeutic role to grammatical analysis: "Here as elsewhere in philosophy, analytic techniques help to answer the penultimate questions, while the ultimate ones, being incapable of *answer*, must be come to terms with in some other way."[3] Burrell's view is that by unravelling the penultimate questions we can position ourselves to face squarely the ultimate ones. And this highlights the propaedeutic nature of the grammatical task which he sees as the proper work of philosophy: "At that point logical analysis can take us no further; we are on our own, or need assistance of another sort" (*AGA*, 115). Keeping the preliminary nature of these grammatical exercises in mind, let us now

---

[3]Joel Feinberg, "Action and Responsibility," in *The Philosophy of Action*, ed. Alan R. White (Oxford, 1968), 119, as cited in *AGA*, 115.

turn to Burrell's development of what the opening questions of the *Summa* might mean for philosophical theology.

TAUTOLOGIES: THE LOGIC
OF FORMAL FEATURES

Once Aquinas has asserted the simplicity of God in Q.3 of the *Summa*, he must explicate what that simplicity means for thinking, talking about, and interacting with God. With some impetus from Wittgenstein, Burrell challenges us to a new look at how Qq.3-11 function. His thesis is that Aquinas is not describing the characteristics of divinity, but is giving philosophical expression to the divine transcendence which follows from asserting the simplicity of God. Thus he is establishing "a set of grammatical priorities designed to locate the subject matter as precisely as possible" (*AGA*, 5). However, before we can examine how these grammatical priorities position us for talking about God, we need to confront the formidable problem raised by asserting the divine simplicity: the simpleness of God surpasses the grammar which must be used to express it.

The structure of our language suits the composite structure of our being, i.e., the natural form of human language is to join subject and predicate. Hence we would quite naturally say that "Joan is good" or "Socrates is wise." But such language is only suited to those who have a limited or mannered way of being. A grammatical shock occurs when we try to speak of a non-composite being using our inherently composite language. The simplicity of God is "beyond the range of our linguistic tools" (*AGA*, 15). Therefore, the structural isomorphism which we presuppose between our language and the things of the world is inadequate for discourse *in divinis.* Burrell points to the crux of the issue: "What holds for the universe cannot hold for the 'source and goal of all things'" (*AGA*, 5). So the simpleness of God, the beginning and end of all things, differentiates God from all created things. God is *sui generis* and therefore not an object which could be adequately described by our language. Divine simplicity closes off the possibility of straightforward description. Any attempted description would necessarily describe something other than, or inadequate to, the divinity of God.

Rather than despair of this grammatical impotence, Burrell, through his reading of Aquinas, builds his thesis upon it:

> Aquinas is concerned to *show* what we cannot use our language to *say*, yet there is no medium of expression available other than language itself.
>
> But our language can be a medium of display only in the measure that we become aware of certain features recurrent in our use of it, and then articulate the meaning of this recurrence. When we can expose such a depth structure in our grammar, we are able to use our language to show what we cannot bring it to say (*AGA*, 6).

Burrell's first book was an exercise designed to make us aware of those "certain recurrent features," viz., analogical terms, whose use can point us toward the "depth structure in our grammar." This second book is focused more on how Aquinas shows the way such terms may be applied to God in spite of the inadequacy of any straightforward reference. Since straightforward reference is ruled out, then what is needed is a mode of predication which can go beyond logic without destroying logic. And as Burrell has shown in *Analogy and Philosophical Language,* analogical terms, with their irreducible judgment component, can do just that. That is, they can refer by reminding us that the divine content exceeds the human word which intends to express it.

Since no single predicate is adequate to encompass the divine transcendence, Aquinas adopts what Burrell calls the "principle of complementarity":

> We can speak of simple things only as though they were like the composite things from which we derive our knowledge. Therefore, in speaking of God, we use concrete nouns to signify His subsistence, because with us only those things subsist which are composite; and we use abstract nouns to signify His simplicity (*ST* I.3.3.1).[4]

So for example, we must not only say that "God is wise" (concrete), we must also say that "God is wisdom" (abstract). These complementary assertions allow us to intend both divine subsistence and transcendence.

Burrell's reading tends so strongly toward the apophatic because his primary focus is on the transcendence of God and because an apophatic strand is unquestionably present in Aquinas. Burrell wants us

---

[4]In Burrell's citation (*AGA*, 5), there are a couple of problems. First, he incorrectly numbers the passage. But most importantly, I think that Burrell, still committed to his apophatic reading, stops his citation too soon. For Aquinas continues:

> In saying therefore that Godhead, or life, or the like are in God, we indicate the composite way in which our intellect understands, but not that there is any composition in God (*ST* I.3.3.1).

My understanding of Aquinas here is that we understand something which we cannot express in a single stroke. Referring to the "principle of complementarity" at work here, Burrell's understanding is:

> This amounts to a slightly more appetible way of saying that we do not know how to say what we want to say about God. Or more bluntly, that we do not know what we are talking about (*AGA*, 21-22).

Having alerted the reader to this strongly apophatic tendency which may not always account for everything in the text, I shall refrain from further criticism at this point.

to take paradigmatically Aquinas' claim in the Introduction to *ST* I.3: "Because we cannot know what God is, but rather what He is not, we have no means for considering how God is, but rather how He is not." Focusing on divine transcendence and what that must logically entail, he skillfully applies the lessons of tautologies learned from Wittgenstein.[5] Periodically, Burrell presents reminders of the tactic: "Let tautologies show us the way" (*AGA*, 14). Thus speaking of the characterization of God as *esse* (to-be) he declares: "It is one of those crucial tautologies defining the logical space of God-talk" (*AGA*, 8). How tautologies can define a logical space can be seen in the following: "Tautologies and contradictions are not, however, nonsensical. They are part of the symbolism, much as '0' is part of the symbolism of arithmetic."[6] Applying this to Aquinas' exposition in Qq.3-11, Burrell argues that Aquinas understood quite well that a doctrine of God or a description of the divine characteristics would have been out of place. Instead, Aquinas takes us through the logical contours of the grammar of divine transcendence. Aquinas' arguments for the perfect, limitless, unchangeable oneness of God turn out to be formal features, tautologous corollaries of divine simplicity. As Wittgenstein put it:

> The proof of logical propositions consists in the following process: we produce them out of other logical propositions by successively applying certain operations that always generate further tautologies out of the initial ones. (And in fact only tautologies *follow* from a tautology.)[7]

---

[5]He cites the following passages from the *Tractatus*: 4.4611, 6.12, 6.124, 6.22 (*AGA*, 174, n. 4).

[6]Wittgenstein, *Tractatus*, 4.4611.

[7]Ibid., 6.126.

One theological ramification of these tautologies of divine transcendence emerges when Burrell defends Aquinas against the charge of portraying an allegedly aloof God. Above we saw Clarke defend Aquinas and yet make some adjustments or concessions to the process point of view, particularly in the language of relatedness. Speaking out of his grammatical investigation of divine transcendence, Burrell will yield no ground at all. The charge that Aquinas depicts an aloof Deity mistakes Aquinas' understanding of the characteristics of God with his philosophical analysis of the *formal* features of divinity. In a section significantly titled, "Relating levels of discourse," Burrell deflects this charge against Aquinas by pointing beyond the strictly grammatical:

> Aquinas' grammatical notions (simple, good, limitless, unchangeable, and one) have been taken to picture a self-sufficient, all-powerful ikon of divinity, set off in solitary splendor. I have been arguing all along that such a construct may be ours, but not Aquinas'. Moreover, there are counter-forces to such a conception in his account. These are the more properly religious predicates (perfect, good, present, eternal, and whole) which are suggested by the grammatical notions. The power of these predicates is that they articulate entire dimensions of religious experience. As inherently mythic notions, they possess a structure of their own. So the guidance offered by the grammatical notions tells only a part of the story (*AGA*, 83).

In other words, the charge of aloofness fails to perceive the levels of discourse which are present in Aquinas and thus fails to perceive the different, but closely related work which those levels of discourse are doing.

Grammar only delivers "a part of the story"; yet it points the inquirer to the overtly religious predicates, "inherently mythic notions" and the domain of religious experience, which deliver the rest of the story (or as much of it as can be known). Burrell's belief is that the exercise of confronting the tautologies such as Aquinas presents helps us avoid "the temptation to think that reality is unintelligible. They enable us to see that whatever would explain the quest for understanding could not be comprehended by us" (*AGA*, 75). So attention to grammar guides the inquiry, but by no means do the grammatical, formal, tautologous dimensions culminate inquiry.

While "logical reminders" are not per se enough to sustain an inquiry so strange as the one which attempts to understand something about God, they are helpful in that

> they do give room for the original impulse to proceed. And, needless to say, we are free to think of the quest in other than logical modes. Along with the rest of mankind, the logician too can conceive it in mythic terms.
> Once again, the strictly ancillary role of philosophy appears. Logic cannot initiate the search for the source and goal of all things. . . . something else empowers the inquiry. That can touch us through myth and through musement. We can follow it with our heart as well as our mind. . . . reason may be employed with utmost sophistication in the service of this original impulse of the heart (ibid.).

PHILOSOPHY AND RELIGION--A DICHOTOMY?

During his more apophatic moments, Burrell suggests a dichotomy between the philosophical and mythical domains of religious discourse. The split can be seen when he speaks of "Aquinas' properly agnostic philosophical theology" (*AGA*, 142) as a sheer alternative to his affirmation of revelation. Hence even the modalities of discourse proper to creation are alleged to evidence this gap:

> For even should we recognize ourselves to be God's creatures, that recognition provides no hope of discerning what God is like. If we may speak in a generic sense of a belief in a creator, then believers

and unbelievers would share the same ignorance of that creator's nature. To believe that God reveals himself in Jesus, however, already offers some privileged access to the nature of divinity (*AGA*, 142).

The discipline of the philosophical exercise thus highlights the compelling human need for revelation.

However, this bifurcation may not be as clear and sustainable as Burrell sometimes suggests. At the outset of the above discussion separating logical from religious predicates, Burrell gave us two lists of examples. An alert reading will have detected that 'good' appears in both lists without explanation. Burrell's placement of 'good' in both lists, the grammatical and the religious, may constitute more than an oversight; for in fact, 'good' seems to be equally at home in a grammatical or a religious account. Going beyond what Burrell has concluded, but working from materials which he has provided, we can understand 'good' as a possible transition between his two realms of grammar (philosophy) and religion (myth, musement, and revelation). Indeed, one of the central points of *Analogy and Philosophical Language* was the natural way in which transcendental terms like 'good' were used in different contexts. Additionally, Burrell showed that the everyday use of analogous terms is already quite extended, so that the move to God is not methodologically so far removed from everyday use.

While there is a logical assessment that can be undertaken of 'good', and I believe that Burrell gives us a good one, I also think that 'good' will not sit still long enough for us to get a grammatical hold on it, an insight which comes out of Burrell's first book. What I am suggesting beyond Burrell is that the presence of goodness in human life and language suggests that one need not and must not bifurcate theology and philosophy. Our knowledge of the good is indeed 'analogous', but analogy is particularly suited to relate different levels of discourse and being. As such, the good may indeed be a bridge area between faith and reason, theology and philosophy.

Aquinas offers some support for my position in his investigation of the question of 'good' in relation to 'being' (*ST* I.5.1): *"Utrum bonum et ens sint idem secundum rem?"* (Whether goodness and being are really the same?). As Burrell summarizes his answer:

1. good means desirable
2. what anything desires is its perfection
3. the perfection of anything depends upon how far it has achieved actuality
4. therefore, a thing is good inasmuch as it exists (*AGA*, 28).

Burrell correctly points out that 'actuality' functions as the middle term in this reasoning, as it often does in Aquinas' arguments regarding God's simplicity. Yet I think that this apparently grammatical, logical argument contains a great deal more in its identification of existence and goodness, an identification which Clarke developed at some length in Chapter One above. As Aquinas concludes the *responsio* in I.5.1: "It is clear that goodness and being are the same really. But goodness presents the aspect of desirableness, which being does not present." My point, which is one that Burrell sets up but never seems to make, is that this particular affirmation/identification constitutes the ontological basis for analogical predication. Aquinas clarifies the matter in I.3.5.2:

> [Although] nothing is commensurate with God, . . . he is called the measure of all things, inasmuch as the nearer things come to God, the more fully they exist (*AGA*, 52).

True to his tendency, Burrell immediately backs away from some important implications of the passage he has quoted, classifying this (contrary to his overall assertion regarding Qq.3-11 as fundamentally explicating the grammar of tautologies) as "experiential" or part of Aquinas' "religious form of life" (ibid.). Shying away from the Neoplatonic implications of Aquinas' position, he then offers a rare criticism of Aquinas: "As a theological statement, however, it appears tautological at best and misleading at worst, presuming as it does a scale of proximity to God" (ibid.).[8] Yet it seems to me that what is most interesting about Aquinas' statement is that it provides a point of convergence between the purely tautologous and the purely religious. Let us look again at what Aquinas has claimed:

(1) things exist more fully the nearer they come to God;
(2) God is *Ipsum Esse Subsistens* (Subsistent To-Be Itself);
(3) being and good are really the same, although separable in thought;
(4) God is the cause of all being (*ST* I.8.1).

While Burrell has rightly shown that none of this gives us any algorithmic certainty, focusing on being-action-good in this frame of reference potentially directs our judgments undertaken in speech about God as well as our valuations of the world.

---

[8]In *Analogy and Philosophical Language*, Burrell is often highly critical of Neoplatonism and questionably tries to distance Aquinas from it. Concomitantly with his later, less apophatic reading of Aquinas, Burrell tones down his opposition to Neoplatonism. While Aquinas certainly adapted Neoplatonism to his own original synthesis, we have already seen in Clarke's and Klubertanz's accounts how extensively Aquinas did use it, incorporating it into his more unified version of participation metaphysics (see Chapter 1 above). For some softening of Burrell's aversion to Neoplatonism, see "Aquinas' Debt to Maimonides," in *A Straight Path: Studies in Medieval Philosophy and Culture*, ed. Ruth Link-Salinger et al. (Washington: Catholic University of America Press, 1988), 37-48.

PERFORMANCE, PROPOSITION AND ASSERTION

Ever hesitant to spell out the more metaphysical aspects of analogy, at least in any direct way, Burrell does illuminate how the linguistic appropriation of 'exists' forces us to do more with words than we can explain. Again, he prefers *performance* to explanation: "That something exists (or a situation obtains) demands expression . . . even though no feature of the thing can express the fact" (*AGA*, 45). The problem is that "exists is not a predicate,"[9] and yet Aquinas would say that 'exists' is the most important quality about anything. It is the ultimate perfection, the most proper name for God (*ST* I.13.11); and the measure of something's existence is the measure of its proximity to God (*ST* I.3.5.2). So the stakes are highest precisely where the conceptual grasp is most slippery. As a result, Burrell remains skeptical about explanatory frameworks and "theory-building"; he would have us frankly face this conceptual difficulty and look instead to the performative aspects of terms like 'exists' and 'good'.

Thus he directs our attention to the difference between a proposition and an assertion, where linguistic performance provides what no merely conceptual argument could:

> A proposition asserted looks just like one that is being considered; my act of asserting it has no structural counterpart. Yet it is this act of

---

[9] The thesis of G. E. Moore, "Is Existence a Predicate?" in *Aristotelian Society Suppl. Vol.* 15 (1936) reprinted in Moore's *Philosophical Papers* (London: George Allen and Unwin, 1959), 114-25. More originally, this is Kant's thesis in opposing Descartes' version of the ontological argument. See *Critique of Pure Reason*, "Transcendental Dialectic," Book II, Chap.3, Sec.4, trans. Norman Kemp Smith (London: Macmillan and Co., Ltd., 1929, and New York: St. Martin's Press, 1965).

asserting which provides the proper analogue for the fact that
something exists (*AGA*, 34).

In essence Burrell is arguing that self-involvement (participation) in
language is our best clue to understanding analogy and existence; for a
proposition may be considered at a safe conceptual remove, whereas an
assertion requires an involvement that personally engages the issue and
then takes responsibility for what is asserted. Even though they are
visibly and logically the same, the reality content is higher in an
assertion. Burrell borrows Lonergan's working analogy:

essence: existence :: understanding: asserting (*AGA*, 179, n. 6).

Burrell suggests that Aquinas understood something like this
performative aspect of language in his contention that "a philosopher
differs from a logician . . . in his power to discriminate among contexts"
(*AGA*, 10-11). If analogical terms are those which lend themselves to
use in different contexts, then we can infer that good philosophy (which
would exercise the "power to discriminate among contexts") and good
use of analogy go hand in hand. And this more or less reiterates the
thesis of Burrell's first book: Analogical usage exercises the judgment
of the person using it.

LOCATING THE MOTIVATING INSIGHT: *ACTUS*

Believing that "language offers a nearly transparent metaphor for
understanding" (*AGA*, 150), Burrell consistently examines analogy by
keeping language at the center of his focus. Placing language at the
center includes logical analysis, but is clearly not limited to logic.
Something more is required:

The medievals were no strangers, certainly, to the paradigms of formal logic. They assumed that no proposed argument could contravene these paradigms. This test alone, however, was not regarded as a sufficient one. For besides the universal principles of logic there remain the principles proper to the domain under consideration (*AGA*, 3).

In fact, the medievals would have ridiculed anyone who failed to consider the Aristotelian teaching that each science had its own first principles which were not attained logically. With this historical reminder, Burrell reiterates his awareness of the logical limits of his project and begins to exploit those limits.

So while his account develops from a focus on grammar, not experience, he does acknowledge the mutual interpenetration of the two: "A logical treatment can be guided by our key experiences, as well as shape the way we comprehend them" (*AGA*, 31). In his investigation of Aquinas' use of *actus* (action), Burrell cites the "mixed appeal: to grammar and to our experiences of knowing. An appeal to experience, in cases like these, is never that far removed from the grammatical" (*AGA*, 147). It is as though we might catch something else out of the corner of our eye, but the proper focus of the eye remains language and how it is being used. When Aquinas' treatment of 'intentional' leads Burrell to acknowledge an immaterial "domain called *spiritual*," Burrell remains typically cautious about going too far beyond language's guidance:

It may seem rash to introduce an ontological domain on the strength of a grammatical peculiarity, until we recall that we have no more trustworthy indicators than these. What we must monitor carefully is the manner in which the philosopher goes on to describe that domain. Should he exceed the evidence adduced by the grammar--in this case, that of intentional activity--he may be accused of perpetrating metaphysics, in the nefarious sense. If not, he is simply reminding us of structures or patterns to which our very discourse already commits us (ibid.).

But finally, Burrell tells us that "something is missing in our consideration of Aquinas' philosophical logic" (*AGA*, 115). The missing component turns out to be what animated the analysis in the first place. Burrell calls this original insight, the one which impels the inquiry, the "master metaphor" of *actus* (*AGA*, 116). Again stressing the performative character of this key ingredient of language, and again, as he persistently does, mixing the categories of metaphor and analogy, Burrell asserts:

> As metaphors, these terms are inherently analogous; we use them better the more we realize how using them reveals us to ourselves and shapes the self we will become. In short, inherently analogous expressions are inescapably performative in character (ibid.).

The entire second part of *Aquinas: God and Action* is devoted to understanding Aquinas' use of *actus* in the light of his previous grammatical stipulations.

According to Burrell, Aquinas' *actus* is an opening beyond grammar inserted in the midst of grammar. In fact Burrell contends that *actus* is the one great exception to Aquinas' (and his own) method of indirection: "Aquinas can allow himself to make only one direct statement: God is pure act" (*AGA*, xii).

Burrell first shows how this master metaphor or basic analogy guides Aquinas' logical analyses and then shows how it may be used in facing various problems and challenges. Thus he cites Aquinas' assertions:

> *necesse est id quod est primum ens esse in actu* (what is the first existent thing must be in act) (*ST* I.3.1)

ipsum esse est perfectissimum omnium, comparatur enim ad omnia ut actus (Being itself is the most perfect thing of all, to be compared to everything else as act) (*ST* I.4.1.3)

ipsum esse subsistens ([God is] self-subsistent being) (*ST* I.11.4).[10]

Both Burrell and Clarke centrally focus on these texts from the Thomistic corpus. Clarke, showing how being, action, and good are interrelated, based his whole epistemology upon *actus*. While Burrell's explication of *actus* is quite different than Clarke's, it is not so much an opposing view as a complementary one.

THE INTENTIONAL ACTIVITY OF KNOWING AND LOVING

In addition to telling us that *actus* is the master metaphor which guides the grammatical analysis, he also tells us that "the distinctively human activities of knowing and loving . . . offer Aquinas a paradigm for understanding action more generally" (*AGA*, 116) and that Aquinas' paradigm use of *actus* is intentional activity (*AGA*, 162). Burrell illustrates how knowing and loving lead us on to understand intentional activity which turns out to be the pivotal point in the relationship of God and humankind. If it seems a bit circular to have "knowing and loving" function paradigmatically to understand 'action', which is itself supposed to be the animating impulse to the inquiry as well as the "master metaphor," this would be unlikely to trouble Burrell. For he has persistently argued for a kind of reconnoitering rather than the capturing of a beachhead. His strategy is to trace the circularity of tautologies in

---

[10]Citations and translations are taken from *AGA*, 116.

order to gain an overview of the lie of the land. And as we saw in Chapter Four, acts of judgment break the circularity as the agent becomes self-involved in inquiry.

Burrell wants to disabuse us of the connection between *actus* and accomplishment. *Actus* is not to be conceived as a striving to effect changes in the world. Trying to give us a picture of this unusual notion, he cites the diverse sources of Aquinas' treatment of martyrdom and the superiority of the contemplative over the active life, Wittgenstein's *Tractatus* 6.373 ("The world is independent of my will"), the *Bhagavad Gita* ("Whoever wishes to act authentically must renounce the fruits of their actions), and Ghandi's echo of the *Ramayana* ("Any accomplishment is a miracle") (*AGA*, 163-169).

Regarding this proscribed use of *actus* as accomplishment, Burrell explains:

> Whatever is 'in act,' as Aquinas puts it, need do nothing further to become a cause. Its capacity for acting is inherent, although that power will not ordinarily be evident until some object which it can affect comes within range. At that point, the inherent activity shows itself, and the thing in question becomes an agent. Notice, however, that the agent itself does not change in becoming an agent. It is the object acted upon which is changed (*AGA*, 117).

Some of the theological force of this account can be seen by linking this above statement to Aquinas' account of "The Existence of God in Things":

> God is in all things; not, indeed, as part of their essence, nor as an accident; but as an agent is present to that upon which it works. For an agent must be joined to that wherein it acts immediately, and touch it by its power; hence it is proved in *Physic.* vii that the thing moved and the mover must be joined together. Now since God is very being by His own essence, created being must be His proper effect; as to ignite is the proper effect of fire. Now God causes this effect in things not only when they first begin to be, but as long as they are

preserved in being; . . . . Therefore as long as a thing has being, God must be present to it, according to its mode of being. But being is innermost in each thing and most fundamentally inherent in all things since it is formal in respect of everything found in a thing, as was shown above (Q.7,A.1). Hence it must be that God is in all things, and innermostly (*ST* I.8.1).

Contrary to the typical charge against Aquinas that his God is so transcendent as to be aloof, a God who is *supra nos* ("beyond" or "above us") and thus absent from where we actually live, here we see Aquinas clearly explicate a very different picture. Instead of an aloof deity, Aquinas *relates* the being of God (*Ipsum Esse Subsistens*) to all created being by *actus*, where its effect is not through striving for accomplishment but through *presence to* all that is. Or to repeat Aquinas' way of putting it, "As long as a thing has being, God must be present to it." Furthermore, this divine presence is the "most fundamentally inherent," the innermost presence in all things. In making God so continuously present to all that exists, I think that this passage (*ST* I.8.1) renders one of the more perspicuous accounts of what 'creation' might mean. Burrell rightly affirms that creation is "the central though often hidden element in Aquinas' philosophical discourse."[11]

Wide theological implications which impinge upon our use of analogy are derived from Aquinas' picture of creation. For what is being claimed is that the being of all that is, the world and universe, creation itself, is dependent upon the being in act of God. As Burrell nicely summarizes *ST* I.45.3.2: "The creature itself *is* a relation" (*AGA*,

---

[11]Joseph Pieper, *The Silence of St. Thomas*, trans. J. Murray and D. O'Connor (New York, 1957), 47-50, as cited in *AGA*, 136.

138). The to-be of a creature, its very being, is the reception of the divine activity, the divine outward movement.[12]

Just as Clarke did above, Burrell differentiates the ontological relations within the Trinity from the freely chosen relation of God to the world. In defending Aquinas against the challenge of process thought, Burrell argues for the coherence of Aquinas' grammar which declares a one-way relation of creatures to God but denies a real relation of God to creatures (*ST* I.13.7.4). While our current concern is only tangential as regards process thought, what is important is the elucidation of 'intention', 'will', and 'intellect' which Burrell achieves through the confrontation. Working from a later article of Aquinas, Burrell clarifies the point:

> There is no process or property inherent in divinity which demands or results in creatures. . . . "[God's] relation (*habitudo*) to creatures does not flow from his nature. He does not produce creatures out of the necessity of his nature, but rather by intellect and will (cf. 1.14.8, 1.19.4). *For this reason* we cannot speak of a "real relation" to creatures in God" (1.28.1.3, emphasis Burrell's, *AGA*, 85-86).

Burrell wants us to see that Aquinas is once again running us through the grammar of divine transcendence. In this case it means that creating should not be thought of as an internal property within God. The charge of the process thinkers, that Aquinas' position denies what is most crucial to creatures, Burrell demonstrates to be something of a category error. Their mistake results from confusing the formal features, the logic which follows from God's being *Ipsum Esse Subsistens*, with the

---

[12]This understanding is reminiscent of Clarke's above explication where being is never self-enclosed but displays an inherent movement toward sharing its presence, i.e., it is being in act.

divine intentional activity which does not lend itself to such grammatical deductions.

Within the Trinity "the divine processions are in one and the same nature" (*ST* I.28.1.3); hence they are designated real relations (*ST* I.28.1). Yet something besides intrinsic nature relates God and creatures. As Aquinas asserts: "[God] does not produce the creature by necessity of His nature, but by intellect and will" (*ST* I.28.1.3). From this Burrell gathers that "the creator bears to creatures an *intentional* relation" (*AGA*, 86) and that this kind of treatment invites a personalist development. He then arrives at some of his most forceful conclusions:

> The point of Aquinas' treatment of relations between God and the world would be better expressed, then, by denying that God is naturally related to the world. With such terminology we could accurately parse the equivocal observation that God is not *really* related to it. Such a grammatical treatment remains open to God's *freely* relating to the world. And if so, we are led to think of him as related to the world much more intimately than by virtue of natural process. Thus by denying that God is by nature creator, Aquinas is actually setting the stage for a far more effective affirmation. The relatedness that comes with knowledge and love is of another sort entirely, and the function of these denials is to display that clearly (*AGA*, 86-87).

The freedom of the divine intentionality in so creating the world and humankind, the freedom to relate through knowledge (intellect) and will (love), carves out a noetic space for free human response in intellect and will, knowledge and love. Burrell's paradigm for understanding *actus* recognizes that God, as first and ultimate cause, has created humanity as secondary causes, agents who may also freely function. Thus, "the transcendence of the first cause . . . disposes natural things to act according to natural laws, and intentional beings to act freely" (*AGA*, 101).

Working 'from below', Burrell's first book pursued the question about analogy until it expanded into a question about anthropology. Allowing himself a bit more theological rein, he develops *actus* 'from above', i.e., as a theological anthropology. The development of *actus* provides a pivot between the two approaches, even as it provides a shared activity between God and humankind.

The shift to theological anthropology is further evidenced in Burrell's insistence on 'consent' over 'decision' language (*AGA*, 125-126). At issue between the two terms is the determination of the human *telos*. 'Decision' language is misleading because it gives the appearance of *sui generis* activity. By contrast, if human being is primarily an intended to-be, a creation, then the real activity is the choice (or rejection) of an already existent end which constitutes the highest possible good for humankind, viz., God. The language of consent presupposes the act of creation and acknowledges that our being is dependent and contingent. The *theo*-logic of this anthropology is clear: "The nearer things come to God, the more fully they exist" (*ST* I.3.5.2). If I am more real the closer I am to God, then human fulfillment is a function of movement toward God. Humans who have moved closer to God, and this movement is grounded in intentionality, are freer because they *have* more being in act. The logic of such a movement follows from asserting that God is *actus essendi*, the act of being. If by consent I can move toward God, then I have ipso facto moved toward greater power and possibility. I have become more real because I have approached what is most real and the source of the real.

Having situated the relation of God and humankind in the freely chosen, more than natural, space of intentionality, Burrell's exposition of intellect and will has effectively linked *actus* and *relatio* and rejoins Burrell's account with Clarke's:

> Openness to whatever can be understood distinguishes the human intellect as such, and invites Aquinas to define the 'scope of our intellectual activity [as] being in general' (*ST* I.79.2, *AGA*, 120).

The heuristic process of inquiry requires both an active seeking and an "active receptivity" (*AGA*, 121). There is an unending give and take between the searching intellect and the enormous "scope of our intellectual activity [as] being in general." Truth is pursued in committing oneself to ongoing inquiry, and "a person is never more active than when he or she is actually understanding" (*AGA*, 122). The desire to know and the accomplishment of knowledge, the seeking for understanding and the act of understanding, "provide a privileged instance of how potency and act are internally related" (*AGA*, 121). The phenomenology of speaking and hearing nicely illuminates the dynamic of act/potency and *actus/relatio*:

> While a speaker may cause another to hear, . . . that same speaker cannot cause someone to understand what is being said. The difference lies in locating the active principle. In hearing, it is the speaker who actively activates the hearer; in understanding, the active principle lies within the one addressed.
>
> When Aquinas insists that the act whereby the agent is agent becomes the act of the thing moved, he effectively shifts the stage of the discussion from *actus* to *relatio* (*AGA*, 134).

Through the analogy of knowing and loving, *actus* is our best way of understanding something of the trinitarian existence of God. From Aquinas' distinction that real relations do exist in and among the Trinity, it follows that "God's own life must be thought of as a kind of relating" (*AGA*, 143). Through the pivotal notion of *actus*, creaturely life is also understood as a kind of relating, but a relating through consent rather than through a natural, necessary ontology. In *actus*, which Burrell calls "the best candidate" (*AGA*, 174) to shed some light on "the beginning and end of all things and especially of rational creatures" (*ST* I.2, Intro.), understanding, willing, causing, and relating are intertwined.

Once again, Burrell has avoided giving us a straightforward account of analogy. Instead, he has attempted a two-part performance. Where the first part tried to delineate Aquinas' grammar *in divinis*, and so functioned to prepare us for the second, the second part attempted to apply that grammar in coming to a greater awareness of how Aquinas' most basic analogy, *actus*, is at work in understanding and loving, the basic paradigm for relating God and humanity in the realm of intentionality. Thus he concludes:

> Intentional activity cannot be explained precisely because it functions as the paradigm for every other use of *actus*. Fortunately, however, we all know what it is to understand, in the connatural sense that we know the thrill of getting the point. And that thrill, Aquinas contends, is the best clue we have to our humanity and to its sources (*AGA*, 173).

For all their differences, Burrell and Clarke join forces in their mutual embrace of *actus*, variously developed from their respective readings of Aquinas.[13] As Clarke put it: "All human knowledge of the real is an interpretation of action."[14] Yet where Clarke was more willing to drop the terminology of "real relations," Burrell has shown why it is important to work harder at understanding what Aquinas meant by that language. The point of Aquinas' grammatical restriction is to

---

[13]Given the accounts of Clarke and Burrell, it would seem that any viable account of Aquinas would have to consider the significance of *actus*, something which Jüngel does not do in his polemic against Aquinas discussed below.

[14]Clarke, "Action as the Self-Revelation of Being," 64.

open up a greater possibility--something beyond logical necessity and inherent relationship--something which is originally and freely chosen by God and might also be freely consented to by humankind. Thus more is at stake than mere terminology. The *intentional* action of God creates the possibility of intentional human response through understanding and will. This shared space of mutual intentionality is the possibility of love. Undoubtedly, the genius of creation is the gift of possibility. For, as Burrell has told us, "the thrill of getting the point . . . is the best clue we have to our humanity and to its sources" (*AGA*, 173). Considering the above lessons of grammar *in divinis*, particularly that the divine source of our humanity is pure actuality, *Ipsum Esse Subsistens*, the realm of the intentional and the possible is a remarkably appropriate place to search for the distinctive purpose of humanity.

CHAPTER SIX

DIFFERENTIATING AQUINAS THROUGH ANALOGY

THE SETTING OF THE INQUIRY

In *Knowing the Unknowable God* David Burrell continues his investigation of the Thomist tradition and analogy. This study follows the spirit of Karl Rahner and Vatican II by re-examining Aquinas through his dialogue with other faiths. Burrell's background idea is that Ibn-Sina (Avicenna), Maimonides, and Aquinas can be read as a kind of serial conversation, whose "intellectual intermingling . . . made possible the medieval synthesis which has served as the baseline for Western theology ever since."[1] Burrell uses a historical study of this intermingling "to show how Muslim, Jew, and Christian conspired to fashion a doctrine of God by transforming classical philosophy to display

---

[1]David Burrell, *Knowing the Unknowable God: Ibn-Sina, Maimonides, Aquinas* (Notre Dame, IN: University of Notre Dame Press, 1986), 1-2. Within the rest of this chapter, this work will be cited parenthetically as *KUG*.

divine transcendence" (*KUG*, ix). Appropriating the historical dialogue among these medieval masters gives Burrell a new angle on his continuing quest to express divine transcendence without betraying it in the process. Most important for my purposes, this fresh historical perspective leads him to differentiate Aquinas from his Muslim and Jewish counterparts through the affirmation of *positive* divine attributes based on analogical predication. While all three medieval thinkers seek to display the divine transcendence, Burrell differentiates Aquinas by showing how he went beyond philosophical agnosticism in positive affirmations about God. Hence, this last book incorporates an important shift in Burrell's thinking. This is said not by way of criticism but by way of praise; for it is salutary to see one who has placed so much weight upon committed inquiry and *manuductio* to evidence some progress over the course of his own inquiries.[2]

Before turning to Burrell's specific arguments, let us note his conceptions framing the enterprise of philosophical theology. First he recognizes that the task cannot be undertaken from a neutral, objective vantage point; therefore, he deems it best to acknowledge his own standpoint (and that of all others involved) from within a specific

---

[2]*Aquinas: God and Action* has been rightly criticized for construing Aquinas too much like Maimonides in terms of philosophical agnosticism. See, for example, Mark Jordan, "Names of God and the Being of Names," in *Existence and Nature of God*, ed. Alfred J. Freddoso (Notre Dame, IN: University of Notre Dame Press, 1983), 161-90.

tradition of religious practices and discourse.[3] He then defines the enterprise:

The term "philosophical theology" embraces many of the issues once considered under "natural theology," but with less concern to distinguish between the sources--reason or revelation--and no specific apologetic content (*KUG*, 114, n. 1).

While the goal is theological, the task is the philosophical exercise of "conceptual clarification" (*KUG*, 2). Continuing many of the themes of Burrell's previous works, this third book deepens some of those themes and clarifies others, as it develops a less apophatic tone in treating Aquinas and analogy.

Even though the point is not developed at any length, one of Burrell's most creative insights is his linking of analogy and history, both of which hinge upon judgments regarding *existing* things and people. As he puts it:

Those who can dispense with history must demand a clear, univocal sense for each expression, while those sensitive to historical shifts in meaning can appreciate the need for analogical uses. In any case, a comparative study such as this demands both historical awareness and analogical discernment (*KUG*, 113).

I think, however, that the single most important question of this work, the one that shapes it and gives it purpose, is: "If the interests of distinguishing creator from creation be served by . . . transcendental grammar, what steps need to be taken to articulate the positive side of the creator-creation relationship?" (*KUG*, 71). What is there, if anything, beyond the tautologous grammar of transcendence? Without compromising divine transcendence, what can be *positively* stated about

---

[3]Having done so, Burrell manages an admirably dialogical, non-polemical tone throughout the work, even when preferring Aquinas and implicitly or explicitly criticizing Ibn-Sina and Maimonides.

the Creator-creation relationship? While Burrell's thematic development of *actus* has implicitly provided something of an answer, the questions of this third inquiry lead him to probe the resources of his own tradition in order to specify the positive aspects of analogy.

THE FUNDAMENTAL DISTINCTION BETWEEN GOD AND WORLD

Whether one's tradition speaks of "the Holy One," "Our Father," or "Allah Akbar," the shared philosophical aim of Ibn-Sina, Maimonides, and Aquinas is "to secure the distinction of God from the world, and to do so in such a way as to display how such a One, who must be unknowable, may also be known" (*KUG*, 3). Now although these three writers shared the same desire to distinguish God from the world, the manner in which each went about doing so affected the critical question of how such a transcendent God might also be known. Burrell uses the proffered solutions of Ibn-Sina and Maimonides as a foil to that of Aquinas, showing where Aquinas was able to say more and say it more consistently due to his way of specifying the distinction.

Burrell's characterization of this fundamental distinction points back to his non-theoretical theory of analogy: "For the distinction in question lies at the margins of human understanding and so at the intersection of reason with faith--a locus one may well be aware of without being able to inhabit" (*KUG*, 4). Locating the distinction at the "margins of human understanding" places it beyond what univocal speech can accomplish. Hence Burrell still speaks of 'awareness' rather than the surety of personal possession or habitation. This accords well with his perduring insistence on the determinative judgment component in analogy. So whatever specifications we may succeed in making, analogy will remain "a species of ambiguity" (*KUG*, 112).

ESSENCE/EXISTENCE
A DISTINCTION TO EXPLAIN THE DISTINCTION

As Burrell understands it, the essence/existence distinction was called into service to help us conceive the nature of divinity without stumbling into the error of making it out as one of the set of things *in* the world which it had created. The *principium*, "The beginning and end of all things, and of rational creatures especially" (*ST* I.2 Intro.) cannot be contained, and therefore cannot be conceived, as one of those things. So much for the problem. The historical solutions were variations of treating essence and existence as they could be conceived in God and in creatures. This distinction between essence and existence "finds its roots in Alfarabi, its first articulation in Ibn-Sina, is approved by Maimonides, and brought to a refined status by Aquinas" (*KUG*, 35).[4]

The essence/existence distinction must be versatile enough to go both ways: secure the distinction of the transcendent God yet provide a connection from that Creator God to the creation. Therefore, "one needs a distinction which makes its appearance within the world as we

---

[4]The essence/existence distinction did play a central role in medieval times and in Clarke's retrieval of participation metaphysics which we saw above; but below, Jüngel will develop his polemic against the Thomist tradition by attacking the essence-existence distinction as one of the problematic causes, perhaps even *the* most problematic cause of modern atheism.

know it yet does not express a division *within* that world" (*KUG*, 20).
Burrell finds that the best candidate, and the only viable one for the job
description, is the fact of existence, which appears in the world but does
not distinguish kinds as it does so (*KUG*, 21-22). But once again, this
solution will not sit still for us and allow a neat formulation and
resolution. For as Burrell likes to cite from G. E. Moore, "existence is
not a predicate." So if existence is not a predicate, how can predication
be based upon it?

Reaching back through a long list of conversation partners to
Aristotle, Burrell refocuses the problem in terms of the questions, "What
is it?" and "Is it?" (*KUG*, 20). Noting Ibn-Sina's essentialism with its
attendant problems, Burrell sees Aquinas as inviting us to a kind of
conversion, a conversion which not only starts with the act of existence,
but one which also places "What is it?" (essence) in a subordinate
relationship to the act of existence:

> In short, we are asked to remind ourselves that essences, properties,
> and the like, cannot be the term of our philosophical inquiry, since
> they must be considered not things but constituents of things. It
> should be clear how this invitation moves one in a resolutely
> Aristotelian direction, confirming the individual existing thing, to be
> the paradigm instance of *what is*: substance (*KUG*, 36).[5]

Burrell connects Aquinas' method of dealing with the
essence/existence distinction to his analogical mode of discourse about
God through judgment. Once he has made the unique move of
beginning with and basing all upon *esse*, and since "existence is not a
predicate," at least not in the sense that we could spin out its
ramifications through syllogistic reasoning, then the account must

---

[5]This assessment, helpful though it is, could be strengthened by incorporating
Clarke's treatment of infinity in "The Limitation of Act by Potency," as cited above.

incorporate a degree of ambiguous tension which only acts of judgment can consummate. Continuing the theme of his earlier works, Burrell presents a "performance test," observing the "startling fact" that anything we might say about an object is irrelevant if we do not assert that what we say *is* in fact what obtains. Whatever the propositions may be, "they are all held in abeyance, as it were, awaiting assertion."[6] Taking issue with Ibn-Sina's notion that existence somehow comes to the essence or nature of a thing, Burrell contends:

> Truth, in other words, does not "come to" statements any more than existence "comes to" natures; but represents their culmination as asserted by a responsible knower, much as *esse* represents a thing's coming into existence by the creative power of a gracious God. True propositions are neither found nor do they emanate from a primal set of axioms; they must be asserted by one able to offer suitable warrant on their behalf (*KUG*, 32).

Analogy, in this view, is very much a philosophical *activity*. It is an exercise of responsibility, an act of judgment culminating in the assertion that something is in fact the case--that it is true. As we have seen, the judgment component of analogy, what might be called its active ingredient, argues against the claim that analogy is at root univocal (Duns Scotus). In the agential participation which culminates in judgment, the risk of failure and the potential joy of success point to the moving nature of temporal, finite existence and its intended relatedness to the eternal and infinite God. The wisdom of calling our loftiest expressions--which attempt to relate these various levels of existence-- neither univocation nor equivocation but analogy is fitting with the anthropological situation in which we actually find ourselves.

---

[6]Burrell, *Aquinas: God and Action*, 36.

As Burrell further demonstrates, the simpleness of deity follows from the identification of God as *Ipsum Esse Subsistens*. Divine simplicity is another way of expressing a solution to the distinction between God and the world--one which also could serve to link God and the world. For Aquinas, *esse* is not only the best appellation for God, it is also "the effect proper to the first and most universal cause, which is God" (*ST* I.45.5). If *esse* is what God produces, and all perfections come from God, then *esse* would have to be the sum of all perfections. This way of putting it would let Aquinas have his distinction and connect it to the world too:

> This is precisely what Aquinas insists in showing that the essence of divinity can be none other than to-be: "*esse* (to-be) is the actuality of all acts, and therefore the perfection of all perfections" (*De pot.* 7.2.9). This is what he is enabled to say after having shown in *De ente et essentia* how all existing things, even immaterial ones, can be said to be composed--by a mode of composition one step higher than that of matter to form: essence to *esse*. For once we begin to consider existence as the act proper to essence, then we can link it with perfection (*KUG*, 42).

Noting the primacy and intimacy of *esse*, that nothing extrinsic can be added to it except non-being, Aquinas concludes:

> Therefore *esse* is not determined by another as potency is by act, but rather as act is [limited] by potency. . . . And so this *esse* is distinguished from another *esse* insofar as it is of such and such a nature (*De Pot.* 7.2.9).

Burrell's use of act/potency and essence/existence clarifies how we might speak of God and the world; but most importantly, his adoption of this argument rejoins him to the central thrust of the Neo-Thomist school: participation metaphysics. He again embraces the language of participation metaphysics when he says of Aquinas: "There is then for him no 'existence in itself'; only what *has* existence by contrast to what

is existence--and that contrast formulates 'the distinction'" (*KUG*, 46).
In order to explicate *esse*, Burrell sees two related paths that Aquinas
uses: "the root analogy of potency to act (*actus essendi*) . . . [and]
participation (*ens per essentiam/per participationem)*" (*KUG*, 31). After
citing one of Aquinas' many summary passages on participation, Burrell
comments:

> The being which is subsistent in divinity is to be construed, then, as
> though it were an act, and furthermore an act in which created
> things--even spiritual creatures--participate as "having *esse* rather than
> being their own to-be" (1.3.4) (*KUG*, 31).

Perhaps because of its historical use with emanation schemes, against
which he polemicizes in all three of his books, Burrell never seems quite
comfortable with using participation language. Of particular significance
in his adoption of participation metaphysics is its association with the
positive nature of Aquinas' account, in contrast to Burrell's earlier
apophatic inclination. Evidently, the requirements exposed by his
grammatical probe eventually brought him round to this point of
convergence with participation metaphysics.[7]

Burrell shows that both Ibn-Sina and Maimonides formulated the
distinction, but they did so in such a way that only the uniqueness of
God could be stated. But in elaborating creation as a *sui generis*
activity, where God, the *actus essendi*, produces the *esse* of each
creature and of all that exists, Aquinas has found a way to express more
than the uniqueness of God. And this is what analogy based on
participation does--it expresses the connection while respecting the
distinction. In a pivotal passage, Burrell distinguishes between negative

---

[7]Some participation references can be found in *KUG*, 30-31, 46, 60, 90.

notions, which render an account of divine simplicity, and positive terms, used to predicate the attributes of God:

> What is essential to recognize here is that these two sets of adjectives correspond to different ontological levels, and hence require a separate treatment. Moreover, simpleness, and the notions which Aquinas will link with it--limitlessness, unchangeableness, and unity-- are all to be understood negatively, whereas he will defend a practice of predicating positive attributes. *Considerations of analogy, then, properly enter with such attributes*; yet the demand for attention to analogous uses of language will be established as one establishes "the distinction" through these formal features of divinity (*KUG*, 47, emphasis added).

So here we have a vital link: analogy enters with positive attribution. Nonetheless, it enters upon a stage set by formal features of grammar *in divinis* which constantly prevent the temptation to essentialize, to possess the attribution conceptually, to own a univocal core of meaning. That is, the formal features prevent the tendency to univocation if permitted to work with and guide our application of analogous terms. And this insight, the need for informed performance in using analogy, is certainly one of Burrell's finest contributions.

INDIVIDUALITY, RELATIONS AND CREATION

Among Burrell's three protagonists, Maimonides plays a key transition role in seeking an account which could show God's providential care for individuals. Maimonides' dissatisfaction with Aristotle's reported view, that "God's providence ends at the sphere of the moon" (*KUG*, 20), sparks Burrell's search for how Aquinas will take this "most precious" sphere of human life and connect it to his account of divinity. The search is for a way to affirm something more than the structural permanence of the species. The individual life, in all its vulnerability, must also be valued.

Burrell contends that Aquinas chose as his starting point a design "to secure the reality of individual things" (*KUG*, 30) and that this starting point is closely related to his analogous treatment of *esse*. In affirming the value of the individual life, we thereby offer even greater praise to the creator of that life:

> We cannot cede to the temptation to denigrate created things to exalt their creator. For it amounts to an even greater praise to affirm a creator able to constitute creatures to function as agents in their own right, having existence as a gift, to be sure, but *de jure*, as it were (*KUG*, 34).

Aquinas' desire to secure the reality of the individual can also be seen in his opposition to Ibn-Sina's theory of knowledge. Ibn-Sina opted for a kind of realism in which the intellect was illuminated by the "agent intelligence" in its reception of essential forms (*KUG*, 29). The passive nature of this account threatened the activity inherent in Aquinas' secondary causes, i.e., in human agents. Burrell's claim, drawn from Aquinas, is that human knowing culminating in judgment is our highest activity. The freedom of intentionality, both divine and human, comes into play here. For where Ibn-Sina put forth a triad of "emanation, essence, reception," Aquinas wrote in terms of "creation, *esse*, and judgment."[8]

Seeking an account of what God might know about particulars, Burrell shows how adopting a practical model of creation (as opposed

---

[8]Etienne Gilson, "Pourquoi S. Thomas a critiqué S. Augustin," *Arch. d'Hist. Doct. Litt du* M-A 1 (1926) 5-127, as cited in *KUG*, 29.

to a theoretical or speculative one) lets Aquinas elaborate God's relation to individuals. Although Maimonides had the original inclination to shift from the speculative to the practical model of creation, it was Aquinas who was able to unify that model with other questions at issue:

> Shifting the mode of knowing from speculative to practical, not only extends God's knowing to singulars, but grants it an intentionality *par excellence*: God knows the particular manner in which each individual participates in the divine essence, and so can be said to know the *ratio* proper to each thing--"indeed the singular essence of each individual" (*KUG*, 90, citing from *De Ver.* 2.7).

Intimately present to the individual as the source and maintenance of its *esse* (*ST* I.8.1), God is thereby availed of intimate knowledge of each individual.

Human life and relationships. While Burrell wants to follow Aquinas in affirming the integrity of the individual, he certainly does not advocate individualism. Indeed, he situates the reality of the individual in its various relationships: first, in its relationship to the *principium*, "the beginning and end of all things, and of rational creatures especially" (I.2 Intro.); second, in its relationship to the world (attitude); and third, in its relationship with other humans (*KUG*, 7, 22). We remember Burrell's point above: "The creature itself *is* a relation."[9]

By considering fictional characters and creations, further light is cast onto *esse*. For instance, we could describe a unicorn, but it would be a different matter entirely to relate to one. Similarly, we might gain something from an encounter with a literary character, and such a fictional character could not be said to be an illusion, but attempting to

---

[9]*Aquinas: God and Action*, 138, in turn drawn from *ST* I.45.3.2.

have a relationship with it would be an illusion.   This highlights
Burrell's stress on what escapes direct philosophical formulation but
remains crucial to the enterprise of inquiry--existence:

> The human spirit, it is true, can enter into many sorts of
> relationships, one of which is knowing or describing something, yet
> the sense in which human relationships are treasured is one which
> presupposes the reality of each of those relating (*KUG*, 22).

So what is presupposed, but too often ignored, turns out to be of
preeminent importance.

Still, it is not easy to pin any of this down, and if we did do so,
we would not have captured anything worthwhile.   The elusiveness of
esse, yet its being at the root of what we value the most, should
convince us of the need for Burrell's inquiry as a procedure, or the
manuductio.   Even relation "remains the most elusive of Aristotle's
categories, not properly an accident for its being is not *in* but *ad*; which
is to say that it does not exist *in* another so much as 'between' the
relata" (*KUG*, 23).   We might say that the reality of a relationship, its
'betweenness', must be enacted, actually lived, just as the reality of a
statement hangs in abeyance, awaiting its assertion by a responsible
knower, and a bank check is worthless unless signed and dated by a
responsible party.[10]   Relationships resemble these other illustrations,
for they too must be affirmed in word and/or deed.   Within the
intentional realm, this involves something like the relation of potential
to actual.

---

[10]The illustration that an unasserted statement is like an unsigned check is from
Polanyi, *Personal Knowledge*, 28.

Creation vs. emanation.   Throughout *Knowing the Unknowable God,* Burrell criticizes emanationist accounts, using Ibn-Sina's in particular as a foil to Aquinas' account of creation. Emanation involves necessity and thus can be grasped through conceptualism or essentialism. But because creation involves intent--knowledge, will, and judgment--it must be grasped through participation, self-involvement. Another clear divide is Ibn-Sina's acceptance of the Aristotelian eternal world, upon which creation imposes forms, from Aquinas' Christian doctrine of *creatio ex nihilo.*[11] The clean beginning of *creatio ex nihilo* neatly differentiates nothingness from the divine *actus essendi* and the creaturely being which is produced from God's intentionality in creation. Ontologically, God is distinguished from the world. Through intentionality, God is freely related to the world.

The deistic relation, watchmaker: watch :: God: world, does not adequately express Aquinas' portrayal of the relation of Creator to creation. For Aquinas, God maintains an "intimate presence to each individual" (*KUG*, 93). Reiterating Aquinas' key passage, Burrell declares:

> It is this feature which also connects the creator with all of creation: "since the essence of God is *esse* itself, it is proper that created *esse* be the effect proper to God"; but *esse* is that which is most inward to each thing and most profoundly within all things . . . so God may be said to be in all things, and intimately so" (1.8.1). Where the emanation scheme supplied a formal and imaginative connection, Aquinas reaches for an even more intimate linkage by making a move beyond formal structures to the very to-be of things (*KUG*, 49).

---

[11]In an otherwise favorable review, Burrell has been criticized for not bringing out this fundamental historical difference between Ibn-Sina and Aquinas. See Raymond L. Weiss, review of *Knowing the Unknowable God* in *Journal of Religion* (1988): 302-305.

Contrary to the agnostic tendencies in his earlier works (and vestiges still linger in this last study), Burrell's repeated affirmation of this Thomistic passage has surpassed philosophical agnosticism. Neither Aquinas nor Burrell remain philosophically agnostic in asserting this account of the divine presence. And as we have learned from both Clarke and Burrell, presence, especially divine presence, is not neutral or self-contained. The presence of God is the divine being in act. As such it makes all the difference to the world and the individuals to whom it is present as creator and maintainer of their own dependent, contingent act of being.

Commenting on the ephemeral nature of our individual lives in the world, lives which do not exhibit the same lastingness as structures or species, Burrell again uses literature to make his point: "We can readily discriminate great literature from trite or formulaic imitations by its singular capacity to render the individual present to us" (*KUG*, 21). Two insights can be drawn from this literary "making present." First, it instantiates the practical model of creation as it appears in the products (literature) of secondary causes (human agents). Second, in rendering the individual character present to us, it is demonstrating the power of the act of existence through the narrative creative imitation of human *esse.*

FURTHER IMPLICATIONS FOR ANALOGY

Maimonides, Burrell tells us, preferred to separate his philosophical predication from the admittedly anthropomorphic usage of the Torah. Aquinas, on the other hand, develops the use of analogy as a "middle ground" (*KUG*, 53), which permits him to unify his manner of predication with his overall project. We have already noted how Burrell saw that Aquinas' use of analogy let him render a positive account of divine attributes where Maimonides had to remain in the silence of philosophical agnosticism (*KUG*, 47). Recalling Burrell's first study, which showed how analogical terms functioned quite naturally in different contexts, Burrell now makes a fascinating suggestion, linking the analogical, the spiritual, and the capacity to relate:

> This capacity, moreover, to relate (potentially) to all there is, is what defined mind for the medievals--intellect and will--as a spiritual power. *Spirit* referred not in the first instance to an unfamiliar mode of existence, but to a capacity for relating on different levels and across the space-time parameters endemic to bodies (*KUG*, 23).

Thus 'spirit' and 'analogy' share the common feature of relating to and on different levels, 'spirit' being thought of as a capacity and 'analogy' used as an instrument to express that capacity.

As we conclude this examination of an account which has consciously used logic with the hope of surpassing logic, preferred performance to theory, and demanded our committed participation in the inquiry, Burrell's insight into the way we actually do theology might help us think about where we are and where we have been:

> It turns out that we seldom, if ever, reason *to* God's existence, but rather retrospectively retrace our tracks to satisfy ourselves of the cogency of the individual steps which cumulatively brought us to where we are (*KUG*, 6).

Burrell's concluding remarks continue to inveigh against those who would try to tame analogy by reducing it to univocation:

> What seems to most modern writers to be the only way to offer analogy respectability would have rendered it superfluous for Aquinas. (Much like those analysts of metaphor who keep trying to spell them out non-metaphorically. Were their project realizable,

metaphors would remain as decoration only.) What makes analogical expressions at once respectable and valuable to Aquinas is our use of judgment (*KUG*, 112).

Because analogy always involves *us* in judgment and responsibility, we could characterize using it as 'the analogical act'.

Analogy involves "an activity of altering . . . understanding" (*KUG*, 57); for we use it in expressing that which transcends any one level or context. Presumably, or at least hopefully, that which alters understanding alters it toward a greater understanding. Hence, something greater than understanding alone must be involved in the alteration. And this something greater, which comes to expression in the analogical act, might truly be called 'spirit'.

CHAPTER SEVEN

INTERLOCUTORY REMARKS

GRAMMATICAL ISSUES

The Conflation of Analogy and Metaphor.

While Burrell has shown how analogical terms function, and even specified some differentiations from metaphor, he has persistently interchanged metaphor and analogy as though they were identical. So if we apply his own notion of looking at use rather than theory, then Burrell's use demands a warrant which is never forthcoming. He assumes that language is inherently metaphorical, observes that both metaphor and analogy require the active judgment of the one who uses them because their use is more like a performance than a strict theory, and then often employs the terms interchangeably. Now while I would agree that there is a certain play in language, a play which keeps language as flexible as the life of its users, I do not think that the presence of play or ambiguity affects the more traditional arguments for distinguishing univocation, equivocation, and analogy.

Let us begin by examining some of Burrell's many statements which conflate metaphor and analogy. Pursuing his strategy that if we became more aware of the free play of words in our ordinary usage, we would see that our God-language is not different in kind, Burrell explores similarities which occur in ordinary speech. Looking through his Wittgensteinian lens (particularly *Investigations*, ##182-183, 602ff.), Burrell says of similarities and analogies: "What is significant here is the fact that we can recognize them where we have no notion of how to formulate them, and that we are continually discarding the less relevant of them in favor of others."[1] But I must take issue with his point precisely because theology, perhaps more than any other discipline, is decidedly *not* "continually discarding" its analogies, metaphors, and discovered similarities. Granted, there is continuing debate in most religious traditions, but Muslims still read the Koran, Jews the Torah, and Christians the Bible. Never mind that these contain some antiquated and inadequate speech forms. Virtually all religious traditions, whatever their openness to progressive expressions, typically show more of a conservatism with religious language. Even apart from putatively sacred texts, words like 'good', 'true', 'beautiful', 'loving', 'just', and 'merciful' appear throughout the religious literature over the millennia of recorded writings. So while one would be correct to speak of adjustments, nuances, interpretative shifts, and perhaps an occasional revelation, most of the central terms for most religious traditions do not

---

[1]Burrell, *Analogy and Philosophical Language*, 125. In the remainder of this chapter, this work will be cited parenthetically as *APL*.

get continually discarded. If I am right about this, then it would follow that Burrell may also have overlooked some underlying structure(s) which this common usage implies.

A second important part of Burrell's view of language as inherently metaphorical is his blurring of the boundary between univocation and analogy which we saw above: "We dare not continue to claim a perfectly adequate division between univocal and analogous usage" (*APL*, 220.) While he can justifiably claim that there is considerable play in many univocal terms, further analysis will show that this observation does not weaken the distinction between univocation and analogy. Whether or not strictly univocal terms exist, univocation still performs a vital function in our language, even if it is only a theoretical one. Ultimately at issue is the independent categorial location of analogical terms. My view is that in order to sustain the independence of analogy, the theoretical position of univocation is required, though not total rigidity in actual use. The function of this 'theoretical' univocation is to establish one pole of the spectrum of *intentional* possibilities, the other being equivocation. Granting that ordinary usage is often inclusive of some metaphorical "crossing over," we can simply locate ordinary usage close to, and in the direction of, but not necessarily identical with, theoretical univocation. In forming these categories the *intention* of the speaker is decisive. While formal accounts cannot provide algorithmic certainty, even Burrell ends up allowing three clear intentional categories: univocation, equivocation, and analogy. Consider his description of how the origin of metaphorical usage depends upon established usage:

We could not "cross kinds" to advantage were such crossings the usual thing--for them [sic] we could neither call it crossing nor would we have any kinds to cross (*APL*, 221).

So Burrell too recognizes the need for a univocal pole, or something akin to it. Furthermore, he notes the tendency of metaphors to lose their crossing function and settle down into ordinary or univocal usage: "Thus are univocal terms often born" (ibid.). This settling-down effect constitutes a gravitation toward what I have called the theoretical pole of univocation. So while the blurring that Burrell has demonstrated requires an adjustment of the categories of univocation and equivocation, it does not affect the analogical category in any strong sense.

In fact, the most important inference from Burrell's stimulating treatment of these issues, but an inference which Burrell does not draw, is that analogical terms never settle down while metaphorical ones always do. The fact that both metaphor and analogy incorporate some ambiguity is not sufficient grounds for categorial conflation. The shared ambiguity is no more than an indicator of human contingency, which has more to do with our finite, ontological status in relation to an infinite Creator God than to a linguistic category.

Yet Burrell punctuates his account with such misleading statements as "analogous terms are at root equivocal and hence not to be trusted in argument."[2] With Burrell, I would readily grant that analogy should not be employed as an argument but as a mode of speech--the best one available for speech about God. As we saw above with Neo-Thomist accounts of analogy, something else must do the work which analogy is then called on to express. So more precisely, my objection is only to the first part of Burrell's statement that "analogous terms are at root

---

[2]Burrell, *Aquinas: God and Action*, xii, hereafter cited parenthetically as *AGA*.

equivocal." Now what Burrell does show rather well, particularly in his first two books, is that analogous terms uniquely possess the capacity to "be used properly in utterly diverse contexts" (*AGA*, 122.). This capacity, as we have seen in both Burrell's and Clarke's accounts, prevents them from being rigorously defined. They retain a certain "stretch" capacity. But Burrell takes this capacity for transcontextual use, the stretch capacity, and concludes that deep down they must be metaphors:

> Yet our reliance on paradigm instances when we actually use analogous expressions shows that they never quite cease being metaphors (ibid.).

Similarly, in introducing *actus*, he refers to it as one of the "master metaphors," and then again asserts a categorial conflation: "As metaphors, these terms are inherently analogous" (*AGA*, 116). And in yet another assertion, with sweeping implications if correct, he suggests that *esse* is metaphorical: "In this metaphorical sense, then, 'to-be' is the predicate of predicates" (*AGA*, 36). Since this claim cuts against Aquinas' fundamental treatment of the issue, and since Aquinas plays the central role in all three of his books as the one so grammatically astute, then it seems that Burrell at least needs to recognize this dissonance with Aquinas and give greater warrant for his own departure. For in contrast to Burrell, Aquinas contends: "All univocal predications are reduced to one first non-univocal analogical predication, which is being" (*ST* I.13.5.1). Burrell and the many other modern writers who have contended that language is inherently metaphorical can do so only by ignoring Clarke's "embarrassing little 'is.'"[3] Is there anything

---

[3]Clarke, "What Cannot Be Said in St. Thomas' Essence-Existence Doctrine," 21.

equivocal or metaphorical about existence? What value would any other quality possess without existence, without life itself?

Carefully considered, being is neither univocal nor equivocal. It is common to all that is--infinite, uncaused being in God, finite, created, responsible being in humankind. Being, the gift of life itself, underlies and enlivens all other qualities of which we may speak. Yet while being is common to God, humankind, horses, dogwood trees, and rocks, it is not common in the same manner. When we say that "God exists" and that "my daughter exists," we mean what we say literally. However, "exists" is being differentially applied to an infinite and a finite context. Therefore, it is inaccurate to say that being is univocal. Instead, terms which are at home on such different levels qualify as analogical predicates. Hence, while I agree that *esse*, being, is "the predicate of predicates," Burrell's assertion that being is metaphorical does not follow. Metaphorical terms acquire their punch by being skillfully forced to play away from home (to borrow Burrell's own phrase), taken out of their normal context. But to say that something or someone *is*, involves no equivocation; it is not metaphorical because there has been no unusual crossing of contexts. When I say that I have a good horse and that I worship a good God, in neither case do I equivocate. In neither case is a word forced out of its normal context. Nonetheless, different ways of existing are sharply highlighted in the infinite God and the finite creation which that infinite God has created. To be a creature is to exist dependently, conditionally, and with limitations. Since being does not distort its meaning when spoken of on its different levels, it is rightly thought of as analogical. Indeed, this is the test of all analogical predicates: that they, like being itself, can be used on different levels of being without distorting their meaning.

EXTRINSIC vs. INTRINSIC PREDICATION

Conflating metaphor and analogy, as Burrell has done, ignores the distinction between extrinsic and intrinsic predication and the closely associated placement of the prime analogate. Yet these concerns are vital to the discussion.[4] Although the issues are rather convoluted, I shall attempt some clarifications, since the extrinsic/intrinsic distinction can enforce the boundary between metaphor and analogy.

First, while Burrell has provided an excellent reading of Plato with his notion of the engaged, committed inquirer, and has skillfully developed that notion with his *manuductio* reading of Aquinas, he has taken a good idea too far when he asserts that the prime analogate is located in "the questioner's awareness of his own existence" (*APL*, 150). By contrast, Aquinas specifically classifies as metaphorical the predication which recognizes the creature as prime analogate:

> All names applied metaphorically to God, are applied to creatures primarily rather than to God, because when said of God they mean only similitudes to such creatures. For as "smiling" applied to a field means only that the field in the beauty of its flowering is like to the beauty of the human smile by proportionate likeness, so the name of "lion" applied to God means only that God manifests strength in His works, as a lion in his (*ST* I.13.6).

---

[4]See Klubertanz, *Aquinas on Analogy*, 45-46. Also see Lyttkens, *The Analogy between God and the World*, 247, 333, 335. Lyttkens makes a good case for intrinsic predication without ignoring counterexamples in Aquinas' corpus.

As Aquinas points out, 'lion' can be predicated of God only in a secondary, extrinsic sense.   Unlike analogy, this metaphorical predication is context dependent. We would hardly say of the revelation on the cross, "God is a lion"; in fact, one often speaks of the 'Lamb' in this context. On the other hand, there is no context in which we would deny that God is good. 'Good' qualifies as an analogical predicate because its use can transcend a given context. One may quite correctly state that God is good and that a given human mother is good.

One of the strongest features of this analogical theory is showing how *God* can be the prime analogate for a given perfection intrinsic to both God and creatures. The analogical expression of these intrinsically realized perfections is ultimately warranted by an account of creation and the subsequent relation of God and humankind. Thus Aquinas argued:

> But to other names not applied to God in a metaphorical sense, the same rule would apply if they were spoken of God as the cause only, as some have supposed. For when it is said, "God is good," it would then only mean, "God is the cause of the creature's goodness"; thus the term "good" applied to God would include in its meaning the creature's goodness. Hence "good" would apply primarily to creatures rather than God. But as was shown above (A.2), these names are applied to God not as the cause only, but also essentially. For the words, "God is good," or "wise," signify not only that He is the cause of goodness or wisdom, but that these exist in Him in a more excellent way. Hence as regards what the name signifies, these names are applied primarily to God rather than to creatures, because these perfections flow from God to creatures (*ST* I.13.6).

A crucial distinction is thereby elaborated: analogical terms are used with the distinctive claim that God and humans share the perfection, God in the infinite essence of divine being, and creatures, "because these perfections flow from God to creatures." God's merely being the cause of a perfection in humans would only permit metaphorical predication of the quality to God. In order to attribute the predicate analogously, God must also possess the perfection "in a more excellent way." Thus two conditions must be met in the most serious claims of analogical predication: 1) God is the cause of the perfections that creatures possess; and 2) both parties, God and creatures, possess the given perfection intrinsically, although God does so preeminently.

Aside from one or two passing references, Burrell does not appear to confront this evidence directly, and in ignoring its import while seizing upon less positive statements of Aquinas, he is led to some strongly apophatic conclusions, particularly in his first work:

> If God must remain outside of any genus, he is properly unknowable. Such an assertion would seem to end in pure agnosticism. Yet Aquinas refuses to settle for that and goes on to drive a wedge: then God must be improperly knowable, namely by analogy (*APL*, 126).

Now if Burrell wants to employ "properly" and "improperly" as he does, I think that he owes a clear refutation of its normal Neo-Thomist usage, or at least, more justification of his own. In the conventional Neo-Thomist usage,

> an analogy is called "proper" if the perfection is intrinsic to each of the analogates in question, and "improper" or "extrinsic" if the perfection is present in only one of the analogates.[5]

Second, and far more importantly, it seems that if Burrell were right about analogy representing "improper" knowledge of God, then this would remove the *raison d'etre* of analogy for Aquinas, viz., discourse that is fitting, or proper, to the creature's unique setting as a subject of creation and revelation, but discourse that still avoids the twin evils of

---

[5]Klubertanz, *Aquinas on Analogy*, 7, in his section titled "Traditional terms and definitions." Burrell acknowledges this general usage in *APL*, 11-12.

either presuming too much, as in univocation, or of admitting to the "Fallacy of Equivocation" (*ST* I.13.5). Third, while Burrell rightly recalls Aquinas in saying that "God is not in any genus," that is not all that Aquinas says on the subject:

> All created perfections are in God. Hence He is spoken of as universally perfect, because He lacks not . . . any excellence which may be found in any genus (*ST* I.4.2).

In a short but *a propos* commentary on Burrell's second book, John Milbank observes:

> Burrell does not recognize that there is a tension between his notion of a 'grammatical' approach to the unknown beyond the known, and the very different idea that throughout his writings Aquinas is spelling out the specific 'grammar' of Creation *ex nihilo* in which the 'unknown' and 'known' are specified together according to a particular religious assumption about ultimate reality . . . . Burrell's own exposition in fact veers between these two different notions-- grammar as giving the transcendental possibility of a negative specification of the unknown, and grammar as explication of the culturally-specific meaning-presuppositions involved in the logic of creation *ex nihilo*.[6]

If analogical predication is our best way of talking about God, it need not claim any 'privileged access'. It only claims a knowledge which neither reduces to a univocal core nor evaporates in equivocation when God and humankind are "specified together"--i.e., understood to share a given quality. So while Burrell's first work tends to be somewhat unbalanced in speaking of alternatives like "pure agnosticism" or "driving a wedge," it is certainly to his credit that his last book ends up speaking about Aquinas adopting the "middle ground" of analogy in

---

[6]John Milbank, "'Between Purgation and Illumination': A Critique of the Theology of Right," in *Christ, Ethics, and Tragedy: Essays in Honour of Donald MacKinnon*, ed. Kenneth Surin (Cambridge: Cambridge University Press, 1989), 169.

order to present a more positive account of God by distinguishing "genuinely analogical uses from those which could only be employed metaphorically."[7]

By this later admission of analogy as a distinct and positive means of speaking of God, Burrell can then differentiate Aquinas from what he takes as the more agnostic approaches of Ibn-Sina and Maimonides. I take Burrell's reversal on the separation of analogy and metaphor as highly significant; for when it comes down to specifying any positive knowledge of the divine which is not completely context-dependent, no matter how modest the claim may be, analogy is the best candidate for such expression. Indeed, it may be the only candidate, as long as we remember that analogy is used not to establish faith, but to express it. In this latter account, Burrell has self-corrected some of the earlier imbalances which I have criticized. This self-correcting movement within his corpus actually demonstrates the methodological principle with which he began his first study--the willingness of the engaged inquirer to let himself be led by the logical and perhaps extra-logical forces at work in a Socratic-style investigation.

'ACT OF' LANGUAGE

Attempting to penetrate what Aquinas is up to in speaking of existing as an act, as the *actus essendi*, Burrell cites some interesting examples of 'act of' language, fails to draw the real significance of these examples, and then somehow manages to arrive at the most important

---

[7]Burrell, *Knowing the Unknowable God*, 53.

conclusion in spite of it all, the awareness of *presence*. Following his usual modus operandi, Burrell hopes to find a clue to the more profound matters by looking at normal usage:

> Actually we seldom speak of the 'act of' anything, and 'act of existing' will prove the oddest expression of all. Act of appears to be largely a solemnity used to signal important events or identify act with agent, as in, "You are witnessing the act of signing the peace treaty with Japan," or, "he saw the act of murder." This usage is closely allied with 'in the act of' which is used to pinpoint temporal connections: "As I came in, he was in the act of pouring a drink." What is interesting about these cases is that act of [sic] and in the act of [sic] are superfluous (*APL*, 147-148).

As Jüngel will argue below, 'act of' language is hardly "superfluous." On the contrary, what is going on in these examples is an *intensification*, an announcement, alert, or warning. 'Act of' functions as an intensifier which recreates the *event* nature of the specific action. It is really not unlike Burrell's very good account of the difference between a statement and an assertion. "Witnessing the act of signing the peace treaty" places the witness within the event, makes him or her *present* as a participant. It is as though one penetrates time in a new way by such 'act of' expressions. It is not just that something has happened, will happen, or happens; it *is* happening. Thus its existence is being asserted in an intensified manner which tries to unite event, speaker, and hearers. When we "pinpoint temporal connections," we may not transcend time, but we at least vivify it and perhaps are ourselves vivified as we are drawn more into the present so that we are wholly *present to* what is transpiring. Anyone who has ever experienced the power of communion has become present at the pinpoint of temporal connections.

To his credit, Burrell does get to at least part of the import of *presence* and *present to* from examining Aquinas' remarks:

Our mind cannot understand itself in such a way as to immediately apprehend itself; rather it is the case that in apprehending something else, it arrives at a knowledge of itself (*De Ver.* 10.8, as cited in *APL*, 152.)

While Burrell does speak of the category of "presence" and "being-present-to" (*APL*, 152), it is strange that he would deny their heightened grammatical expression in 'act of' language.

TAUTOLOGIES--ANALYTIC AND SYNTHETIC PROPOSITIONS

One of Burrell's most interesting contributions to understanding the *Summa*, Qq.3-11, is showing how Wittgenstein's tautologies can illuminate what Aquinas is doing. However, Burrell has erred in contending that Aquinas' use of *actus* is one of those tautologies: "By insisting that 'whatever is is in act,' [Aquinas] offers one of those illustrative tautologies" (*AGA*, 117). Properly understood, tautologies constitute analytic propositions from which other propositions necessarily follow. But in linking existence with *actus*, Aquinas has made a synthetic rather than an analytic move. As we saw in Clarke's discussion above, 'existence' can perhaps be considered in and of itself (although Aquinas really does not do so). But if existence itself is existence in act, then as action it is no longer something unto itself; it is part of being present to others, making a difference somehow, and being part of an interacting universe. Speaking in terms of action opens up the discussion, leads the concept away from itself, and lends itself to combination and interaction. (While there is an obvious anachronism in applying Kant's terms to Aquinas' exposition, this should be no more out of order than applying Wittgenstein's.) In other words, grammatical analysis alone is insufficient to the task of understanding *actus* since by *joining* existence to act, we are no longer dealing with branches of a single concept.

THE NEGLECT OF PARTICIPATION

The most serious problem which I find in Burrell's work is the failure to confront directly Aquinas' extensive treatment of participation metaphysics as the basis of analogy. These problems are most evident in his first two books, because once again, in his last work, *Knowing the Unknowable God*, Burrell has begun to recognize the presence and importance of participation for Aquinas. Having taken the more modern route of the linguistic turn, Burrell seems to have ignored some of the best work in the Neo-Thomist tradition. Perhaps Wittgenstein, whom Burrell and many others credit with freeing them from a sort of 'bewitchment', also casts a bewitchment of his own.

Burrell's first two books are sprinkled with strongly apophatic statements and various attacks upon Neoplatonic concepts. Yet if Clarke is right in what we considered above, then Aquinas' unique and original appropriation of the Neoplatonic tradition is one of the keys to his use of analogy. Furthermore, the absence of 'infinity' in Burrell's treatment of Aquinas' grammar *in divinis* is a glaring omission directly stemming from the avoidance of participation metaphysics. This omission is all the more noteworthy when we consider that the first part of Burrell's project in *Aquinas: God and Action* was to elucidate the grammar of the

Summa, Qq.3-11, and Q.7 is exclusively devoted to "The Infinity of God."

John Milbank, who wants to incorporate something like Burrell's linguistic doctrine, likewise faults him for not seeing Aquinas' dependence on participation:

> For Aquinas the possibility of analogy is grounded in this reality of participation in being and goodness. Analogy is not, for him, primarily a linguistic doctrine, even if . . . it must become so for us-- though not in a manner which persists in the transcendentalist illusion that a 'semantic' account of analogy can be given before an ontological account of participation.[8]

Language must express its debt to that which makes it possible in the first place, which is very much like Clarke's understanding of what analogy does. Milbank further criticizes Burrell for attributing his own incomplete understanding to Aquinas:

> 'Good' offers us a semantic depth not because this word already happens to have this character within some sphere of ordinary secular language which Aquinas could never have conceived of, but because actual, given human being is involved in some indefinition in relation to God. Against Burrell one must say that to ascribe real degrees of perfection to being, indeed any use of evaluative perfection-terms, *already* assumes a metaphysics of participation, such that grammar here grounds itself in theology, not theology in grammar.[9]

Milbank's point, that grammar must be grounded in theology and not vice versa, is not inconsistent with Clarke's earlier criticism of Wittgenstein, viz., that even a form of life must be grounded in the metaphysics of action.

---

[8]John Milbank, "Between Purgation and Illumination," 171.

[9]Ibid., 172.

SUMMARY REMARKS

Burrell has provided fresh insights into analogy, both in his many successes and in what I take to be his occasional shortcomings. My criticisms notwithstanding, Burrell has still made a lasting contribution to understanding analogy.

Most importantly, he has shown how the "systematically vague" nature of analogous terms is appropriately fitting to the anthropological condition. Capitalizing upon the ambiguity in Aquinas' metaphysics of *esse*, he has linked the "middle ground" of analogical use to judgment. In short, he has shown that if the evaluative element in analogical language (and human life itself) were to be tamed by some algorithmic, essentialist scheme, then that which we value most in human life and relationships would have been removed. Taken as a whole, his work is an eloquent refutation of the idea that analogy is at root univocal. Applying methodological insights learned from Wittgenstein, Burrell's extended treatment of judgment, commitment, and the self-involving nature of inquiry clarifies much of what takes place as analogy is actually *used*.

Yet the espoused guidance of Wittgenstein can be both blessing and burden. On the blessing side of the ledger, the narrower focus on use within a form of life avoids the dizzying aspects of an unaided focus on being itself. Undoubtedly, this more limited field, especially at the beginning of Burrell's inquiry in *Analogy and Philosophical Language*, aided his development of how judgment functions in analogy. The major disadvantage is that Wittgenstein chose not to venture into the kind of areas which Aquinas and Neo-Thomists generally see as most vital. Hence, at key moments of the inquiry Wittgenstein's guidance goes "on holiday." For example, when Burrell extensively develops Aquinas' "chief analogy" of *actus* in *Aquinas: God and Action*, and when he further adopts participation as the basis for positive predication about God in *Knowing the Unknowable God*, he has entered metaphysical and epistemological terrain which clearly surpasses Wittgenstein's scope. At these decisive turns, the guide is no longer Wittgenstein but Aquinas; or more precisely, Aquinas and Burrell's own good judgment rendered as an event in the inquiry.

PART THREE

EBERHARD JÜNGEL'S CRITIQUE AND ANALOGICAL ALTERNATIVE

INTRODUCTION TO PART THREE

Eberhard Jüngel undertakes a radical critique of traditional forms of
analogy; for in his historical analysis, he sees analogy, particularly
Aquinas' use of analogy, as the expression of a hidden agnosticism.
Jüngel is convinced that 1) inherent flaws within the metaphysical
tradition led inevitably to the atheism of modern times; and 2) analogy
was the not so innocent means of masking and thus temporarily avoiding
those inherent flaws. Assessing the modern situation, Jüngel believes
that "the word 'God' . . . . threatens to become a more and more
inappropriate word."[1] He is concerned lest

> our talk about God does not end up silencing him. Compared to
> atheistic thoughtlessness, this is the much greater danger for theology
> and for the Christian faith: that God will be talked to death, that he
> is silenced by the very words that seek to talk about him (*GMW*, vii).

---

[1] Eberhard Jüngel, *God as the Mystery of the World: On the Foundation of the
Theology of the Crucified One in the Dispute between Theism and Atheism*, trans.
Darrell L. Guder (Grand Rapids, Michigan: William B. Eerdmans, 1983), 3. In the
remainder of this introduction, and in the following chapter, this work will be cited
parenthetically as *GMW*. Also see Jüngel, "God--As a Word of Our Language," in
The Liberating Word, ed. Frederick Herzog, trans. Robert Osborn (Nashville:
Abingdon Press, 1971), 21-45.

Jüngel perceives that the inappropriateness of theism, especially the rationalistic foundationalism of the metaphysical tradition, must generate the atheism in which so much of the modern world now finds itself.[2] Jüngel attempts to find a *tertium quid* beyond theism and atheism: "Atheism can be rejected only if one overcomes theism" (*GMW*, 43). In contrast to the above accounts of analogy, accounts which capitalized upon ambiguity, he seeks specific and "*unambiguous* talk about God" derived from the humanity of God, from a christologically informed anthropomorphism (*GMW*, vii, emphasis added).   Seeking the unambiguous as he does, Jüngel consistently polemicizes against the tradition of negative theology.   Significantly for this present study, he includes Aquinas as one of those apophatic theologians.

Jüngel's constructive proposals arise out of his strong christological allegiance as well as the failures which he perceives in the theological and philosophical tradition.   Methodologically, Jüngel links his systematic discussion with historical analysis:

> Sweeping criticism, moreover, does not change the criticized traditions, but rather permits them to expand even further under a minimally altered surface. A differentiated appreciation of our

---

[2]What Jüngel has assumed as a given, viz., the atheism of the contemporary world, is actually more controversial. As Ted Peters has argued:

"Our modern age is right now undergoing rapid and dramatic change. A newer post-modern sensibility seems to be emerging. Post-modernity is not atheistic. It is quite religious, even mystical. There is a resurgence of religious consciousness all over the world, Germany included. . . . In many ways the excesses of scientific atheism have become old hat. A new religiosity is rapidly taking its place." See Peters, Review of *God as the Mystery of the World*, in *Currents in Theology and Mission* 11 (1984): 313.

While I think that Peters is generally right about the contemporary situation, Jüngel's more somber assessment is still accurate for the academic world, and perhaps most importantly for Jüngel's thesis, for the church. A new and general "religiosity" may very well be underway without engaging Christian theology.

historical sources will lead, on the other hand, to an ultimately radical controversy with it (*GMW*, ix).

Jüngel's work raises radical controversy with Aquinas and the metaphysical tradition. In this controversy, which is developed as a dispute about analogy, fundamental issues of theology and anthropology are debated.

CHAPTER EIGHT

JÜNGEL'S ANALYSIS: THE APORIA IN DOCTRINAL AND ANALOGICAL EXPRESSION

THE GENESIS OF THE *APORIA*

The theological failure of metaphysical signification. Instead of a "sweeping rejection" of either theism or atheism, Jüngel seizes upon the modern world's rejection of God as the key to the nature of God. By encountering the aporia which became manifest in the nineteenth century, he believes that he can find an authentic doctrine of God. Hence he is sharply critical of theology's refusal to address the death of God while continuing to embrace what he sees as the fragments of a defeated metaphysic.

Instead, Jüngel wants us to follow Luther (theologically) and Hegel (philosophically) in an honest assessment of the death of God. Jüngel refers to the death of God on two related levels: first, in the sense of metaphysical failures leading to modern atheism; second, in confronting the death of God as a historical event in the cross of Christ.

195

Jüngel would have us remember that Tertullian, a theologian, first developed the concept, not later philosophers such as Nietzsche. By developing his doctrine of God and his metaphysics from the cross, Jüngel would like to reclaim the death of God for theology.

The metaphysical tradition could not think through the death of God because it had defined God as omnipotent, impassible, imperishable, and *supra nos* ("above us" or "beyond us"). In such conceptions of God were hidden seeds of disintegration which inevitably led to atheistic responses. Pointedly, Jüngel considers the essence/existence distinction (which Clarke and Burrell use so extensively) as the chief culprit. Tracing the history of the Scholastic discussion, Jüngel delineates how what was at first a merely rational distinction between the essence and existence of God eventually led thought (i.e., philosophy) to assert itself between the essence and the existence of God. Once it had assumed this position "between God and God," as in Descartes, then thought attempted to become its own ground. It began to develop itself through self-reflectivity, through return to itself. It is this focus on the self which Jüngel contends is the source of the modern aporia: the unthinkability, the unspeakability, and finally, the silencing of God.

While the Scholastics needed to make a rational distinction in order to develop their metaphysical doctrine of God, Jüngel notes that they always asserted simultaneously the oneness of the existence and essence of God. It was always assumed that God had created both the things to be known and the human intellect which knows them. "In God, thought had a guarantor not only for the context of all things but also for the coherent context of thinking and being." In this God-enveloped context, "truth was regarded as the 'equation of intellect and thing'" because created things had previously existed in the divine intellect (*GMW*, 105-106). In this metaphysical conception (particularly that of Anselm of Canterbury) God was conceived as a *necessary being*, a conception that Jüngel will contest in his exposition of God as love.

Jüngel sees the metaphysical tradition as innately diseased, but one of its worst symptoms is the attempt to understand God through words of signification instead of grasping God in the word of direct address.[1] Jüngel's thesis is that the metaphysical God described through the signifying power of words goes hand in hand with *necessary being* and gives rise to a constellation of fatal problems.

Citing Anselm's famous formulation of God, "That than which nothing greater can be conceived," Jüngel elaborates his contentions:

> That means that God is *over everything*, and thus he is *above us*, he is *absolutely superior* to us. That is the only way in which he can be considered.
> The 'thing signified' (*res significata*) by "God" would then also have to be absolutely superior to human *thinking* and *comprehending*. And that is the reason why "God is not capable of definition." What the word "God" provides for our *thinking* is then basically impossible to think through, cannot be grasped by thinking, and thus can be grasped only as something incomprehensible. At least, that is implied by a broad tradition with its language usage, a tradition which theology has largely followed in its dogmatic formulations (*GMW*, 7-8).

It is this inability to define the essence of God, to say something definite and positive about God, that disturbs Jüngel. Thus he launches an extended polemic against apophatic theology because it signifies God as above and eventually as out of this world. His critique of Thomistic analogy is directed against the theory of predication which aims to

---

[1]This point is hardly original in Jüngel. See, for instance, H. Richard Niebuhr, *The Meaning of Revelation* (New York: Collier Books, 1941), 112 et passim.

protect this metaphysical notion of God *supra nos*. Negative theology in particular, as well as the broader theological tradition which has operated on much the same principle, asserts the existence of God as so absolutely superior to us that the divine essence remains necessarily ineffable. And this ineffability leads to the disturbing silencing of God that Jüngel sees in the modern world.

The Philosophical manifestation of the aporia. Historically, Jüngel sees the problem taking its fatal turn in Descartes' *cogito ergo sum*. With this move Descartes resituates, re-*places* the grounding of the human self in thought. Human existence is now grounded in human thinking. Descartes' principle of doubt throws the self back upon itself as the guarantor of its own existence. However, Descartes must then call upon the metaphysically conceived God *supra nos* to guarantee continuity for the self-grounded ego. *Les jeux sont faits*. God, the one metaphysically understood to be above and beyond me, is now needed as a component of the human ego system. The locus of God's presence is now understood *through* me, and the aporia begins to surface. Problematically, the self-grounding 'I' implicitly guarantees the existence of God whose essence is completely above and beyond the human 'I':

> *The clearly and distinctly comprehending human ego becomes the place of presence in general.* Only the ego can be present in a total way (*GMW*, 124, Jüngel's emphasis).

Jüngel sees this shifting of the primary locus of presence to the human thinking ego as "man appropriating God"; "man is responsible for God" (*GMW*, 125). He now formulates the aporia:

> (a) In that the essence of God is represented (imagined) by me, the existence of God is secured through me.
>
> (b) With regard to his *essence* God is the almighty Creator, who is necessary

> in and through himself and through whom I am (both in general and
> in terms of what I actually am).
> (c) In terms of his *existence*, however, God is through me, in that *his*
> existence can be understood only as representedness through and for
> the subject, which "I" am (*GMW*, 125).

By reasserting the traditional doctrine of the unity of the essence and
existence of God and by adding his ontological proof for the existence
of God, Descartes tried to conceal this contradiction between an essence
above the self and an existence through the self. Yet the implication of
the aporia remained, leading to the inevitable failure of modern
metaphysics, a failure whose precondition was the medieval/Scholastic
conception of God, and whose ramifications were to be played out in the
philosophical responses of Fichte, Feuerbach, and Nietzsche.

Thus Fichte responded that we should not think God because, as
understood through the *cogito*, thinking is a "mortalizing predicate." In
order to preserve the metaphysically understood divine essence, to avoid
a "mortalizing predicate," we must not think God.

Feuerbach's response to the aporia was that we only truly think
when we think God. But to think the essence of God we must first deny
God's existence so that humankind may be elevated to the conceived
infinity of God. (According to Jüngel, Feuerbach thus violates Kant's
minimum standard of non-contradiction, since a God conceived without
existence could not be God at all.) In foregoing the existence of God,
Feuerbach tried to seize the essence for humanity.

Finally Nietzsche asks, "Could you conceive a God?"[2] In asking
this question, Jüngel sees him as the most rigorous in facing Anselm's
"That than which nothing greater can be conceived." Nietzsche simply

---

[2]Friederich Nietzsche, *Thus Spake Zarathustra; A Book for All and None,* in *The
Complete Works of Friederich Nietzsche,* 99, as cited by Jüngel, *GMW*, 146.

leaves God inconceivable and advocates the Superman in God's stead.

Let us now consider how this analysis of the historical development of the aporia affects the doctrine of analogy.

THE APORIA CONCEALED BY ANALOGY

In "The Problem of Analogous Talk about God," Jüngel displays the aporia generated by the philosophical and theological traditions in their use of analogy. In spite of his stated desire to avoid "sweeping criticism," he does fire off an accusation of theological irresponsibility: "Theology, instead, should have seen its responsibility in preventing such philosophical developments from ever happening" (*GMW*, 281). As the prelude to his own positive proposal, Jüngel wants to expose the problematic in previous applications of analogy. Much is at stake in this analysis; for if he is right about the failure of the tradition, and if he is also right in claiming that

> there can be no responsible talk about God without analogy. Every spoken announcement which corresponds to God is made within the context of what analogy makes possible" (*GMW*, 281),

then his own constructive claim for analogical predication would have imperial ramifications for theology. In any case, we now have both Catholic and Protestant agreement on the necessity of analogy. The on-going dispute now centers around how analogy is to be done.

The Analysis of Kant. Suspecting a problem common to Aquinas' and Kant's use of analogy, Jüngel centers a great deal of his analysis on Kant. As Jüngel portrays him, Kant attempts to solve the aporia with his use of analogy. On the one hand, the critique of pure reason establishes strict boundaries of understanding based on perceptual experience, boundaries beyond which responsible statements could not be made. On the other hand, even though God must be beyond the categories of understanding oriented toward the world, the idea of God is indispensable if we are to avoid the notion of an infinite world. Most importantly, the idea of God is *necessary* to insure Kant's moral project, since the ultimate proportion of virtue and happiness cannot be determined within the limits of this world alone: "Thus we need the idea of a God who is distinct from the world without being able to say on the basis of our experience as what the essence of this God is to be defined" (*GMW*, 263).

Given the commitments of his systematic thought, Kant's problem is that "the concept of God remains meaningless" (ibid.). As Kant formulates the problem:

> If we represent to ourselves a being of the understanding by nothing but pure concepts of the understanding, we then indeed represent nothing definite to ourselves, and consequently our concept has no significance; but if we think of it by properties borrowed from the sensuous world, it is no longer a being of understanding, but is conceived phenomenally and belongs to the sensible world.[3]

Kant's setting of the problem is similar to the problem Burrell (and Aquinas) has addressed in *Knowing the Unknowable God*: how to preserve the transcendence of God (the distinction of God from the world) and yet relate God to the world.

Kant's proposed solution is to form our concept of God, who has already been defined as beyond the world and thus remains unknown,

---

[3]Immanuel Kant, *Prolegomena to any Future Metaphysics*, ed. L.W. Beck (Indianapolis and New York: The Bobbs-Merrill Company, 1950), 103f., as cited in Jüngel, *GMW*, 263-264.

by analogy with empirical conceptions which may legitimately be known. According to Jüngel, Kant adopts a position which moves him toward the Thomistic analogy of proportionality:

> We limit our judgment merely to the relation which the world may have to a Being whose very concept lies beyond all the knowledge which we can attain within the world. For we then do not attribute to the Supreme Being any of the properties in themselves by which we represent objects of experience, . . . but we attribute them to the relation of this Being . . . to the world.[4]

Kant can then assert that he has avoided a "dogmatic anthropomorphism" but has achieved a legitimate "symbolical anthropomorphism," one which "concerns language only and not the object itself."[5]

Jüngel strongly objects to such "symbolical anthropomorphism" because being limited to statements about relations, it leaves God, as God is *in se*, unknown.   Hence Jüngel concludes: "The infinite difference between God himself and human (anthropomorphic) talk about God, is not silenced, concealed, or circumvented, but rather is directly expressed" (*GMW*, 265).   The rift between the thinkability and the knowability of God has only been enlarged, not overcome. For Kant's use of analogy "does not signify (as is commonly understood) an imperfect similarity of two things, but a perfect similarity of relations between two quite dissimilar things."[6]

Looking at Kant's various examples, e.g.,

God: world :: watchmaker: watch
God: world :: shipbuilder: ship,

Jüngel notices that the examples are used to express dependence.

---

[4]Kant, *Prolegomena*, 105f., as cited in Jüngel, *GMW*, 264.

[5]Ibid.

[6]Kant, *Prolegomena*, 106, as cited in Jüngel, *GMW*, 265.

Furthermore, the analogy of relationships is always that between cause and effect, grounds and consequences. Hence there is a definite ordering between them. From this Jüngel concludes that Kant has actually intermixed two different kinds of analogy which the theological tradition had generally distinguished--the analogy of proportionality and the analogy of attribution.

Continuing to build his case for the similarity between Kant's grounds for analogy and Aquinas', Jüngel then examines the use of analogy in Aristotle, once again finding these two basic types of analogy--proportionality and attribution. The import of Jüngel's exegetical effort is now becoming clear. If he can show that the broad metaphysical tradition, whatever the particular terminology employed may be (since Kant does not explicitly adopt the terms but does seem to adopt the use), ends up utilizing these types of analogy, then he can show that whatever aporia is generated, or at least supported by its use, applies to all cases. Hence if Aristotle, Kant, and most significantly for our present purposes, Aquinas, all employ analogy along the same fundamental lines, and if such usage only highlights the problem of the speakability of God, then a completely different understanding and employment of analogy would be called for. And as we shall see below, that is what Jüngel has in mind.

The Analysis of Aquinas.   Jüngel strategically places his analysis of Aquinas between his exegesis of Kantian and Aristotelian analogy and his subsequent criticism of Kant. Just as in Kant and in Aristotle, Jüngel finds the following framework more or less operative in Aquinas:

1. the analogy of proportionality;
2. the analogy of attribution; with either,
   a. a dominant relation of the many to the one; or,
   b. a dominant relation of the one to the others.

While most of his exegesis centers on the analogy of attribution, Jüngel will again try to show that Aquinas, like Kant, has actually intermixed the two forms.

With regard to the analogy of proportionality, Jüngel cites the work of the German Catholic scholar, G. Scheltens. Scheltens' research had indicated, as had the work of George Klubertanz, that although Aquinas stressed the analogy of proportionality in *De Veritate* (1256-57), he then discontinued its use. While Jüngel takes note of Scheltens' work, it is significant that he does not incorporate its implications into his reading of Aquinas. Although he is not very clear on this point, he does seem to admit that this research has counterimplications to his argument:

> If the interpretation which I now present is correct, then the material here will have to be evaluated in a more differentiated fashion" (*GMW*, 271, n. 33).

Below we shall in fact consider some of those counterimplications.

Working from Aquinas' well-known passages on analogy, Jüngel connects Aquinas' analogy of attribution to the analogy of proportionality. Jüngel observes that the renowned health example includes subtle distinctions between the hermeneutical first thing and the ontic first thing: "'healthy' is predicated of medicine and urine in relation and in proportion to health of the body, of which the former is a cause and the latter is a sign" (*ST* I.13.5). The one thing to which others are ordered is a first thing not in the ontic order, but in the order of knowing. Likewise, Jüngel reminds us that, for Aquinas, the order of language follows the order of knowing. So in the order of knowing, the health of the body is the first thing; while ontically, the medicine which is the cause of health in the body is the first thing. (The urine, which has been around in this perennial illustration since Aristotle, receives pride of place in neither order.) Jüngel also mentions what is well-known in the Thomistic tradition--that talk about God cannot utilize the analogy of attribution where the many are related to the one because this would either place God in the same series as the other analogata, or would relate God to a third and higher principle. (So in our above enumeration, 2a is rejected.) Furthermore, if God can only be known from his effects as the cause of those effects, then Jüngel again rightly understands that Aquinas saw this as problematic (*ST* I.13.6), for the attribution of the quality would remain merely extrinsic. Jüngel concludes:

> The actual theological analogy of naming is given for Thomas only when the 'one thing' which as the common element in different things is the hermeneutical reason for the analogy of naming, first subsists in God himself and *therefore* in the creatures caused by God (*GMW*, 275).

For example, God would have goodness (more accurately, *be* goodness), by virtue of having his own being. Then God distributes this goodness to the creatures whom he has caused. But in order to understand this analogy, a conceptual reversal is necessary; for the goodness which God possesses first by his being, is first known and named by its possession in the creature. (As we saw above, this conceptual reversal is often discussed in terms of *res significata/modus significandi*.)

Still, what is most interesting and most controversial in Jüngel's account is the way Jüngel links Aquinas to Kant. Jüngel attempts to warrant this linkage by claiming that the conceptual reversal used in the analogy of attribution "is thus connected for Thomas, in point of fact, with the first model of analogy of naming (which derived from rhetoric), the 'analogy of proportionality'" (*GMW*, 275). Jüngel's objective is to show that:

1. both Kant and Thomas were using the same two models of analogy--proportionality and attribution;
2. both Kant and Thomas had to mix these two forms to avoid an obvious emptiness;
3. in spite of the admixture of the two forms, both Kant and Thomas fail to provide an authentic way to let us speak about God.[7]

Although Jüngel's warrant for this reading is less than lucid, he seems to reason as follows: In the analogy of attribution, the "'one thing' [viz., God] *relates itself* to the common element" in that God both has the common perfection by God's being (for God 'having' necessarily means 'being') and causes the common perfection to exist in the creature, although the creature has the common perfection in a derived and imperfect manner. Since the creature is the "other thing" and yet has the common perfection at least to some degree, Jüngel essentially equates this common possession of a given perfection to an elaborated restatement of the analogy of proportionality:

> The so-called 'analogy of attribution' has drawn into itself the so-called 'analogy of proportionality' when the issue is analogous talk about God" (*GMW*, 276).

Putting all this as simply as possible, Jüngel sees a latent presupposition in the analogy of attribution--i.e., God has a given perfection to God's being as the creature has the same perfection to the creature's being.

---

[7]The point of Burrell's concern in *Analogy and Philosophical Language*, i.e., formal schemes are really empty of content, can be felt as Jüngel attacks the formal scheme of proportionality as he sees it implied in the analogy of attribution. This raises two issues: 1) Did Aquinas in fact have this kind of scheme? and 2), If he did not, then how did he, and how should we, utilize analogy? It is interesting that Jüngel, Clarke, and Burrell all offer ways of understanding analogy without proportionality.

And this reading amounts to:

$$a:b :: c:d$$

or, the analogy of proportionality. Actually, Jüngel's reading is similar to many Catholic interpreters who followed Cajetan's exegesis of Aquinas. Jüngel further observes: "This factual intermingling of the two analogies is declared in Catholic textbooks to be indispensable for the knowledge of God and for the corresponding talk about God" (*GMW*, 276). So it is not as strange as it first might seem when Jüngel claims: "We are dealing here with a connection similar to that found in Kant" (ibid.).

The polemic against God supra nos. Once Jüngel has traced the common ancestry of the two types of analogy to Aristotle, and has shown that both Kant and Aquinas employ both types, he continues his polemic against the metaphysical tradition, both in its philosophical and theological development. He wants to bring the concealed aporia out of the closet, the aporia which led to the silencing of God:

> The question to be decided is whether God is speakable only as the
> one who actually is unspeakable, and can be made known only as the
> one who is actually unknown. Within the framework of analogy, the
> problem has confronted us up to now as the question of how human
> talk about God could be possible without a "humanization" of the
> divine essence which is inappropriate to God, since . . . . language
> in its lingual character is oriented to the world and thus is told by the
> world how it is to speak? (*GMW*, 277).

Jüngel protests against the speakable which only says that God is unspeakable and against the known which only claims that God is unknown. Jüngel's concern reminds us of Burrell's early apophatic readings of Aquinas, even the title of Burrell's third book, *Knowing the Unknowable God*. Thus the criticism which is directed at Kant, who, without question, allows the naming of God only as the unknown, also strikes Aquinas if he is read as apophatically as Burrell sometimes does.

The stringent logic of such a metaphysic functions to keep God *out* of the world. This Kantian (and allegedly Thomistic) solution was designed to protect God from any anthropomorphic talk--dogmatic anthropomorphism. However, since it ends up increasing the distance of God from human speech, it is a pyrrhic victory. For in being limited to statements which make God known in language only (symbolical anthropomorphism) and not as God is *in se*, the essence of God remains a disturbing unknown:

> Thus the theological critique to be directed against the great accomplishment of this metaphysical tradition focuses on the fact that in its obtrusiveness the unknownness of God has become an unbearably sinister riddle. For it is intolerable to live in the awareness of a condition which comes into view only in order to disappear again into unknownness. It is difficult enough for a person, within his earthly conditionedness, to have an unknown father, as a procreator but not as a father. . . . the analogy of attribution defines so precisely the unknownness of God that it vastly increases that unknownness into God's total inaccessibility. That fact is not softened, but rather hardened by the formulation of concepts 'on the analogy of proportionality,' based on the presupposition of the so-called 'analogy of attribution' (*GMW*, 278).

So seen, the very accomplishment of the metaphysical tradition is also its profound theological weakness. Being able to speak about a God who is always *supra nos* creates a greater problem than it has superficially solved.

Noting that Kant was particularly responding to the metaphysical skepticism of Spinoza, whose concept of divinity necessarily excluded humanity, just as being a square excludes being a circle (*GMW*, 280), Jüngel directly attacks this "suspicion of absurdity" as antithetical to the Christian faith on both hermeneutical and christological grounds.

Jüngel's contrasting proposal is to maintain a distinction between God and humanity through the logic of faith, not through the metaphysical doctrine of God *supra nos*. Thus he declares and demands:

> There is christological reason to ask whether there is not a God-enabled, a God-required, even a God-demanded anthropomorphism which moves far beyond the naiveté of "dogmatic" anthropomorphism as well as the skepticism of "symbolic" anthropomorphism. Briefly: is there a theological use of analogy which corresponds to faith in the incarnation of God? (*GMW*, 280).

Where the metaphysical tradition had avoided anthropomorphism, Jüngel attempts to discover a christological anthropomorphism and an accompanying metaphysics which allows the speakability of God.

JÜNGEL'S DOCTRINAL ALTERNATIVE

Jüngel understands the purpose of theology as understanding, thinking, and *saying* what we believe. As we saw in his criticism of the tradition, he sees theism and atheism as two sides of the same coin. The metaphysics worked out in *God as the Mystery of the World* begins by hearing the atheistic criticism of theology, linking the death of God metaphysically considered to fundamental problems in the theological tradition's understanding of God, and then offering a *tertium quid*-- thinking God in a new way on the basis of the certainty of faith, that is, as faith confronts uncertainty.

In order to avoid the sterile God of metaphysical certainty, authentic faith must confront doubt. In this sense the certainty of faith is not comparable to the certainty of understanding. As Robert Scharlemann recently put it, faith must be something like "not-understanding."[8]   Without collapsing the distinctness of either faith or understanding, Jüngel wants to show the task that each must perform in their theological relationship.

For Jüngel faith is a going out from the self to trust another. Because it is a going out of the self, faith deprives the self of security grounded in the self.   The thinking which finds its path in following faith must oppose the Cartesian methodology of doubt, return to self, and foundational *self*-certainty.   If faith (theology) does not lead thought (philosophy), then thought inevitably turns back upon itself in the self-reflectivity of the *cogito*.   By leading thought away from itself in its going out to the other, faith effectively prevents thought's reflex action of self-contemplation and the self-deception of attempted self-security. Instead, by relating the self to the other, faith functions to guarantee the distinctness of each one, be it a human and God or two humans.

Jüngel connects the self-directedness of thought to the typology of signification and the other-directedness of thought to the typology of address.   When used in signification function, words signify ideas, and ideas signify things.   The metaphysical God of signification is inherently prone to the metaphysical death of the Descartes-Fichte-Feuerbach-Nietzsche syndrome.   Ironically, Jüngel is making the point that the doctrinal understanding of God as necessary being, *supra nos*, and imperishable, is in fact the cause of the metaphysical death of God. Jüngel's alternative doctrine begins by looking to the *historical* death of God in the confrontation of being with the non-being of the cross.

---

[8]Robert P. Scharlemann, "Fides Quaerens Intellectum as Basis of Pluralistic Method," in *The Whirlwind in Culture: Frontiers in Theology*--in Honor of Langdon Gilkey, ed. Donald W. Musser and Joseph L. Price (Bloomington, Indiana: Meyer/-Stone Books, 1988), 240.

Closing the metaphysical gap: The direct address.   In the address function of words, virtually all of Jüngel's major theses converge. Both his doctrine of God and his methodology of how analogy must correspond to that doctrine are developed out of this address function. Borrowing from the work of Ernst Fuchs, he develops his own doctrine of God through the possibilities of "language event."[9]   Jüngel's questions highlight this connecting thread of his work:

> The question now, however, is whether that to which the word refers must itself exist *beyond* the word, *outside* of the language context in which it is "found." Is the thing which is interpreted by the word itself fundamentally speechless? Does the word fundamentally signalize something which is beyond language? Or is it not at least partially possible that the thing, about which words are spoken, is not what it is without the word? Is there some existing thing which exists only or chiefly in the word event? . . . We must carefully consider whether words always are mere representatives of something else which itself is wordless (*GMW*, 10).

In opposition to the correspondence theory of truth, God is to be grasped authentically *in* the word: "God becomes *thinkable* on the basis of his speakability." Where the correspondence theory and its associated metaphysical conception of God allow a conceptual distance between the one thinking God and God *in se*, the direct address removes this distance. Jüngel illustrates the point by reminding us that successful jokes and invective can get inside a person so that one cannot help laughing, or in the case of invective, cannot help feeling the word so closely that anger, hurt, or shock is produced in us. In these cases "the word includes the person in its meaning and thus approaches him *too*

---

[9]Ernst Fuchs, "Das Sprachereignis in der Verkündigung Jesu, in der Theologie des Paulus und im Ostergeschehen," in *Zum hermeneutischen Problem in der Theologie; Die existentiale Interpretation, Gesammelte Aufsätze* (Tübingen: J. C. B. Mohr [Paul Siebeck], 1965), I, 281ff., as cited in *GMW*, 12, passim.

closely" (*GMW*, 11). The one speaking, the one addressed, and the word spoken, are all drawn into the one language event. The judge pronouncing sentence or lover declaring her feelings to the beloved produces an event in the very act of speaking such words. In this event the word of address affects the whole being of the one addressed.

Jüngel's trinitarian and lingual concept of God presents God coming to God in the word and God coming to humanity in that same word in Jesus Christ. If God is *in* the word, then it follows that the distance fabricated by metaphysical signification actually prevents locating God who has already been placed *above* the world and therefore beyond description. By contrast, Jüngel insists that what the word refers to need not exist beyond the word itself. That which is being interpreted, i.e., God, is not fundamentally speechless. The being of God is what it is as it occurs *in* the word.

Now this alternative might be summarized and highlighted against the tradition as follows:

1. God is *in* the word.

2. Metaphysical signification unnecessarily distances God by conceptually locating God *above* the world and therefore *beyond* what words can describe.

3. The conceptual problematic of modernity, the aporia, results from this humanly fabricated displacement.

4. In the historical death of God on the cross, in the actual confrontation of being with non-being, theology should look first in order to think God.

Participation in the lingual event. Where the Neo-Thomists offer an understanding of participation through creation, Jüngel presents a notion of participation through the lingual event which joins God and God as well as God and humanity. Jüngel claims that God

> not only speaks in order to communicate something; rather, he speaks in order to communicate himself and thus to make possible fellowship with himself and to provide a new way to participate in his own being (*GMW*, 12-13).

From various Scriptural warrants, Jüngel indicates that the word contains a power because it is a person:

> It is in the power of the word that he raises the dead, according to Romans 4:17, and he calls what is not into being. As the word he becomes flesh (John 1:14) and dwells among us in order to communicate himself. In his word, God goes out of himself. As such, he is the one who speaks, who expresses himself, who states his being. In speaking he shares and communicates himself (ibid.).

Because God is the one who speaks, and who speaks first, because God's being is shared as God is spoken, then the one who is addressed can participate in the being of God through and in that address:

> Faith is participation in God himself. Certainly faith does not force itself into a position *between* God and God. It is the essence of faith to let God be who he is. But if faith does participate in God himself, without penetrating God in such a way that it forces itself between God and God, then God's being must be thought as a being which allows that it be participated in, that is, a being which turns *outward* what it is *inwardly*. This happens in the word and only in the word of God (*GMW*, 176).

Jüngel, Clarke, and Burrell all want to show how God may be distinct from the world and yet related to it. However, where Clarke and Burrell variously develop the essence/existence distinction, Jüngel emphatically rejects it. Instead, Jüngel takes the theological high road, calling for direct participation in the language event brought about by God's coming in the word directly addressed to us. In light of his direct participation theory, Jüngel cannot see the "merely rational" distinction between the existence and the essence of God as an innocent methodological instrument.

Jüngel might sum the case up as follows. First, the attempt to understand God metaphysically has to assert thought between God and God in order to get itself started in the first place. This flawed beginning is the ancestor of the problems leading to the historical aporia. On the other hand, in understanding God only through the direct address which God has spoken in his word, there is no place, no conceptual space, for thought to insert itself and assert itself between God and God. Most importantly, there is no need for thought to do so; its function is fulfilled in thinking God *in* the word.

God's being is in coming. Following Karl Barth, Jüngel's earlier work portrays God's being in *becoming*.[10] In *God as the Mystery of the World*, Jüngel shifts his emphasis and develops the thesis that God's being is in God's *coming*. Jüngel links his account of faith's outward movement to the classic doctrine of *creatio ex nihilo*; for in the creative act, God goes out from God's self into non-being. Jüngel's various themes coalesce around the core thought that God's being is disclosed in the outward movement from God's self. Thus Jüngel sees the cross as the greatest confirmation and disclosure of *creatio ex nihilo*; for in the historical death of God, the being of God is revealed. The cross of Christ discloses the divine self going out to the nothingness of death and perishability, just as the *creatio ex nihilo* of the world began in God's

---

[10]Eberhard Jüngel, *The Doctrine of the Trinity: God's Being is in Becoming*, trans. H. Harris (Grand Rapids: William B. Eerdmans, 1976).

self and went forth creatively into the nothingness. The metaphysical God *supra nos* cannot die, cannot perish, and cannot be coherently thought as part of this world. But if God has come to God's self in the word of Jesus Christ, and simultaneously come to humankind in that same word, then we must learn to think God anew on the basis of that crucified one. If God is identified with the suffering and crucified one as a word *in* this world directly addressed to this world, then an inconsistency is revealed in the metaphysical conception of a God who must remain impassive and unaffected in being above this world.

For Jüngel, theological reflection is on safe ground only when it looks for understanding *in* the word. The being that is expressed in the word, in the world creation *ex nihilo*, and in the *creatio ex nihilo* of the cross, is divine being which characteristically goes out from itself. Similarly, faith is a personal trust which goes out from the self. Something is at risk in going out from oneself, even being itself. Thus Jüngel's point about the death of God on the cross of Christ: here something stupendous, divine being itself, was risked in encountering the non-being of death. We must no longer think God in terms of super-worldly power, but look to this going-out nature of God revealed in the divine blend of weakness and strength of the cross. Looking to the cross, where God is located and self-disclosed in and as a word, theology can be unashamed to develop a theological anthropology which can speak God through the correspondence (*Entsprechung*) to divinity which includes humanity. And when theology remains true to this correspondence, then it has learned to speak "a doctrine of analogy which is appropriate to the gospel" (*GMW*, 261). Thus Jüngel quotes Hegel with favor:

> It is absurd to say of the Christian religion that by it God has been
> revealed to man, and to maintain at the same time that what has been
> revealed is that He is not now revealed and has not been revealed.[11]

Hegel's clear statement contains the heart of Jüngel's objection to
apophatic theology: Something essential has already been said; a
definitive word has already been spoken; and theology must discover its
true task, its place of correspondence, in the space opened up to it by
the arrival of that prior word. Let us now examine how Jüngel's
doctrine of analogy accomplishes that correspondence.

---

[11]G. W. F. Hegel, "Lectures on the Proofs of the Existence of God," in *Lectures on the Philosophy of Religion*, III, trans. E. B. Speirs and J. B. Sanderson (New York: Humanities Press, 1962), 193ff., as cited in *GMW*, 261.

CHAPTER NINE

CHRISTOLOGICAL ANALOGY

Jüngel's 1962 article, "The Possibility of a Theological Anthropology on the Basis of Analogy: An Investigation of Karl Barth's Understanding of Analogy,"[1] won strong praise from Barth:

> I . . . must not delay letting you know how pleased I am with this fine work. You undoubtedly express better than I could have done myself what I have thought and think on the subject. The discussion has now passed a turning point and it certainly cannot go back again.[2]

From Barth he takes a strongly christological anthropology. From Ernst Fuchs' notion of "language event," Jüngel develops the address function

---

[1]Eberhard Jüngel, "Die Möglichkeit theologischer Anthropologie auf dem Grunde der Analogie: Eine Untersuchung zum Analogieverständnis Karl Barths," *Evangelische Theologie,* 22 (1962): 535-557. For the remainder of this part of the chapter, this article will cited parenthetically as "Die Möglichkeit." Translations are my own.

[2]Karl Barth, Letters 1961-1968, ed. Jürgen Fangmeier and Hinrich Stoevesandt, trans. and ed. Geoffrey W. Bromiley (Grand Rapids: William B. Eerdmans, 1981), 71.

of words.   His own mature work synthesizes these influences by portraying analogy as a spoken correspondence to the divine/human event of the two natures of Christ.   By combining his two fundamental emphases, i.e., christology and language event, Jüngel attempts to differentiate his own (and Barth's) use of analogy from both contemporary and classical Roman Catholic usage, and thereby to demarcate the "turning point" in the debate about analogy.

ANALOGIA FIDEI (ANALOGY OF FAITH) vs.
ANALOGIA ENTIS (ANALOGY OF BEING)

Barth's theological career was marked by a real shift in his attitude toward analogy.   As he increasingly employed a kind of analogy, some prominent Roman Catholic scholars engaged him in debate over the proper use of analogy, as did Emil Brunner in a well-known theological row on the Protestant side.[3]   On the Roman Catholic side, both Gottlieb Söhngen and Hans Urs von Balthasar claimed that Barth's use of the *analogia fidei* concealed but still implied the use of *analogia entis*. Stressing Barth's theological framework, Jüngel argues that only a

---

[3]Among the many works probing Barth on analogy, see the following. First, for Barth's infamous polemic against the *analogia entis* as the doctrine of the antichrist, see *CD* I/1, xiii. For the roughly contemporary debate with Brunner, see *Natural Theology*, Comprising "Nature and Grace" by Dr. Emil Brunner and the reply "No!" by Dr. Karl Barth, trans. Peter Fraenkel, with an introduction by John Baillie, (London: Geoffrey Bles: The Centenary Press, 1946). For two important Catholic responses and critiques of Barth on analogy, see Hans Urs von Balthasar, *The Theology of Karl Barth*, trans. John Drury (New York: Holt, Rinehart, and Winston, 1972), 73-150; and Gottlieb Söhngen, "Wesen und Akt in der scholastischen Lehre von der participatio und analogia entis," *Studium* 11 (December, 1955): 649-662.

misunderstanding of Barth permits seeing the *analogia entis* and the *analogia fidei* as compatible and mutually implicit, as two species of the same genus. Jüngel asserts to the contrary:

> If the two genitives, "*entis*" and "*fidei*" are not to be understood in the sense of different species to a common proximate genus, but if in the first place the analogy concept is respectively constituted and made precise through its genitive, then the opposition of the *analogia entis* and the *analogia fidei* has to do with as unrelenting a contradiction as the opposition of righteousness from the law and righteousness from faith (apart from the law) ("Die Möglichkeit," 537).

The "decisive innovation" which Jüngel sees in Barth's anthropology, and consequently in Barth's use of analogy, is that the doctrine of humankind is determined christologically. To ask what the essence of humankind is, to answer what it means to be human, we must look to that "place of light" (*helle Ort*) which the human Jesus provides:

> The human Jesus is therefore the condition of the possibility of knowledge of the essence of humankind generally. Why? Because the humanity of the human Jesus has its factual correspondence (analogy!) in the humanity of humankind generally. And because the correspondence between the humanity of humankind generally and the humanity of Jesus has each in its turn its objectively necessary correspondence in the relationship of the humanity of Jesus to the divinity of Jesus (ibid.).

From the dual nature of Christ Jüngel draws the following implications:

> a) The relation between God and the human Jesus corresponds to the relations in the innergodly being.
>
> b) The relation between the human Jesus and humankind in general corresponds to the relation between the human Jesus and God.
>
> c) The relations among humans in general correspond to the relation between the human Jesus and humankind in general.
>
> d) The relations among humankind in general correspond to the relations in the innergodly being and essence.
>
> e) The relations between God and humanity in general correspond to the relations in the innergodly being and essence.

f) Other relationships of order correspond to the relationships of order existing in the structure of humanity's being as body and soul ("Die Möglichkeit," 541-42).

Because all these analogies have to do with relationships, and because all these relationships are authentically displayed in Jesus Christ, Barth sometimes calls this the *analogia relationis*.

As the proper determination of what humankind should be, it is the human Jesus who is the image of God, the *imago dei*. Jüngel follows Barth in limiting the understanding of Gen. 1:26-27 to the humanity of Christ and not to all humans generally, other than through Christ. This limitation takes us further down the path of understanding analogy christologically--and only christologically. Because it corresponds authentically to the divinity of Jesus, the humanity of Jesus is said to be the true image of God; therefore, "the being of the human Jesus is the ontological and epistemological ground of all analogy" ("Die Möglichkeit," 538).

Barth characteristically looks to this one source, to this one "being of light" (*Hellsein*), which is the being of Jesus Christ. Here he sees a solid starting point, a sure guide, and a reliable correspondence to the divine nature. In the two natures of Christ is also the Barthian basis of a doctrine of participation. Jesus not only reveals the essence of God to humankind, Jesus also reveals what human essence actually is, because that essence of humanity is determined not by humanity itself as a *causa sui* endeavor, but in the relationship of humanity to God and to other humans as the covenant partner of God. Since human essence is christologically determined, it must be understood, if it is to be understood at all, through its christological relationship. True humanity is a correspondence to, a participation in, the revealed essence of humanity in Jesus Christ.

The question, "What is this true humanity which corresponds to and participates in the humanity of Christ?" can also be posed as, "What is the essential nature of the human Jesus?" As Jüngel takes the point, it is "being for" and "being with" God and a being for and with fellow humanity. It is revealed only and always "as relational being" ("Die Möglichkeit," 540). As relational essence, the humanity of Jesus corresponds to and reveals the threefold essence of the being of God. Even the analogy between the essence of God and the work of God is revealed in this one place of light, in the humanity of the human Jesus; for the reconciling work of Christ for his co-humanity acts to restore the eternal covenantal relationship for which humankind was created. The inner being of God is likewise revealed as a turning to others in love:

Here we are dealing with the ground of all analogies, namely with the "divinely-essential correspondence and resemblance between the being of the human Jesus for God and his being for fellow humankind. This divinely-essential correspondence and resemblance consists in that the human Jesus' being for humanity reiterates and reproduces the inner being, the essence of God himself, and precisely therewith verifies his being for God."[4]

Thus Jüngel insists that the personal, relational, christological approach to analogy cannot be understood as *analogia entis*. Methodologically, at the least, he has differentiated the christological approach to analogy from the approach to analogy through the metaphysics of being.

---

[4]*KD* III/2, 261, as cited in "Die Möglichkeit," 539. Jüngel elaborates this notion of being for others in *God as the Mystery of the World*, 368-373, where he affirms Karl Rahner's notion that the immanent and the economic Trinity are one and the same essence, an understanding derived from the "Crucified One."

Christology, covenant, and creation.   Regardless of methodological approach, do the two kinds of analogy, *analogia entis* and *analogia fidei* end up with similar results?   The answer depends largely upon how the doctrine of creation is treated.   Here again Barth and Jüngel separate their analogy concept by contending that analogy cannot be undertaken as a doctrine of creation apart from and prior to a christological starting point.   Thus creation is not understood through shared participation in *being*, but through the covenantal, personal, and trinitarian implications of christology.   Hence the analogy is not in being, but "as a being for . . . or a being with," as

> attested to and revealed through a correspondence, which we have come to know as an analogy between the being of the human Jesus for God and his being for humankind. Therefore, we can speak here of an analogy of analogies ("Die Möglichkeit," 540-41).

Between the Creator and the creation is an original antithesis which yields analogies of order (*Ordnungsanologien*) found in nature, e.g., the structure of the cosmos as heaven and earth and the structure of human being as body and soul.   These relationships exhibit an "irreversible ordering" as in an above and a below, a life-giver and a life-receiver, and an invisible and a visible.   In these analogies of order revealed in nature, Jüngel sees this important distinction:

> The belonging together of body and soul is of nature, while the belonging together of Creator and creature is of grace. Therefore, in the phenomenon of analogy, nature and grace are connected to one another ("Die Möglichkeit," 541).[5]

---

[5]In spite of protestations to the contrary, it is interesting to note how close this summary comes to some venerable as well as contemporary Catholic views on the relation of nature and grace, specifically, of the analogy between the *logos* in the cosmos and the *Logos* incarnate in Jesus Christ. See Jean Richard, "Théologie évangélique et théologie philosophique à propos d'Eberhard Jüngel," *Science et*

Advocates of *analogia entis* have long maintained the analogy between nature and grace, but Jüngel contends that the convergence on this point is merely superficial--the vital difference is in how the analogies of nature and grace are determined.

Opposing his determination of analogy to Hans Urs von Balthasar's and Gottlieb Söhngen's claim that *analogia fidei (relationis)* included *analogia entis*, Barth exclaimed: "No correspondence and resemblance of being, no *analogia entis*!" ("Die Möglichkeit," 543).

Seconding Barth's insistence that the two ways of conceiving analogy do not include one another but remain in stark contradiction, Jüngel contends: "The difference will depend upon the understanding of the relations of covenant and creation" (ibid.). The decisive move begins by privileging covenant (*Bund*) in its link with creation: "The ontological determination of the human being as being-together with other humans corresponds to the determination of humanity as the covenant partner of God" (ibid.), and is completed by understanding covenant through christology. From this viewpoint the question of being can only be raised correctly when it is raised with the relational purpose of created being, and this purposive "being for" and "being with" is grasped by first looking to the "place of light," where humanity and divinity are joined in Jesus.

Jüngel summarizes Barth's extended and complex treatment of the relationship between creation and covenant as follows: "The creation is the outer ground of the covenant, while the covenant is the inner ground of the creation" ("Die Möglichkeit," 543). In this regard the ontological problem gives rise to the theological problem; for the relationships of "nature and grace, condition and history, structure of being and event, continuity and contingency, general and concrete" play themselves out in this interrelationship of covenant and creation (ibid.).

The outer ground, i.e., creation, functions like the stage upon which the action of a play takes place.[6] Extending this metaphor Barth (and Jüngel) would say that the play is not devised for the sake of the material theater, but the theater is constructed for the sake of the play. Whatever meaning we may discover is to be sought in the play, *on* the stage, not *in* the stage itself. In Jüngel's more opaque terms,

> The creation cannot determine the covenant. Nonetheless it is the outer ground for it. The covenant cannot exist without the creation. Yet it is the inner ground for it. The coordination of the outer and inner ground is therefore in the understanding that the inner ground itself presupposes the outer . . . . Through the covenant, the creation is thus the made possible possibility for it. The inner ground makes possible the outer ground and in so doing creates the possibility of the inner ground ("Die Möglichkeit," 544).

Because the purpose of creation is the covenant, covenant is the presupposition of creation. The meaning of creation is relational being, a "being for" and a "being with" which is revealed christologically.

For Barth the key to *analogia relationis* is not in a discovered commonality (*Zwischen*) between God and creation, but between God and God. Barth begins not with patterns, but with persons, specifically with the election of the one divine-human person, where God says Yes to God and God says Yes to humankind. The election of Jesus precedes and is the presupposition of the divine act of creation. The stage of creation is constructed to fit the covenantal, relational purpose already

---

[6]See Barth, *CD* III/3, 48.

chosen in Jesus. In the person of Jesus, divinity and authentic humanity meet, and the divine affirmation is spoken:

> In the double election of Jesus Christ grounding the *analogia relationis*, which in turn guarantees the ontological structure of the being of humankind, on the ground of [this] analogy is a theological anthropology of ontological relevance possible ("Die Möglichkeit," 550).[7]

By this "analogy of analogies" centered in the unique union of the two natures of Christ, is the only meaningful and permissible analogy possible.

Human talk about God can attain responsibility by saying yes where God has already spoken his Yes--in God's revelation in Christ. On the basis of this divinely predetermined affirmation, Jüngel follows Barth in resisting the *analogia entis*:

> That is the main point, in this correspondence of yes to Yes, the essence of the *analogia fidei* as opposed to the *analogia entis* finally to demarcate ("Die Möglichkeit," 554-55).

Jüngel holds that the *analogia fidei* is the proper form of the speech of faith; for its personal medium is the mode of revelation, and revelation is the basis of appropriate theological speech. Jüngel takes from Barth the emphasis upon the prior *speech* of God as the condition of successful human speech about God: "God speaks--the human corresponds. Thus is he the image of God. Thus is theological anthropology possible" ("Die Möglichkeit," 552). For Jüngel, the knowledge which faith seeking understanding may discover rests on a *spoken* correspondence to the Yes of God. Hence, his analogy concept always includes the

---

[7]Jüngel drops 'election' as a theme in *God as the Mystery of the World*. Instead, while adopting the basic outline of Barth's position on analogy, he nuances Barth's more Calvinistic emphasis on election with his own Lutheran predilections.

ontological movement of self-communication which becomes a social essence through the vehicle of speech.

JÜNGEL'S PROPOSAL: THE GOSPEL AS ANALOGY

A new appraisal of anthropomorphism. Jüngel understands analogy as the expression of the gospel which portrays the essence of God in *human* words. Hence, he rethinks and reappraises the anthropomorphic nature of our speech. For the apophatic tradition the ever-present anthropomorphic factor in human statements about God had been an obstacle to be avoided. But Jüngel wants to reverse this trend by openly embracing the anthropomorphism which cannot be successfully hidden, and in his view, should not be ignored. Historically, clumsy attempts to circumvent anthropomorphism had contributed to generating the aporia; but in Jüngel's proposal, the divine essence must be authentically spoken in human speech. So we recall the affirmation of Hegel's insight:

> It is absurd to say of the Christian religion that by it God has been revealed to man, and to maintain at the same time that what has been revealed is that He is not now revealed and has not been revealed.[8]

Jüngel is demanding that theology take seriously its own claim that God has been revealed in Jesus Christ. The target is again negative theology, which, in order to preserve the concept of the superiority of God, maintained the greater distance and the greater mystery of God.

---

[8]G. W. F. Hegel, "Lectures on the Proofs of the Existence of God," in *Lectures on the Philosophy of Religion*, III, trans. E. B. Speirs and J. B. Sanderson (New York: Humanities Press, 1962), 193f., as cited in Jüngel, *GMW*, 261.

In contrast, Jüngel asserts repeatedly the greater nearness of God and that "God is to be grasped as a mystery which is communicable in and of itself in language."[9] The argument hinges on what one does with mystery. Negative theology indicates that God remains a mystery *supra nos*, unconditioned by this world. But for Jüngel, the mystery is not in divinity considered through abstract metaphysical signification, nor in humanity considered generally; instead, the mystery is in the linkage of the divine and human nature, in the one person of whom the gospel speaks. That God has spoken in human words offers seriousness and direction to the theological task: theology must correspond to the leadership which God has already provided in the incarnation of Christ. The mystery and the anthropomorphism which speaks this mystery are christologically derived. This christological factor transforms the possibilities of human speech:

> What needs to be done is to arrive at an understanding of human talk about God which does not merely tolerate anthropomorphism, or which finds its inappropriateness appropriate because of the way in which it expresses the complete differentness of God, but which applies positively and from the outset the anthropomorphic structure of human speech (*GMW*, 260).

What determines the way analogy functions is the doctrine of God which it is called upon to express. In the case of negative theology, analogy is asked to portray the inexpressibility of God as superior to, beyond, and unconditioned by this world. Jüngel's project is

> to contradict it, and in its place seek to develop another view of the analogy between God and man, but our reason for doing so is that biblical talk about God forces us to define in a new direction that classical doctrine of analogy (ibid.).

---

[9]Jüngel, *God as the Mystery of the World*, 260. For the remainder of this chapter, this work will be cited parenthetically as *GMW*.

Because of the christological possibility for analogy, Jüngel rejects Kant's options of "symbolical" or "dogmatic" anthropomorphism. Instead, Jüngel transvalues anthropomorphism through the two natures of Christ:

> There is christological reason to ask whether there is not a God-enabled, a God-required, even a God-demanded anthropomorphism which moves far beyond the naiveté of "dogmatic" anthropomorphism as well as the skepticism of "symbolic" anthropomorphism. Briefly: is there a theological use of analogy which corresponds to faith in the incarnation of God? (*GMW*, 280).

Jüngel is pressing the gospel claim that "God has shown himself to be human in the execution of his divinity" (*GMW*, 288), and the divine revelation *in* humanity forces a revaluation of human speech:

> To think of him as one who speaks, to speak of him as one who speaks, is not a "dogmatic anthropomorphism," which comes too close to God, but rather the result of that *event* in which God becomes accessible as God in language, which the Bible calls *revelation* (*GMW*, 288).

The two prongs of Jüngel's thesis, christology and the hermeneutics of understanding God as God in human words, depend upon "the certainty of a God who is human in his divinity. God is thinkable as one who speaks because and to the extent that he is human in and of himself" (*GMW*, 289). If God can only be understood apart from every human and worldly component, then God becomes alien to all things human and worldly; and that misplaced understanding generates the aporia.

DEFINING GOD AS LOVE

Because love "expresses the divine essence more stringently," Jüngel places it at the center of his doctrine of God. Other attributes, such as divine omnipotence and supremacy over the world, are radically subordinated to the concept of love (*GMW*, 260). Most importantly, if God is grasped as love, and if love means self-communication, then the apophatic tradition of God's inexpressibility and unspeakability is refuted.

By his explication of God as love, Jüngel clarifies his notions of "the worldly non-necessity of God" and that "God is more than necessary" (*GMW*, 24-35, 378, 380).[10] For example, it would be strange to say that it was *necessary* to love one's grandmother, fiancée, or child; for something greater than necessity is present in love. Moreover, thinking God through divine love (which Jüngel explicates as comprising both eros and agape) allows Jüngel's metaphysical preference for possibility (potentiality) over actuality. This renders what may be the most significant difference from the Thomistic concept of God; for although Aquinas likewise stresses and elaborates the divine *caritas* (love) as the chief theological virtue, Aquinas couples that stress on the divine love with a clear metaphysical preference for divine simplicity,

---

[10]Above, we saw that Burrell's exposition of Aquinas' *actus* also stressed the non-necessity of the relationship and thereby placed the possibility of love at the center of God's relation to humankind.

God being conceived as pure actuality.[11]   Against the Aristotelian/Thomistic privileging of act over potency, Jüngel argues:

> Love without possibilities is no love. Rather, love is full of creative possibilities. It is this as the unity of life and death for the sake of life which the loving ones can never exhaust, a unity which God revealed in the unity with the Crucified One (*GMW*, 339).

Thinking of love as ontological movement, Jüngel declares that "God comes from God" (*GMW*, 381). God comes neither from being nor from non-being; instead, God is truly *causa sui*--God comes from God. However, just because God comes from God does not mean that God is to be understood as a solitary being: "To believe in the eternal Father means . . . to acknowledge God as a social essence, namely, as an essence who *vouchsafes* fellowship, as the sovereign of being who permits *participation* in being" (*GMW*, 382). So once again participation in being is key to understanding analogy, but Jüngel's participation doctrine is not based on the *being* of God and humankind but on the "social essence" of God who is love. In this social essence manifested in the Trinity, God comes to God as the Father who comes to the Son and as the Spirit who is the relationship of that relationship of coming.

But Jüngel claims even more can be said about the divine essence grasped as loving, social essence, coming from itself and to itself. For God not only comes to God within the Trinity; God also comes to humankind in Jesus Christ (*GMW*, 383). Thus Jüngel affirms Karl Rahner's insight that the immanent Trinity (God coming to God) is the

---

[11]Above, Clarke suggests: "The simplicity of God must be adjusted to whatever is required in order to fit the simplicity proper to the perfection of a *loving personal being*" (*Philosophical Approach*, 102).

same essence as the economic Trinity (God coming to humankind). In both instances the essence of God is shown to be social: "God's being as such is in coming" (*GMW*, 388). The revealed essence of God and the authentic possibility of humankind are shown to be other oriented:

> But where God is experienced as the one coming to the world and thus coming nearer and nearer to man (as individual and genus!), nearer than man can be to himself, there the experience of not having oneself becomes an experience of anthropological expansion (*GMW*, 391).[12]

How does God get closer to me than I am to myself?--through a self-communication of the God who is love, a self-communication which penetrates and thereby expands our being as God's self-communication is experienced as an eventful arrival. Thus Augustine could say: "Thou wert more inward to me than my most inward part."[13]

For Jüngel, only the direct address function of words has this power to reach our most inward depth. When a word of direct address has been *spoken*, an *event* takes place which might reach me, enter me, penetrate to deeper levels than I had previously been, and radically change who I am. While some words can excite fear or anger within us, the word which reaches us as a self-communication of love invites us to share in its expansiveness of being.

---

[12]Jüngel's parenthetical exclamation "(as individual and genus!)" appears to be another condensed effort to show that the *analogia fidei*, as Jüngel is developing it, continues to stand opposed to the *analogia entis* of the Thomistic school. One of the fundamental principles of Aquinas, viz., God is not in any genus, is apparently being called into question. Jüngel's portrayal of the divine essence as the one who comes and the one who has come as Jesus argues for understanding God as individual in that one person, and as genus in the authentic humanity revealed in that one person.

[13]*Confessions*, bk. III, ch. VII/11, NPNF, 1st ser., I, 63, as cited in Jüngel, *GMW*, 296.

If love is both the essence of God and the essence of what humankind is called to become, then we can begin to understand how "not having oneself becomes an experience of anthropological expansion"; for the person who has himself can only do so as she or he would have a thing, in the illusory attempt at self-possession. Jüngel's theological anthropology actually attempts a new kind of metaphysic, what might be called an ontology of love. This ontology does not begin with the human self, but with the divine 'self' whose very self-essence is a social essence, a coming to the other, and a going out to humanity in the *creatio ex nihilo*. Thus the basis for authentic humanity is the christological 'being with' and 'being for':

> In love, *having*, because it is inherently also a being had, becomes a *being*. . . . the event of love is the most intensive event of self-withdrawal and of new and creative self-relatedness. It may be adequate to articulate love as that event in which an I can no longer exist for itself, so that it exists in connection with a Thou to become a We, and thus is really and properly an I in an unsurpassable sense. For that reason, the love relation radiates out beyond itself and penetrates society not only to create its own institutions and orders within it (such as the family) but also to question critically all the existing orders and institutions in favor of the conquest of love in all the areas and objectifications of human existence. In the event of love, man corresponds to the God who has come to the world in both the most intensive and extensive ways. For this God is love. In the event of love man is at his most mysterious, not because he is at his most ununderstandable when he loves and is loved (that is always true, in a certain sense), but because he, as lover and beloved, corresponds to the God who reveals himself as love and who as love works invisibly. In the event of love, God and man share the same mystery (*GMW*, 392).

In this shared mystery revealed in the words and in the Word that Jesus Christ is, the correspondence has been created where human words may speak authentically about God.

THE NECESSITY OF ANALOGY

Jüngel has brought renewed interest to analogy with his criticism of more traditional doctrines along with his insistence that theology cannot exist without analogy:

> There can be no responsible talk about God without analogy. Every spoken announcement which corresponds to God is made within the context of what analogy makes possible (*GMW*, 281).

However, the necessity of analogy only intensifies the debate about its proper use. While Jüngel remains very critical of *analogia entis*, he also criticizes his Protestant tradition for having misunderstood what *analogia entis* is actually doing. The Protestant misunderstanding is typified by Barth's infamous remark: "I regard the *analogia entis* as the invention of Antichrist, and think that *because of it* one cannot become Catholic."[14] The younger Barth and other Protestants saw *analogia entis* as an attempt to grasp God in Promethean fashion by establishing a natural theology and anthropology. Jüngel rightly points out the colossal misunderstanding in this criticism of the Catholic doctrine and its actual intention.

Tracing Barth's change of mind on the issue, Jüngel asserts that the real problem was not that *analogia entis* brought God and humankind too close, the problem was that it kept them too *distant*, thereby worsening the aporia in which the tradition found itself. Thus the more mature Barth, who had discovered the vital role of analogy in the christological *analogia fidei*, exclaimed: "We need it, we need it through the whole affair" (*GMW*, 282). So the issue for all concerned is not whether to use analogy, but which analogy. Barth's earlier polemic

---

[14]Karl Barth, *CD*, I/1, xiii.

against *analogia entis* is clearly a misunderstanding. Whether or not the later views of Barth (and Jüngel) constitute a different misunderstanding is a more difficult question which will be considered below.

Jüngel's polemical strategy, as we have seen, is to use Kant as a foil and then to link Aquinas to Kant. In Kant's use of analogy, the aporia remained because the precise determination of God's essence remained unknown, empty. God's essence could be articulated through analogy, but this only intensified the problem, since what was being articulated remained unknown. Such talk about God, "symbolic anthropomorphism," is inauthentic talk because it says nothing about God's being. Jüngel's real objection against Kant, and implicitly against the Thomistic tradition, is not that it attempts to do metaphysics, but that its metaphysics is inadequate to the theological task.

> *What remains unthinkable is that God himself relates in this relationship, relates to himself* and at the same time to the world.
> . . . What can be formulated here is the knowledge of the unknowability of God. In order to know God's unknowability, something must in fact be said about God. If this were not possible, then not even the unknowability of God could be known. . . . Analogy serves, therefore, to make expressible in speech the unknowable God in his unknowability (*GMW*, 283).

Linking Kant to the general purpose of *analogia entis*, Jüngel reformulates Kant's position as x:a=b:c, where x is the unknowable God and b:c represents the set of relationships within the known world. Jüngel correctly argues that there is a perfect similarity of relations which is surpassed by a greater dissimilarity of the related things. He shows that what is here lingually related exhausts its potential in that purely linguistic analogy of naming. The problem is that this analogy is dominated by unknown relations which are presupposed as nonlingual. Hence we are left with a way of speaking about God which enables us to speak at the price of not knowing the most important factor of our thought--the nature of God. To the degree that the *analogia entis* has contributed to this situation, Jüngel sees it as the exact opposite of what Protestant polemics have made it out to be:"Analogy thus understood has doubtless the advantage of being the most thoroughgoing *hindrance* to a closed system which forces together God, man, and the world" (*GMW*, 284). If Jüngel is right that *analogia entis* utterly prevents God and humankind from being thought together and that "there can be no responsible talk about God without analogy," then the real task of analogy is to express a way that God and humankind can be thought together. And that is just what Jüngel attempts to do.

THE ANALOGY OF ADVENT

Taking the formula which generated the Kantian aporia, x:a=b:c, Jüngel applies his doctrine of God to it and develops what he calls the analogy of advent. If God (x) is the One who comes to the world (a), then the world-relationship (b:c) is given a new correspondence as it appears in the eschatological light of the divine arrival:

> In the event of the analogy x → a = b:c God ceases to be x. He introduces himself in that he arrives. And this his arrival belongs to his very being which he reveals as arriving. But this is possible only when this arrival itself takes place as an arrival-in-language so that in such an analogy not only the *relata* but also their relations to each other and their correspondence are lingual. Briefly put: the gospel is to be understood as the event of correspondence (*GMW*, 286).

As is his wont, Jüngel speaks of the advent of God in two related ways: first, as the historical event in which God arrived as the Word, as

Jesus; second, as the lingual renewal which recurs when and as this first event is directly addressed in spoken words. This lingual event happens whenever human words correspond to God; it is the gospel experienced as a spoken event. The word is the lingual vehicle for the being of God, who is revealed as the one who comes, as the one whose being is an overflowing, a going out to the other in love.

Jüngel explicates this linkage of the word which speaks of God's coming and the original event of God's coming with a short exegesis of 1 Cor. 1:18: "For the word of the cross is folly to those who are perishing, but to us who are being saved it is the power of God."

> Talk about God which speaks of the death of Jesus Christ on the cross is drawn here into the event of which it speaks, in its being as discourse. The event character of this event, its *dynamis* ('power'), is shared with the speech which speaks of it (*GMW*, 287).

Where the metaphysical tradition, working in the signification function of words, generally presupposed that the real relationship to God remains nonlingual, unknown, and may only be expressed as mystery, Jüngel, working in the direct address function, makes the opposing claim that the mystery is *in* the expression of being which occurs *as* the gospel is spoken. This amounts to a lingual participation in the divine being.

In order for the *analogia fidei* to take place, the Word of God, not by a priori conformity to the context of human language, but by its own prior action, establishes a locus of truth, a place of eventful correspondence, which can *ex post facto* be encountered within the context of human language.[15]   However, what can potentially be encountered in our language is not something which human language

---

[15]See Jüngel, "God--As a Word of Our Language," 25-45.

inherently possesses. It is something which *comes* into our language. We might call this a lingual application of the doctrine of grace:

> The event of the Word of God within the limits of our language brings with it its own truth. And our talk about God, our linguistic use of the word "God," becomes true insofar as it reaches into the realm of this truth and consequently into the context of the Word of God. To reach this realm of truth means nothing other than to expose oneself to the limit that God's Word establishes within the limits of our language.[16]

As we expose ourselves "to the limit that God's Word" has already established within our language, Jüngel's central notion of analogy is again indicated: a God-created correspondence where we learn to say yes where God has already said Yes.

Jüngel's metaphysical explications are worked out from a self-consciously, non-foundationalist perspective (*GMW*, xiv). He is not only concerned about philosophical attempts at self-grounding, but also about theological ones. He wants to protect the event character of truth from being superseded by dogmatic formulation (signification): "The true theologic proposition threatens always to outflank the truth as event, and to this extent it is inevitably and always at the point of becoming untrue."[17] There is a perpetual struggle between the event/address character of truth and the human tendency to codify, encircle, and ultimately possess truth. Jüngel's metaphysics of love, in which both God and humankind have their being in sharing their being, neatly fits the word as the bearer of self-communication. Past and present, time and eternity, are joined *in* the event which encounters us in language:

---

[16]Ibid., 41.

[17]Jüngel, "God--As a Word of Our Language," 40.

> All depends on *God's* coming to word whenever we, through God's
> Word, receive the power of faith and thus of speech. When faith
> happens, there is an eternal time gain that articulates itself in a
> temporal speech gain . . . . the word "God" finds expression in
> speech when the Word of God defines its limits within the limits of
> our language.[18]

With this striking phrase, "speech gain" *(Sprachgewinn)*, Jüngel is
virtually attributing a lingual creation to the Word of God. Just as God
is thought to be the Creator of the world of matter, so is God the
Creator of new possibilities of meaning, possibilities which humans may
actualize in the *event* of speaking the gospel, i.e., in corresponding to
the lingual space provided by this speech gain of the Word of God.

   Jüngel has now presented a new warrant for his opposition to the
view that the analogy of faith and the analogy of being are compatible.
The problem is that the *analogia entis,* in its predilection toward
description in signification terms, lets itself too easily "outflank truth as
an event." For Jüngel, truth either exists as event or not at all: "Man
is not of himself analogous with God. God is as such without analogy
in all that exists" (*GMW*, 386). There is however, a God-created
analogy, a correspondence, to which humankind may come in faith.
This is the "place of light" in which the relation of God the Father to
God the Son corresponds to the relation of God the Father to his human
children. The identification of God with the man Jesus and our current
identification with the man Jesus brings God into language. The
significance of the historical event of the life and death of Jesus "must
become an event itself" (*GMW*, 387). In this event our language gains

---

[18]Jüngel, "God--As a Word of Our Language," 45.

the power to correspond to God, not just to speak about God, and the event of "speech gain" then impinges upon human ontology:

> In Jesus Christ, indeed, God has become *addressable as* God and we have become *addressable as* his earthly children. But in the Holy Spirit, God has become *expressible* as God. To express God as God always means to present one's own humanity in such a way that the entire person is drawn out of itself. This happens in the power of the Spirit (*GMW*, 387).

In this event of being drawn out of ourselves, our humanity is ontologically determined. The self is fulfilled by moving away from the self toward the One whose arrival establishes authentic humanity as "being with" and "being for."

Jüngel contends that the analogy of naming,[19] as based on the analogy of being, expresses lingual relations which are merely secondary over against the external relations which are named but not really contained within that naming. In the contrasting analogy presented as language event, "God relates himself to the world and to man and thus is expressed in language" (*GMW*, 289). In this lingual linkage opened up by the arrival of God as the human Jesus, the relata are all profoundly changed. Humanity is established in a christological light, the world is illuminated in an eschatological light, and through suffering the death on the cross, the alleged imperishability of God is refuted. The God to whom Jüngel's analogy corresponds is not the God *supra nos*, but the God of love whose essence is revealed in going out to others.

For Jüngel, analogy has to do primarily with possibility--the possibility of divine arrival; the possibility of hearing the word directly

---

[19]Question 13 of Aquinas' *Summa Theologiae* is called *de nominibus Dei* (the names of God).

addressed; the possibility of ontological expansion because of what has been heard; the possibility of theological authenticity through correspondence to the locus of divine arrival in Christ; the possibility of lingual renewal through human speech which accepts and thus corresponds in its own thought to the point of power, the "place of light" which has already been divinely established; and finally, the possibility of love. Love, which is the outward movement of the being of God, communicates the divine self *in* the word which addresses its other. The death of God on the cross of Christ indicates that such self-communication is also precarious, yet creative possibilities are diminished and finally negated when something is held back. In that case the address would lack the directness in which speaker, hearer, and world may be joined together. But in Jüngel's analogy of advent, the being of God is in the word; and we are challenged to participate in that same word of expanding possibility.

PART FOUR

CONCLUSION

CHAPTER TEN

CRITICAL COMPARISONS, EVALUATIONS
AND SYNTHESES

Jüngel's work has provoked a great deal of commentary, even though
much of that commentary, to one degree or another, has been critical of
his efforts on analogy and of his treatment of the larger issues which
analogy raises. By examining some of the critical responses to Jüngel,
we can now begin to evaluate the larger issues which the debate over
analogy has raised.

ANALOGY IN THEOLOGICAL CONTEXT

In his defense of Barth, Jüngel tells us that in order to understand
Barth's use of the *analogia fidei* (analogy of faith), one must consider
the concept as it is developed within its theological context.[1]
Methodologically, this request (or warning) seems only fair. Similarly,

---

[1]"Die Möglichkeit," 535-36.

John Webster, whose overall evaluation is quite friendly to Jüngel, complains that theological debates between cultures and/or traditions

> are not infrequently marred by the generality of their description. Because they rarely attend to the details of particular texts and are insufficiently aware of the historical developments from which these texts issue, such accounts do not lead to anything more than rough characterisations which inhibit rather than promote exchange. . . .
> The larger purpose of this essay is, then, to suggest that mutual suspicion and misunderstanding is most effectively dispelled by close study of examples of theological writing from a particular tradition, with an eye to distinct theological procedures and larger theological commitments.[2]

In essence, Jüngel and Webster are calling for fair theological play in interpreting another's tradition; yet the question must be raised whether or not Jüngel himself has followed this procedure in investigating Aquinas' use of analogy.

As it turns out, both Catholic and Protestant, French and English writers, have faulted Jüngel for his treatment of Aquinas on analogy. My own view is that Jüngel's linkage of Kant and Aquinas was a bold move that did not quite come off; however, it is a fruitful failure in that it has so well highlighted the basic issues at stake in analogy. Furthermore, while Jüngel may not have grasped the best in either Aquinas or Neo-Thomist analogy, he may have served that tradition well by pointing to certain dangers of interpretation (one of which might be instantiated in David Burrell's early treatment of Aquinas).

---

[2]John Webster, "Eberhard Jüngel on the Language of Faith," *Modern Theology* 1:4 (July 1985): 253.

In "Analogy according to E. Jüngel, Critical Remarks: The Stakes of a Debate,"[3] Gérard Rémy seconds the methodological motion of Jüngel and Webster by linking the use of analogy to larger theological issues:

> Analogy, however, must be appreciated as a bodily part of the system of thought in which it functions. Therefore it is important to resituate the meaning and intention of Thomistic analogy in the type of intellectual undertaking which St. Thomas adopts for his treatment of God. Similarly, the criticisms of Jüngel can only be truly significant when undertaken in the aim and theological concerns which are his. The problem of analogy thus provokes an enlargement of the debate, capable of making the real stakes appear.[4]

So everyone seems to agree on two things: (1) theological analogy must be understood in its broader theological context; (2) because analogy expresses larger doctrinal commitments, a great deal is at stake. Now let us consider the various points of debate which Jüngel has engendered.

KANT AND AQUINAS--A TENDENTIOUS LINKAGE?

The overwhelming evidence from Neo-Thomist research of the last generation has pointed to an evolution of Aquinas' use of analogy over the course of his career. In the light of Fabro's, Klubertanz's, Montagnes's, and Clarke's work showing the importance of participation in the Thomistic corpus (see Part One above), one can only be surprised

---

[3]Gérard Rémy, "L'analogie selon E. Jüngel. Remarques critiques: L'enjeu d'un débat," *Revue d'Histoire et de Philosophie Religieuses* 66 (1986/2): 147-77, my translations.

[4]Ibid., 164-65.

to find this central theme glossed over and largely ignored in Jüngel's analysis of Aquinas.   To hold Aquinas accountable for an analogy of proportionality which Jüngel sees implied by his use of the analogy of attribution (when Aquinas himself makes no use of proportionality in his last thirty-three works) and to ignore or fail to grasp Aquinas' consistent employment of causal participation constitutes a serious shortcoming in Jüngel's engagement of Aquinas.

Had Jüngel confronted Clarke's portrayal of the *positive* nature of God's infinity in Aquinas' work, where *actus*, the inherent outward movement of being-in-act, functions similarly to the divine movement which Jüngel himself advocates, a more subtle critique might have been forthcoming.   But when Aquinas' central themes go unaddressed in Jüngel's analysis, important areas of potential agreement are neglected; and the engagement becomes unnecessarily polemical.

The impact of such omissions largely vitiates Jüngel's critique of Aquinas' metaphysics; for the appraisal of infinity is so different in Plato and Aristotle than in Aquinas, and so different again in Kant, with whom Jüngel links Aquinas' use of analogy, that even when similar terminologies are employed, they actually signify very different things. Where Jüngel correctly notes that Kant conceived infinity "as only the (empty) essence of the concept,"[5] he fails to address Aquinas' very different appraisal of infinity.   Instead, Jüngel criticizes the Aristotelian influence as leading to the agnostic analogy of proportionality, criticizes the Neoplatonic influence for its negative theology, and fails to realize that both streams of thought are fundamentally revalued as Aquinas

---

[5]Jüngel, *God as the Mystery of the World*, 73.

employs them in his unique synthesis of the positive infinity of God as *actus essendi* (act of being).

The Suspicion of anachronism. Countering Jüngel's polemic against the apophatic tradition, the Québecois scholar Jean Richard offers some important correctives to Jüngel's linkage of Kant and Aquinas:

> It seems to me that there is a misunderstanding which arises from a certain lack of historical perspective. At the outset of any discussion, one must recognize that the problem of the knowledge of God presents itself in very different terms in antiquity and in the modern epoch. The two situations are so different that the solution of former times can be experienced as the present malaise. Formerly, the possibility of a knowledge and a discourse about God presented no difficulty; it was an established fact. But precisely because of that, the need was felt to protect the transcendence and the mystery of God against every overly literal interpretation of Scripture.[6]

The problems of the mid-Thirteenth Century and the late-Twentieth are indeed quite different.   Apophaticism within the confident, theistic rationalism of the Thirteenth Century and apophaticism during the Enlightenment's skeptical rationalism move in different directions. The former protects the freedom and the transcendence of God; the latter aggravates the sense of divine absence by contributing to what Jüngel has called the unspeakability of God. With regard to the contemporary context, Richard agrees that "agnosticism will now be the great danger."[7]

---

[6]Jean Richard, "Théologie évangélique et théologie philosophique à propos d'Eberhard Jüngel," *Science et Esprit* 38:1 (1986): 20, my translations.

[7]Ibid.

However, Richard once again finds Jüngel's account historically insensitive to the varying roles which reason played in Aquinas and Kant:

> One must raise again here the suspicion of anachronism. Kantian agnosticism does not have the same meaning as that of ancient negative theology. Between the two is the advent, the rupture, of critical reason.[8]

The crucial contextual difference is that the modern unspeakability of God stems from an autonomous rationality in science and technology; therefore, we now are faced with a different problem calling for a different solution. In Richard's proposal, faith will certainly play a role, "but it will also be necessary, and perhaps even at the outset, to explore the different dimensions of reason, in order to avoid reducing it to its scientific and technological dimensions."[9]

Complex causality in Aquinas. Jüngel has correctly associated Kant's use of analogy with what might be called an 'outside' notion of causality. This outside relation to God is portrayed in Kant's examples of watchmaker:watch and shipbuilder:ship. Kantian analogy thus depicts a causal relationship which leaves God external, *supra nos*, and ultimately unknown. On the other hand, Aquinas believes that God can be known from God's effects; hence a very different claim about causality and reason is being made.

In comparing Aquinas' use of analogy to Kant's, Richard specifies three fundamental differences:

---

[8]Richard, "Théologie évangélique et théologie philosophique," 22.

[9]Ibid.

First, "analogy" in St. Thomas signifies first and foremost "relationship." But because in theology this relationship of God to the creature is a relationship of causality, and because in this first cause which is God all created perfections must pre-exist in an eminent way, in this case "analogy" ends up meaning "resemblance" between the Creator and his creature. One already recognizes here an important difference with Kant. Second, all the absolute perfections, like wisdom and goodness, can be said of God analogically. But the principal case of analogy in theology is without a doubt the denomination of God as "being," from which arises the importance of the *analogia entis* in Thomistic theology. *St. Thomas thereby resolves a major problem of negative theology and at the same time founds the possibility of an affirmative discourse about God.* . . . The doctrine of analogy permits St. Thomas . . . to affirm . . . a relationship of God to being, in so far as Creator of all being. Now this relationship of creation itself implies that all the perfection of being pre-exists first and foremost in God in an eminent manner. There is hence a fundamental ontological resemblance between God and every creature, which justifies naming God from that which is. Third, there follows yet an important epistemological consequence. For one also finds in that the fundamental justification for an ontological discourse about God. One will be able to speak of God in relation to being--as source, foundation, and power of being. One will also be able to speak of God as being while using ontological concepts like "essence" and "existence." It can be seen that the entire language of philosophical theology finds itself in principle justified by that.[10]

Although there remains a great deal that cannot be said, Aquinas confidently affirms that participatory knowledge of God can be analogically expressed. Quite unlike Kant, Aquinas' analogy concept expresses what we might call an 'inside' understanding of divine causality. And this is precisely the import of participation in Thomistic analogy--the creature partakes of, participates *in*, the created perfections

[10]Richard, "Théologie évangélique et théologie philosophique," 22, emphasis added.

of the Creator. God does not remain entirely outside creation, above it, and unspeakably *supra nos*. God and creatures are both differentiated and specified together, but Aquinas uses analogy to go beyond negative theology in "an affirmative discourse about God."

Rémy sees a dialectic in Aquinas between nearness and distance, the knowability and the unknowability of God. This dialectic is played out in a "symbiosis" between divine causality and exemplarity for which analogy serves as the medium.[11] Rather than an aporia, a dynamic attraction between Creator and creature is portrayed as the source of inexhaustible human potential.

John Milbank has similarly criticized Jüngel for failing to see how the central importance of participation in Aquinas affects causality and reason. Milbank insists that in spite of the apparent similarity to Kant, Aquinas is profoundly different

> because Aquinas thinks of divine causality in terms neither of sufficient reason nor of efficient causality alone, but rather in terms of a complex unity of formal-final-efficient causality which suggests that as all being is from God, then everything in some sense pre-exists within the fullness of the divine simplicity (*ST*, I Q.13 a.3, a.5, Q.12 a.11, Q.6 a.4) (or within the divine *Ars* that is the second person of the Trinity). Hence, to know God as cause is not just to know him as cause of the good, but also to propose him as the perfection of goodness, and in a certain sense as the exact, perfect reality of one's *own*, human being (*ST* 1 Q.6 a.1 ad. 2).[12]

Not only has Milbank seen the richer concept of causality at work for Aquinas, he has also pointed out an obvious but important fact: Aquinas is writing with theological commitments to the Trinity, commitments which Kant does not share. Theological commitments and rationality

---

[11]Rémy, "L'analogie selon E. Jüngel," 163.

[12]Milbank, "Between Purgation and Illumination," 171.

overlap in Aquinas' notion of causality. Reason and multi-layered causality are interwoven in his doctrine of creation.

Theological anthropology in Aquinas. For Jüngel, as for Barth, any truly theological anthropology would have to be accomplished christologically. Once the anthropological conception has been christologically determined, then we can and even must be willing to speak of God anthropomorphically. Hence he develops analogy as a correspondence (*Entsprechung*) of faith, the *analogia fidei*, and opposes it to the Roman Catholic, Thomistically based *analogia entis*. Yet what would become of the Protestant resistance to *analogia entis* if closer investigation showed that it too were based on a theological anthropology that could include strong christological affirmations?

Before returning to Catholic commentators, virtually all of whom understand Aquinas as working with just such a theological anthropology, let us consider Milbank's views. Noting that being is "sheer givenness" for Aquinas (a phrase he borrows from Burrell), Milbank contends that Aquinas' use of the *essentia/esse* distinction

> effectively "eschatologizes" the notion of teleology throughout every level of reality, a move which can then be understood as a preparation for the theology of grace. That which is aimed for, especially as regards human beings, is always, also, that which is "superadded" (*ST*, 1 Q.5 a.1 ad. 3, a.4 ad. 2).[13]

This eschatological teleology permeates every level of reality, including reason, and is a "preparation for the theology of grace." But it is also evidence that reality is already imbued with grace: "From his fullness we have all received, grace upon grace" (Jn. 1:16). Praising the first

---

[13]Milbank, "Between Purgation and Illumination," 170.

grace of created reality should hardly be construed as wandering from the christological "place of light." To the contrary, it is rendering additional praise in discovering the unity and order present in the patterns of creation, a *logos* which arises from the *Logos* which would eventually be made flesh. All lines of correspondence ultimately converge in the trinitarian center of the Son. What point would be served by cutting off all but one of those lines? To the degree that actual things and beings have a share of creation, they are already good; yet for humanity, there are "superadditions" of goodness which

> involve . . . further acts of intellectual synthesis, further strengthening in virtue, further insights into the truth that virtue as especially charity is not merely perfection in us but a constant spilling over into the strengthening of others after the pattern of the divine creative perfection itself.[14]

In fact, this "spilling over" actually resonates rather well with Jüngel's development of love, the essence of God, as a coming to the other.

Contesting the view that Aquinas employs an anthropological foundation, Milbank further separates Aquinas from Kant:

> There is for Aquinas no grounding of the good in a given, self-transcending rational nature. Instead, to define humanity as located in the increasing imitation of divine goodness, and of divine being, is to have a wholly theological anthropology.[15]

Yet Jüngel's reading of Aquinas makes proportionality more basic than attribution in Aquinas and thus

> fails to reckon with the way in which, for Aquinas, any predication of being or goodness to finite things already refers to a dynamic

---

[14]Milbank, "Between Purgation and Illumination," 170.

[15]Ibid.

ontological tension in which they are constantly drawn forwards towards the divine perfection.[16]

Expressing this "dynamic ontological tension" between God and humankind is one of the major functions of Aquinas' analogy.

Similarly, Rémy has argued (*pace* Jüngel) that the human mind is not left in a state of capitulation before the unspeakability of God.[17] Instead, it seeks

> the opening of the mind to a mystery which surpasses it. Far from being interrupted in order to yield to a silence imposed by the unknown, the investigation of St. Thomas is carried out in the very difficult and demanding framework for which human reason is disposed.[18]

In the act of comprehension, the concomitant realization that a great deal is left uncomprehended is a paradoxical indicator that one is on the right track. In this view analogical predication neither strictly defines God nor leaves God defined only as the undefinable. Instead, analogy captures the on-going tension between Creator and creature.

Grace and interruption. Aquinas' strong doctrine of grace is often underestimated, yet grace dominates the syntax within which his metaphysics operates. For example, his entire account of the theological virtues is dependent upon divine intrusion, as seen in his recurrent

---

[16]Milbank, "Between Purgation and Illumination," 163. The idea of "being drawn forwards" is much like Burrell's development of *manuductio*.

[17]While Aquinas inherits and to a degree utilizes apophatic theology, his response to the question, "Whether Affirmative Propositions Can Be Formed about God?" (*ST* I.13.12), clarifies the metaphysical basis upon which he positively employs analogical predication. See above, Chap.2, especially 61-62.

[18]Rémy, "L'analogie selon E. Jüngel," 163.

citations of Lam. 5:21: "Turn thou us to thee, O Lord, and we shall be turned."[19] Aquinas' divine "turning" bears some similarity to Jüngel's notion of divine "interruption"; for both recognize a divine interest and relationship of potential particularity to the world, a particularity which Kant does not acknowledge. However, in Aquinas the specific divine action *restores* the human being, the *imago dei*, to its original orientation and purpose. In Jüngel's account, the specific divine action creates something new to which human allegiance and speech may then correspond, viz., the Christ event which in turn presents the only true *imago dei*. In spite of these different emphases, neither Aquinas nor Jüngel would be coherent without divine grace, divine activity in human affairs. On the other hand, there is no place for such divine activity in Kant's various writings.

DIVERGENT ESTIMATIONS OF
THE POWER OF LANGUAGE

Strong disagreement remains about how final a category language itself is, a category in which analogy necessarily must function. Upon investigation, at least three types emerge: Kant's, Jüngel's, and Aquinas'. Jüngel has correctly argued that Kant's notion of analogy is embedded in language of a very limited capacity. In the "symbolical anthropomorphism" which Kant allows as permissible use, analogy expresses everything that can be known in language; yet the real object

---

[19]See, for example, *ST* I.23.5 and *ST* I-II.109.6.

remains unknown to us outside of language. There is a strong and ultimately determinative 'leftover' in Kant's estimation of language. Jüngel, on the other hand, tremendously escalates the possibilities of language. For him, God is not an object outside language to which language distantly refers; God *comes* into human language. In the divine advent, which is always expressed as direct address, there is no leftover. The being of God is communicated *in* the word with revelatory force--the event nature of analogy.

In Jüngel's event nature of analogy, truth is "fundamentally the interruption of the human life-connections."[20] In this fertile notion of truth as interruption of human language and world relations, Jüngel's event-language takes on progressive ethical implications. Divine advent in language always brings something new, something which exceeds previous human limits of understanding:

> Whilst the language of faith is not literally descriptive of actuality, it is not thereby referential to *less* than actuality but to *more* than actuality, precisely because it is metaphorical language. The suspension of literal reference allows the linguistic identification of states of affairs beyond the actual.[21]

Jüngel's view, developed in opposition to Aquinas' essence/existence doctrine, keeps the *actuality* of God, humankind, and world thoroughly distinct from one another. But in the event of correspondence, his view yields the closest *possible* intimacy:

> To say that the Kingdom comes "*as* parable" is to say that its relation to the world is tangential, and, in one sense, indirect: the Kingdom is not adjectival upon the world and so has come to speech indirectly.

---

[20]Jüngel, "Anrufung Gottes als Grundethos christlichen Handelns," in *Barth-Studien*, 330, as cited in Webster, 267.

[21]Webster, "Jüngel on the Language of Faith," 261.

> Thus the world-relation of the Kingdom as it occurs in parable is
> *eschatological*: the Kingdom is in the world only insofar as it tears
> apart the world's temporal structures *ab extra*.[22]

By rupturing inadequate temporal structures, divine advent opens up and
organizes new 'linguistic space' into which human thought may enter
and there speak a true analogy of correspondence. More can be said
because divine interruption has expanded human language.

In contrast to Jüngel, Aquinas contends that what can be said is
limited by language. Whatever we say, and with the use of analogy we
can say some things truly about God, God will remain more than can be
expressed by the vehicle of human words. The priority in Aquinas is
ontological rather than lingual. As the infinite actuality, God is the
source, sustainer, and goal of creaturely participation. By definition,
participation, i.e., having a share of, cannot be total and infinite;
nonetheless, participation can be increasingly substantive. Much of the
tension within the analogy concept seems to reside within this two-part
message of 'yes--but not entirely'. So Aquinas declares:

> No name is predicated univocally of God and of creatures.
>   Neither, on the other hand, are names applied to God and
> creatures in a purely equivocal sense (*ST* I.13.5).

The function of analogy is to avoid these two extremes of excess and
deficiency--saying either too much or what amounts to nothing at all.

The problem which Aquinas sought to resolve, and with which we
too must struggle, is how theological language, and that still means
human language, can adequately express something about the infinite
God. Jüngel has ably shown that theological language must not commit
itself to a metaphysics which cannot speak the event of the cross. But

---

[22]Webster, "Jüngel on the Language of Faith," 257.

in focusing so exclusively upon the cross, particularly upon the death of God, and then joining that focus with a Heideggerian preference for potency over actuality, does Jüngel thereby suggest a lessening of the substantive infinity of God? As we saw above in Clarke's work, one of Aquinas' historic achievements was to combine a positive, substantial concept of God's infinity with creaturely, finite being. While I support Jüngel's view that our metaphysics must be able to account for the divine action on the cross, if he has relinquished divine infinity in order to do so, then as many problems are created as solved by such an account.[23]

Aquinas' analogy expresses an ontological differential between infinite and finite. For him, analogy is not based upon some present or potential power of language, but on a prior ontological communication in nature. As Richard states:

> The ultimate foundation of the value, correctness, and truth of our theological language must obviously be of the ontological order. If there can be verbal communication between man and God, then there is first a prior ontological communication from God to man by the very fact of creation.[24]

Given perfections are first experienced by creatures through the limited mode of their creaturely participation; however, since God is all these perfections in the infinite mode of the divine act of being, and as such

---

[23]It is not altogether clear to me what Jüngel's view of infinity is in these matters, since he does not explicitly discuss infinity with regard to analogy or Aquinas. As with Burrell, so too with Jüngel, the omission of this aspect of divinity detracts from the overall account.

[24]Jean Richard, "Analogie et symbolisme chez saint Thomas," *Laval Théologique et Philosophique*, Commemorative of the Seventh Hundred Anniversary of the Death of St. Thomas Aquinas (October 1974): 392, my translations.

the source, sustainer, and goal of these perfections which we first know as creatures,

> there is thus a veritable ontological communication from God to the creature. And this communication is itself that of participation. The very fact of participation no doubt implies a kind of ontological downstepping, in the sense that these perfections will be received by creatures according to a limited and finite mode. But they no less retain the mark of their divine origin, and they refer to it constantly by a transcendental orientation of their entire being.[25]

As we come to know a perfection in a limited way, this limited knowledge also orients us toward the infinite source of the perfection. The differential between our mode of knowing and the origin and divine fullness of the referent (*res significata*) is the source of Milbank's "dynamic ontological tension" and Richard's "transcendental orientation of [our] entire being." Thus understood, analogy is anything but a static concept; as an expression of creaturely participation in the divine, it is brimming with dialectical implications of both present achievement and 'not fully', 'not yet'. The relationship with God provides an inexhaustible depth of semantic meaning for analogical predicates, but this same relationship forbids "any semantic resting place."[26] The profundity of divine ontological communication provides an ascending possibility for all aspects of human development. At the same time, the "ontological downstepping" indicates something of divine pedagogy; for the infinite/finite tension generates the potential of creaturely achievement and the actuality of human responsibility.

Seen in this light, the problem of language about God is a function of our on-going incompleteness. In the very discovery or realization of

---

[25]Richard, "Analogie et symbolisme chez saint Thomas," 392-93.

[26]Milbank, "Between Purgation and Illumination," 172.

a given perfection, say goodness, we are turned, re-oriented and reinvigorated toward the divine source of that goodness. Milbank nicely captures this sense of on-going movement:

> Actual, given human being is involved in some indefinition in relation to God. . . . to ascribe real degrees of perfection to being, indeed any use of evaluative perfection-terms, *already* assumes a metaphysics of participation . . . . Thus to have some knowledge of virtue, of perfection, is imperfectly to know one's humanity, which is only absolutely comprehended in the divine inclusion--as *esse ipsum*--of all *differentia*.[27]

This indefinition draws humanity forward toward ever greater participation in created *esse*. Thus, at the heart of his analogy concept, Aquinas' participation doctrine includes a "teleological development" which is colored by a certain "religious-moral self-dissatisfaction."[28]

Aquinas really is a contrast to both Kant and Jüngel. Like Kant, he has a 'leftover' beyond what the human creature can legitimately say. But unlike Kant, Aquinas' doctrine of participation does not leave the creature in an unknown relationship to the divine. The *principium*, the beginning and end of all things (*ST* I.2 Intro.), is also intimately present to each existing creature (*ST* I.8.1). Besides, Aquinas' leftover is not unknowable *simpliciter*; it is just unknowable all at once. So here again, Aquinas' analogy is a middle way between Kant's logical agnosticism and Jüngel's definitive essence.

---

[27]Milbank, "Between Purgation and Illumination," 172.

[28]Ibid.

EVENT, PERSON, AND RELATIONSHIP

LANGUAGE AND PERSON

In his synthesis of christology and hermeneutics, Jüngel adopts Ernst Fuchs' notion that Jesus is "the parable of God."[29] Balking at this understanding of Jesus, Rémy asks: "Is a person reducible to a category of language?"[30]

Jüngel is not defenseless on this point. His explication of God as love, as a going out to the other, is fitting with an escalated possibility for language, since language also involves a going out from one self to another. The Prologue of John, especially when *logos* is translated as "Word," lends further strength to his thesis that the being of God is communicated *in* and as the word. Additionally, Milbank suggests that when language is undertaken before the transcendent Jesus Christ

> language is also "like God," and our linguistic expression mirrors the divine creative act which is immanently contained in the *Ars Patris* that is the Logos. "Analogy of being" becomes "analogy of creation" because our imitative power is a participation in the divine originative-expressive capacity.[31]

These views are typical of the total investment which many modern theorists place in language. Nonetheless, which is more like God and which is more fundamental for humankind? Language, or persons?

In his debate with Karl Barth, Emil Brunner defended the use of *analogia entis*, not because of anything *in* language itself, but because

---

[29]Jüngel, *God as the Mystery of the World*, 289.

[30]Rémy, "L'analogie selon E. Jüngel," 157.

[31]Milbank, "Between Purgation and Illumination," 189.

the capacity for language, language itself, and relationships of responsibility, exist in and between *persons*.[32] In this construal, person, itself based upon the *imago dei*, is a more fundamental category than language. Language and responsibility, including responsibility for language, are earmarks of what it means to be a person; but it is more accurate to say that persons have language than that language is like persons, or even the more extreme, "language is 'like God.'" Language is one differentia, but not the sole differentia, of the species. Language does not exhaust everything in God, nor does it exhaust everything in humankind, created as the *imago dei*.

Brunner contends that two interdependent revelations, one in Jesus Christ and the other in the "theater of nature," are clearly attested in Scripture. Hence, he argues, this is not an either/or issue: "The question is rather how the two revelations, that in creation and that in Jesus Christ, are related."[33] Fundamentally, this is the perennial question now disputed in our present debate: How should analogy function theologically? And even more specifically, What is the relation of creation and christology? Brunner's retention of a revelation in nature, even though "understood correctly only in faith," leads him to affirm the *analogia entis*, linking the notions of person, *imago*, and incarnation:

> The *analogia entis* is not specifically Roman Catholic. Rather is it the basis of every theology, of Christian theology as much as pagan. The characteristic of Christian theology, and somehow also the difference between Roman Catholic and Protestant theology, is not the issue *whether* the method of analogy may be used, but *how* this is to be

---

[32]Brunner, "Nature and Grace," 24, 34, 55-56.

[33]Ibid., 26.

done and *what* analogies are to be employed. The determining factor in Christian theology is the energy with which the fact that God is a subject is--in contrast to other analogies--maintained in theology. This determining factor rests upon the doctrine of the *imago dei*, which can be adequately understood only in the incarnation of God.[34]

Although Brunner vies with the best of the Protestants on the ravages of sin (Barth), he contends that the possibility of being addressed by God, as well as the possibility of human responsibility, rests upon the formal *imago* being unaffected by sin, even though sin has rendered it materially dysfunctional. In its retention of the formal image of God, humankind is

> the only legitimate analogy to God, because he is always a rational being, a subject, a person. . . . Father, Son, Spirit, Word--these all-important concepts of Christian theology, of the message of the Bible, are concepts derived from personality.[35]

Not unlike Burrell, and especially like Clarke (See "'Person' as Primary Analogate," above in Chapter Three), Brunner places 'person' at the base of the analogy between God and humankind.

CREATION, STRUCTURE, AND SIN

According to Jüngel,

> the one who develops the metaphor and "discovers" the parable must be gripped by the same proportion which will later grip the hearers of his speech. What distinguishes him from them is that he *first of all discovers* the engaging correspondence and then expresses it.[36]

---

[34]Brunner, "Nature and Grace," 55-56.

[35]Ibid, 55.

[36]Jüngel, *God as the Mystery of the World*, 291. Jüngel claims that analogy "causes the character of address found in metaphor and parable" (ibid., 290).

But what does it mean to say that someone can "discover" a parable or an "engaging correspondence"? Does this not commit Jüngel, by the implications of this language, to an underlying structure which is discoverable? In turn, does this not entail recognizing something like an *analogia entis*? In one sense, we have just restated the question that Catholic critics repeatedly put to "Barthian" Protestants: Is there not presupposed a doctrine of creation which enables human speech and any sort of correspondence in the first place?

Rémy faults Jüngel for not addressing with sufficient clarity,

> the problem of the articulation between the Kingdom as an eschatological or supernatural reality and the linguistic means that it employs in order to call the hearer, but which belong to a different order, a natural and human order.[37]

While Jüngel has offered an explanation in both *God as the Mystery* and "God--As a Word of Our Language" of how God's advent creates a new possibility for language *(Sprachgewinn)*, the original possibility inherent in human language is left hanging and unclear.

An important point of disagreement in the debate between Brunner and Barth centered around the question of *Wortmächtigkeit* (the capacity for words).[38] In his reply to Jüngel, which looks a lot like Brunner's reply to Barth, Richard independently uses two of the foundations of Brunner's position: the inherent capacity for speech and the *imago dei* of Gen. 1:26-27:

---

[37]Rémy, "L'analogie selon E. Jüngel," 158.

[38]Barth apparently misquoted Brunner on this issue, accusing him of affirming a natural *Offenbarungsmächtigkeit*, a capacity for revelation. See the introduction by John Baillie in *Natural Theology*, 8-9.

> Jesus Christ can only be the analogical Word of God if humanity is already fundamentally the image of God, if human language already possesses the fundamental capacity to express God analogically.[39]

The Richard/Jüngel debate, a kind of déjà-vu with regard to the Barth/Brunner debate, highlights many of the issues at stake. In support of Jüngel, we speak a differentiated, richer language because of what Jesus proclaimed and what has been proclaimed about him. On the other hand, Jesus can hardly be said to have created a new language, at least not without denying the fundamental import of incarnation into *human* life.

If however, we are to take the incarnation seriously as a theological theme, then Jesus cannot simply be reduced to words which he has spoken, words spoken about him, or just to his death. What Jesus did, how he participated in a particular social location, and the effect which his *living relationship* had upon those who knew him must likewise be considered. These expanded criteria call into question Webster/Jüngel's notion that

> the Kingdom is not adjectival upon the world and so has come to speech indirectly. Thus the world-relation of the Kingdom as it occurs in parable is *eschatological*: the Kingdom is in the world only insofar as it tears apart the world's temporal structures *ab extra*.[40]

From the Prologue of John, Richard makes the opposite case:

> The logos can only come among its own, it can incarnate only in a world which is already its expression; put differently, the logos of the universal creation is itself manifested in the world only in the person of Jesus Christ.[41]

---

[39]Richard, "Théologie évangélique et théologie philosophique," 23.

[40]Webster, "Jüngel on the language of Faith," 257.

[41]Richard, "Théologie évangélique et théologie philosophique," 23.

While Jüngel's approach captures the newness and the distinctiveness of the divine advent, it seems to do so by ignoring the obvious. That is, if humanity could not already speak and were not in some manner already responsible for its judgments, points upon which Brunner has insisted, then God would have to be in the business of constantly creating in a virtually pointilistic fashion. But according to Aquinas (and Brunner), the perduring structures of creation, including the *imago dei*, have not been destroyed by sin, even though sin has disordered and disoriented humanity from its proper object--God. Hence Aquinas' repeated plea for being re-*turned* (Lam. 5:21).

The issue of continuity, whether and how much the patterns of creation have been disrupted by sin, underlies much of this discussion. A. M. Fairweather summarizes Aquinas' position:

> The teaching of Aquinas concerning the moral and spiritual order stands in sharp contrast to all views, ancient or modern, which cannot do justice to the difference between the divine and the creaturely without appearing to regard them as essentially antagonistic as well as discontinuous. For Aquinas, no such opposition obtains between God and the world which he has made. Any evil which disrupts the continuity of human endeavor after self-realization in God is due to corruption, not to nature, and such corruption is never absolute.[42]

For Aquinas, there is a friendlier tone between the reason derived from created nature and the superimposed gifts of grace:

> The gifts of grace are added to us in order to enhance the gifts of nature, not to take them away. The native light of reason is not obliterated by the light of faith gratuitously shed on us. Hence Christian theology enlists the help of philosophy and the sciences. Mere reasoning can never discover the truths which faith perceives;

[42]A. M. Fairweather, General Introduction to *Nature and Grace: Selections from the Summa Theologica of Thomas Aquinas*, The Library of Christian Classics (Philadelphia: The Westminster Press, 1954), 21.

on the other hand, it cannot discover any disagreement between its own intrinsically natural truths and those divinely revealed. Were there any contradiction, one set or the other would be fallacious, and, since both are from God, he would be the author of our deception, which is out of the question. In fact the imperfect reflects the perfect; our enterprise should be to draw out the analogies between the discoveries of reason and the commands of faith.[43]

This passage demonstrates not so much a strong continuity as a sense of harmony and complementarity between faith and reason. The theological task, aided by reason and the sciences, is "to draw out the analogies." Aquinas is fond of declaring that even "the philosophers . . . proved many things about God" (*ST* I.13.5), along with Rom. 1:20:

Ever since the creation of the world his invisible nature, namely, his eternal power and deity, has been clearly perceived in the things that have been made. So they are without excuse.

As we shall see below, the issue for our contemporary discussion is not just the potential dialogue between philosophy and theology but the potential dialogue among science, philosophy, and religion.

Rémy observes that the opponents of *analogia entis* presuppose that sin has nullified the rational ingredient which this analogy utilizes:

The theological motif which could emasculate the rational use of analogy would be the corruption of the natural human faculties by sin, which causes these faculties to be paralyzed or to deviate from their use. As great a part of the truth that this pessimistic vision may contain, its radicality is hard to harmonize with the theology of creation.[44]

In line with Aquinas, Brunner, and Richard, Rémy counters this "pessimistic view" with the notion that sin neither destroys the original

---

[43]Exposition, *de Trinitate*, ii.3, as cited in *Theological Texts*, 7.

[44]Rémy, "L'analogie selon E. Jüngel," 174.

power of the divine creation nor the possibilities and responsibilities of humankind created in the image of God.

Interestingly, Jüngel does not say a great deal about sin in *God as the Mystery of the World*. What he does say comes rather late (225), and although a creative outworking of his metaphysics, it does not in and of itself argue against the *analogia entis*; it argues *differently* from the metaphysics that would support *analogia entis*. That is, where the *analogia entis* is primarily concerned with being and human participation, Jüngel is primarily concerned to show that God must be understood in the encounter of being with non-being. For Jüngel the cross is no mere accident of history, something which particular historical circumstances dictated, and which Jesus, being subject to those circumstances, had to undergo. Instead, the cross of Christ is the paradigmatic instance of the definitive encounter with darkness in which the nature of God is revealed as a "being for" and a "being with." Divine being moves into nothingness for the sake of being, for life. As Jüngel has developed this theme, all encounters with the divine would reveal this same being-in-going-out.

Hence Jüngel defines sin as that which opposes the outward movement of being that realizes itself only as it goes out to the other. The direction of being is the crux: "Sin is nothing other than the compulsion toward oneself into which man places himself."[45] Since the self must follow God in the movement away from the self, movement back toward the self amounts to movement toward nothingness:

> Sin is the *intensified power of nothingness*, that nothingness into which God goes out and out of which he calls his creation into being,

---

[45]Jüngel, *God as the Mystery of the World*, 359.

an empowerment *to the level of a power summoning back to
destruction.* Sin makes nothingness into something; it builds up
nothingness into an anti-deity. And it does this by keeping God out
of the struggle between being and non-being.[46]

To be sure, Jüngel does not deny the Reformation theme of divine
justification of the sinner; however, he does rework it in the context of
his singular metaphysics, contending that sin is man's attempt "to justify
himself as *coming* from nothingness (instead of being created from
it)."[47] In this respect the self-reflective movement of the Cartesian
cogito constitutes something like the chief metaphysical sin.

Given Jüngel's explication of sin, he does not really need to
follow Barth's view that sin totally corrupts the *imago dei.* Since the
opposing interpretations of the *imago dei* become underpinnings for the
conflicting paradigms of analogy, possibilities for increased dialogue
might enter at this point.

THE MISSING CATEGORY
OF RELATIONSHIP

Jüngel so strongly emphasizes movement and event that he avoids
speaking of perduring relationships. Jüngel's thesis that "God is more
than necessary" fits well with his exposition of God as love, but a
problem begins to emerge when, contending for the non-necessity of the
parable, he declares: "It was also`not necessary to call Jesus God's

---

[46]Jüngel, *God as the Mystery of the World*, 225, n. 73.

[47]Ibid.

Son."[48]   Any sense of stasis is being denied in order to benefit his
understanding of divine being in movement toward non-being.

Furthermore, as Jüngel argues for similarity over dissimilarity
against Erich Przywara, Jüngel ignores the obvious category of
relationship which could have greatly clarified the entire discussion.
Jüngel really wants to bring God and humankind as close as possible
without falling into Feuerbach's conflation. As Barth did, he maintains
that God's identification with the man Jesus was the event which
preserves the distinction (between humanity and God) as it provides the
place of intimate correspondence when the event is recreated through
speaking of it. By faith in the Crucified One,

> the Christian faith confesses that God's becoming man, the
> incarnation of the word in Jesus Christ, is the unique, unsurpassable
> instance of a still greater similarity between God and man taking
> place within a great dissimilarity. This event makes clear, however,
> that the difference of such still greater similarity is not a matter of
> relationless identification. That the still greater similarity between
> God and man remains an *event* and only as such is true and real is the
> actual mystery of God which is revealed in the identification of God
> with the man Jesus, an identification which preserves this
> difference.[49]

By so heavily and exclusively emphasizing "event" as that which alone
makes similarity "true and real," Jüngel cannot elucidate the character
of an on-going relationship between humankind and God. Not unaware
of this danger, Jüngel counterasserts:

> Event is more than a momentary happening. Events can have their
> history and can make it. The accusation of "existentialistic

---

[48]Jüngel, *God as the Mystery of the World*, 291.

[49]Ibid., 288.

punctualism" would simply miss entirely what is being presented here.[50]

This overemphasis on event is only aggravated by the understanding of Jesus as the "parable of God," an understanding which again seems to ignore the category of persons in relationship.

METHODOLOGICAL ISSUES

APORIA, FAITH, AND REASON

What is the relationship between our talk about God and talk about the world, a world whose ethos is increasingly scientific and technological? Jüngel's exposition of the historical development of the aporia focuses almost entirely upon thought as expressed in philosophy and theology, with hardly a mention of the burgeoning discipline of science and its associated technologies. However, if theology is not to become an isolated discourse, then it must engage the rapidly moving science and technology of modern times. Concerned about the proper role of reason, Bernard Lonergan warned:

> The constructions of intelligence without the control of reasonableness yield not philosophy but myth, not science but magic, not astronomy but astrology, not chemistry but alchemy, not history but legend.[51]

The remarkable scientific accomplishments of the past four hundred years have tremendously intensified the question of reason in its relation

---

[50]Jüngel, *God as the Mystery of the World*, 324, n. 22.

[51]Lonergan, "Religious Knowledge," in *Lonergan Workshop* Vol.1, ed. Fred Lawrence (Missoula, Montana: Scholars Press, 1978), 312.

to faith. Can Jüngel's doctrine of advent, which in Webster's words, is "not adjectival upon the world," speak to this contemporary issue? Assuming that dialogue between science and theology is meaningful, is some kind of re-appropriation of Aquinas' complementarity of faith and reason necessary, i.e., some concept of *analogia entis*? For Richard, retrieving reason from its modern orphanage in science and technology is a necessary part of the current theological task:

> In order to protect against [agnosticism], it will no doubt be necessary to have recourse to the virtualities of faith, but it will also be necessary, and perhaps first of all, to explore the different dimensions of reason so that it is not reduced to its scientific and technological dimension.[52]

So while Richard more or less accepts Jüngel's problem, he proposes a very different solution, one which could include the science and technology of our era. The problem of how to think and speak God is closely related to this particular problem of the retrieval of modern reason:

> There can be no doubt that the philosophical theology of the past came to an impasse on the threshold of the modern era. But looking immediately for the solution from the side of evangelical theology would only amount to a short-circuit. One cannot pass directly from the reason of the past to the faith of the gospel, for then the problem of how reason stands in regard to faith remains intact. It is necessary first to go from the reason of the past to the reason of the present, in order to see how today, as well as yesterday, faith in God can be thought and expressed.[53]

Construing *analogia entis* and *analogia fidei* as competing paradigms may effectually obstruct meaningful dialogue between science and

---

[52]Richard, "Théologie évangélique et théologie philosophique," 20.

[53]Ibid., 20-21.

theology. If science and theology, each of which exerts a profound influence upon its contemporary adherents, go their separate ways, then this separation will further contribute to a deleterious and dangerous compartmentalization of contemporary thought.

In his critical response to Jüngel, Rémy imagines a " *'disputatio scholastica'* between St. Thomas and Jüngel. " In this disputation,

> the real stakes appear to us to be found in the relation between creation and revelation, reason and faith. Do these two orders of reality find themselves in a conflictual relationship? Is a conciliation desirable and possible and under what circumstances?[54]

Generally speaking, the paradigm of *analogia entis* asserts that conciliation between faith and reason, science and theology, *analogia entis* and *analogia fidei*, is desirable and possible. Thus seen, *analogia fidei* is only incompatible with the *analogia entis* by the misconstrual of an unnecessary polemic, one which expands a revelatory starting point into a catch-all category. Rémy finds the one-sidedness of Jüngel's analogy a kind of revelatory reductionism:

> Thus analogy finds itself transposed to the specifically Christian level of parable as the event of revelation. . . . By that analogy is even seen as the equivalent of sacramental reality. But it is important to count the cost of such a transposition; for stripped of its value on the rational level, analogy becomes the prerogative of biblical revelation, outside of which it falls into insignificance.[55]

At issue is the independent value of reason, (Aquinas and Rémy), the value of human language apart from the *Sprachgewinn* (Webster), and the retrieval of reason in a technological society (Richard). Rémy thus questions Jüngel's transposition of analogy to the event of revelation:

---

[54]Rémy, "L'analogie selon E. Jüngel," 148.

[55]Ibid., 154.

"Doesn't one pass from the level of objective knowledge to that of the subjective relation with God in the Christian existence?"[56] Allowing that the cross must play a fundamental role, even one that determines Christian specificity, Rémy nonetheless demands: "Does it follow that it is exclusive of other mediations? Its place, albeit central, would it not be registered in a larger economy of revelation?"[57] We too must ask: Is the cross the only pattern of creation? If there are other patterns, is the cross the imperial lens through which all others must be seen? Or, does this imperial vision deny God the freedom and the possibility of coming to humanity in another way in another epoch?

PHILOSOPHICAL AND EVANGELICAL THEOLOGY

En route to answering these questions raised by Jüngel's work, Richard focuses on the methods of philosophical theology vis-à-vis evangelical theology and how each is implicated in *analogia entis* and *analogia fidei*. Richard finds Jüngel's account in *God as the Mystery of the World* methodologically flawed in that it begins by calling for an engagement with the modern world in the language of that modern world, only to preempt the debate by jumping to evangelical solutions in the midst of the fray. Richard demonstrates his point by juxtaposing some of Jüngel's remarks:

---

[56]Rémy, "L'analogie selon E. Jüngel," 157.

[57]Ibid., 169.

> Faith must speak the language of the world if it does not want to become dumb. Therefore, beginning with the age of early Christendom, it had to speak the language of metaphysics as the language of thought at that time if it did not want to deteriorate into thoughtlessness."[58]

Similarly, he supports Jüngel's assertion that the evangelical theology of today must

> recapture the biblical questioning without dropping the questioning of our time which would abandon it to itself. The knot of history must not be cut in such a way that modern thought advances into the future against God and so that Christian faith, emptied of thought, goes its own way.[59]

Richard finds these insights worthy affirmations of a theologian "fully conscious of his responsibility before the thought of his time."[60] So once Jüngel has set out this theological agenda, Richard expresses surprise at his subsequent opposition of philosophical and evangelical theology:

> A theology which is responsive to the Gospel, meaning a theology which is responsive to the crucified man Jesus as the true God, knows that it is fundamentally different from something like philosophical theology.[61]

He then questions the necessity of this opposition with his own solution, reminiscent of Tillich:

---

[58]Jüngel, *God as the Mystery of the World*, 39. Richard cites its French translation (I, 58) in "Théologie évangélique et théologie philosophique," 6.

[59]Jüngel, *God as the Mystery of the World* (I, 170), as cited by Richard, "Théologie évangélique et théologie philosophique," 6.

[60]Richard, "Théologie évangélique et théologie philosophique," 6.

[61]Jüngel, *God as the Mystery of the World*, 154. Richard cites its French translation in "Théologie évangélique et théologie philosophique," 7.

> Evangelical theology and philosophical theology would be conceived as two different types of theology, which distinguish themselves by whether the accent is placed on the pole of the divine word or the human situation, on the pole of the divine address or the human question. That obviously supposes that in the event of the experience of Christian revelation, divine word and human question are intimately united in a relationship of correlation. . . . That would yield two different types of theology, but each of them could call themselves authentically Christian, since both would be accomplished within the framework of the Christian experience of revelation.[62]

Richard's philosophical theology would engage the world as it finds it, and in that engagement, speak an authentically evangelical theology. He calls for two poles in a strict correlation, philosophical and evangelical theology, the evangelical message and the situation of human history, where each one mutually interprets the other. From this perspective, the true opposition is not between evangelical and philosophical theology, but between philosophies which oppose each other and theologies which oppose one another.

Richard strikes hard at Jüngel's methodology, for he construes him as correctly identifying the modern aporia but failing to stay with it in a consistent plan of attack. Much like Rémy's criticism, Richard also sees an unwarranted passage in Jüngel's leap from philosophical to evangelical theology:

> Philosophical theology having led us to an impasse, right away we jump to the heart of the gospel, to the word of the cross, in order to find the adequate solution. But would it not be right to expect the problems of philosophical theology to be accounted for first on the level of this same philosophical theology?[63]

---

[62]Richard, "Théologie évangélique et théologie philosophique," 9.

[63]Ibid., 16.

Richard allows that Jüngel has forcefully demonstrated the breakdown of the old metaphysics maintaining an impassible God *supra nos*. But he believes that his evangelical, neo-Reformation response is likewise insufficient, recommending instead, a more modern and contemporary conception:

> No doubt it is necessary for us to convert anew and incessantly our image of God, and incessantly go from an idolatrous image to a more evangelical image. Yet alongside there is another conversion which must be accomplished incessantly: one going from the past to the present, from a culture already dead to one which has replaced it and in which we are now living. For each cultural mutation, each cosmological and anthropological mutation, also entails a displacement of theology.[64]

Richard sees this displacement, much as does Jüngel, from the medieval conception of an immutable God, with an imperishable heaven looked up to by mortals with imperishable souls, to a modern age which has more or less identified itself with perishability, or at least with perishable things: "The center of gravity is displaced from heaven to earth, from the soul to the body."[65] This anthropological displacement likewise implies a theological displacement, which Jüngel has ably demonstrated. However, once Jüngel, as a strategy for combatting the modern aporia, follows Kierkegaard and Heidegger in attacking the Aristotelian privileging of act over potency, Richard again cries foul over the unpaid methodological debt:

> It is quite evident that this combat takes place in the philosophical arena. In this arena, one must deliver to the end philosophy's fight;

---

[64]Richard, "Théologie évangélique et théologie philosophique," 16.

[65]Ibid.

one cannot slip away at the crucial moment by making an appeal to divine revelation.[66] Authentic theology is constituted of a twofold and interrelated responsibility before God and the contemporary world; for theology, which must be true to God, is evaluated by its performance in the world.

LANGUAGE AND WORLD: METAPHORICAL AND ANALOGICAL OUTLOOKS

Traditionally, analogy has held a privileged rank, in that more is claimed in analogical predication than in metaphorical speech. While Jüngel does not conflate analogy and metaphor, he does closely link them, placing analogy at the base of "successful metaphors." Jüngel describes metaphor so as to imply that it has an underlying structure of analogy (which incidentally, he continues to see as a:b :: c:d):

> "Socrates is a horsefly" says more than "Socrates is a dialectical person"--under the presupposition that one understands the *situation* of the naming process (Socrates torments the citizens of Athens the way a horsefly torments a horse--a:b=c:d).[67]

When Jüngel speaks of discovery and correspondence as the key elements of successful tropic language, he tends to do so wholly within the framework of language itself:

> Something *absolutely alien* would not grip one. What grips us is that correspondence which mediates between the unknown and the already known, the foreign and the customary, the far away and the near, the

---

[66]Richard, "Théologie évangélique et théologie philosophique," 17.

[67]Jüngel, *God as the Mystery of the World*, 293.

new and the old. Analogy grips us. It causes the character of address found in metaphor and parable.[68]

An "engaging correspondence" is available alike to the original discoverer as well as to subsequent hearers, making analogy "an eminently socializing phenomenon."[69]   Yet this account leaves the largest questions untouched: How does language correspond to the created world?   How would we test its authenticity?   Could we even speak a language that was unrelated to material structures and pattern?

Brian Wicker contends that analogy and successful metaphor are unsustainable without an underlying metaphysics. Wicker's delineation of the historical differentiation of metaphor and analogy, and how each has fared in various epochs, sheds light on how metaphor and analogy are related to the world, to one another, and what such relationships imply for theology:

> The classical theorists looked on the use of metaphor with a certain lofty disdain. 'All such arts are fanciful and meant to charm the hearer. Nobody uses fine language when teaching geometry', said Aristotle; and Aquinas seems to have shared something of the same outlook.[70]

As the Renaissance generally moved away from the medieval outlook, metaphor, and the creative possibilities of language itself, took on new worth. In this later vision "metaphor is not just a way of describing things but a way of *experiencing* them." And by Shakespeare's time, it was recognized that "metaphor is a lamp, not just a mirror, held up to

---

[68]Jüngel, *God as the Mystery of the World*, 290.

[69]Ibid., 291.

[70]Brian Wicker, *The Story-Shaped World: Fiction and Metaphysics: Some Variations on a Theme* Notre Dame, IN: University of Notre Dame Press, 1975), 11. Wicker's citations are from: Aristotle *Rhetoric*, III 1404a, and Aquinas *ST* I.1.9.

nature."[71]   Wicker's concern for a natural order independent of what we humans might say is at the heart of the issue.   For if language were really all-powerful, or even most "like God," then those who control language (e.g., academic theologians?) could become all-powerful:

> The recurring temptation to self-indulgence and even dishonesty that goes with a dedication to metaphorical language is far from conquered today. Yet there is a deeper danger even than this: namely that language itself may become a barrier between ourselves and the world, instead of a lamp held up to illuminate it. If all language is metaphorical, as I. A. Richards seems to suggest, then all things automatically tend to become humanised and the world is delivered up to the not always tender mercies of man's own thirst for meaning. We need the corrective presence of the not-human, of the other, of that which is impervious to linguistic manipulation.[72]

The point is not to rid humanity of the poetic vision, but to couple it with the scientific, i.e., that which seeks to *discover* reality, not create it.   The gift of *logos* in the patterns of creation is a check, a balance, upon human tendency to manipulate, rhetorically dominate, and turn the reality of language back on itself.   Ironically, Jüngel's notion of sin as turning back to the self can be used against him at this point.   For while he allows God to enter language, we might say 'from above', he does not speak to the value of science, whose discoveries enter, enlarge, and discipline language 'from below'.   On the other hand, *analogia entis* places humanity in a middle position, related to both Creator and creation.

Unlike Jüngel, who indicates that the analogical basis of metaphor is in language, Wicker contends that the basis of analogy stems from observation of the natural world:

---

[71]Wicker, *Story-Shaped World*, 11.

[72]Ibid., 12.

> For many of the metaphors on which we commonly rely and indeed
> on which officially or unofficially much of the world-view of any
> society is built, rest upon the common recognition of some basic
> analogies. Thus, as Lévi-Strauss points out, much of men's sense of
> cultural identity comes from the transference of facts observed in
> nature to the human situation.[73]

Wicker has done what Jüngel has neglected doing--suggested an
articulation between the language of humankind and the world in which
we find ourselves living. Now this link between language and world
amounts to a "frankly metaphysical, and indeed potentially theological"
conception of nature.[74] Such a metaphysical or even theological view
in turn rests upon one's fundamental notion of causality.

Above, we saw that Kant's strict focus on efficient causality is
much more restricted than Aquinas' "complex unity of formal-final-
efficient causality" (Milbank's phrase). Otherwise put, Aquinas
connected a teleological understanding ('inside' causality) with the divine
being and the act of *creatio ex nihilo*. In fact, this linkage of teleology
with the divine *actus essendi* and *creatio ex nihilo* functions as the basis
of Aquinas' analogical participation, where the larger role of causality
is perceived in nature, linguistic structures, and the relation between
them.

Criticizing those who fail to articulate the relationship between
language and the world, Wicker contends that, without such an
articulation, structural distinctions within language are unintelligible:

> The whole concept of distinctions depends ultimately upon a non-
> Humean concept of causality. Now this fact has particular
> philosophical, indeed, ideological implications. Thus a cause, it might

---

[73]Wicker, *Story-Shaped World*, 21.

[74]Ibid., 31.

be said, is not a relationship but a thing: an agent that brings about some effect by what can only be called its own 'natural tendency' to behave in a certain way. *Pace* Hume, and empiricists and associationists generally, causality therefore involves a metaphysical notion of *Nature*; for according to this theory, agents behave regularly in certain ways by what can only be called their 'nature'. This concept of the natural order made up of the sum of the natural tendencies of agents underlies all those commonsense inferences which exemplify at every turn the principles of analogical reasoning. Thus, a healthy complexion is a *reliable* sign, or analogue, of a healthy man only because we believe there is a natural order, or bond between the two things. And if, *per impossible* such a bond did not exist, it would have to be invented. This seems so obvious a point that its importance may easily be missed: which is that, if true, it rules out from the start the whole farrago of post-Humean associationist thought about causality. It further suggests that the discoveries of structuralism in linguistics and elsewhere are not the neutral, value-free or un-metaphysical propositions they may sometimes seem to be. On the contrary, they imply a whole philosophy of 'Nature' without which the structuralist schema itself would fall apart.[75]

This problematic of linguistic correspondence which does not address the material world is obliquely raised by Webster in one of his only criticisms of Jüngel. Webster is concerned about the standing of human language independent of the "language gain" brought by the divine advent into words:

> For all Jüngel's concern to validate human speech from the prevenient divine Word, there is a real threat of absorption of our language into

---

[75]Wicker, *Story-Shaped World*, 20. While our own discussion has featured a comparison of Kant and Aquinas, Wicker places the great divide between Hume and Aquinas. Since much of Kant's work can be understood as a response to Hume, but one that limited the discussion to Hume's rules of engagement, then Wicker's criticism of the Humean, associationist description of causality serves to corroborate the 'inside' understanding of causality.

the divine speech-act, or at least of the implication that a purely "natural" language is a bastard form of speech.[76]
On the other hand, if human speech is ultimately dependent upon an order in creation, then a divine ontological communication, which makes human speech both possible and meaningful, must precede human lingual communication. Or in other words, *analogia entis*.

Construed less polemically, Jüngel's *Sprachgewinn* might reveal unseen possibilities already present in the original act of universal creation. Thus seen, an articulation between human speech per se and human speech about Jesus Christ at least becomes possible. In this view, *analogia fidei* is not diluted by *analogia entis*; to the contrary, *analogia fidei* is the divinely appropriate fulfillment of *analogia entis*.

ANALOGY AND DIALECTIC: PATTERNS
IN RELIGIOUS LANGUAGE

Commenting upon David Tracy's work, Elizabeth Johnson observes two broad patterns of religious language, analogy and dialectic:

> For those of an analogical imagination, the central clue to the whole of reality is found pre-eminently in the symbol of the Incarnation: the gracious gift of God to the world in that event makes possible the perennial discovery of some order, some harmony, in reality. Those of a dialectic imagination find the central symbol to be focused in the resurrection of the Crucified: the reversal of norms through the power of God in that event opens up the possibility of overturning present disorder and of expecting the genuinely new. . . . In order to do justice to the complexity of reality, each imagination needs to

---

[76]Webster, "Jüngel on the Language of Faith," 259.

incorporate elements of the other, but they remain recognizably distinct ways of grasping the whole.[77] As we have seen, Jüngel advocates an incarnational strategy but actually employs a dialectical reversal, where God's advent is seen as an "interruption" or "disturbance" of current actuality. The reversal is witnessed in the movement toward the non-being and perishability of the cross, which turns out to be the movement in which we have our being. Jüngel's incarnation does not really stay; it provokes a dialectical disturbance of existing order and harmony en route to a new order. Jüngel classifies his project with the overlapping terminology of incarnation and cross, but he carries it out dialectically from the cross while polemicizing against what are in fact more incarnational approaches.

Jüngel's adoption of covenant as the inner ground of creation is helpful, but putting things this way does not carry sufficient polemical weight to justify holding *analogia fidei* against *analogia entis*. While I agree that the patterns of creation are intended for the personal, and the personal is indeed fully revealed in Jesus Christ, these truths in no way

---

[77]Elizabeth A. Johnson, C.S.J., "The Right Way To Speak about God?: Pannenberg on Analogy," 691. Also see David Tracy, *The Analogical Imagination: Christian Theology and the Culture of Pluralism* (New York: Crossroad, 1981), 408ff. Tracy rightly insists that all analogical theologies must retain a negative moment; otherwise, the tensive power provided by the unknown would be lost: "If that power is lost, analogical concepts become mere categories of easy likenesses slipping quietly from their status as similarities-in-difference to mere likenesses, falling finally into the sterility of a relaxed univocity and a facilely affirmative harmony" (ibid., 410). The presence of the unknown does not commit us to agnosticism, but it does mean that "the system is open to correction at every crucial moment in its analogical journey" (ibid., 411). Equally important, Tracy also points out that strongly dialectical theologies of proclamation, such as Barth's, almost invariably end up by incorporating some sense of analogy and manifestation.

nullify Richard's and Wicker's arguments that God's prior ontological communication is what makes linguistic statements possible and meaningful in the first place. The more conciliatory attitude which would combine *analogia fidei* with *analogia entis* allows an account of human striving for perfection, as well as, and in association with, the divine revelation of what truly is perfection. It provides at least the possibility of dialogue with the puissant force of scientific technology and so addresses the concern with which Jüngel began *God as the Mystery of the World*: the speakability of God in a world where God is alleged to be no longer necessary. The pattern which may be scientifically discovered, and the Person who has made the pattern possible, should not be construed as mutually incompatible. Instead, theology must find ways to articulate

> the relation, the analogy, between the logos incarnate in Jesus Christ and the logos as universal Creator. The Prologue of John describes well the relation: the logos can only come among its own, it can only incarnate in a world which is already its expression; put differently, the logos of the universal creation is itself only manifested to the world in the person of Jesus Christ.[78]

---

[78]Richard, "Théologie évangélique et théologie philosophique," 23.

CONCLUDING CONVERSATIONS

COMPARING CLARKE, BURRELL, AND JÜNGEL

This investigation has centered on Clarke, Burrell, and Jüngel because I believe them all to be competent exponents of their particular projects in analogy. Since Clarke, Burrell, and Jüngel have not directly engaged one another on these issues, I have used diverse writers, such as Richard, Rémy, Milbank, Brunner, and Wicker, who have either commented directly upon the main exponents or have commented on the issues they raise. This conclusion will place Clarke, Burrell, and Jüngel in conversation with one another, sharpening substantive disagreements but also pointing out areas of possible agreement which might not be immediately evident.

The first obvious divide is in the writers' attitude toward Aquinas, where Clarke and Burrell are consistently deferential, even when taking issue with him, and Jüngel is consistently critical.[1] It is not so much

---

[1]While this divide seems to fit the historical opposition of Roman Catholic and Protestant views of Aquinas, the current theological situation shows a great deal of mutual appreciation; thus denominational generalizations should be avoided.

that Jüngel has misunderstood Aquinas as that he has not discovered and presented his strongest side. Nonetheless, Jüngel's treatment of Aquinas has not been unproductive. The apophatic, agnostic content which Jüngel saw in Aquinas is not too different from the apophatic, agnostic statements which Burrell makes in his first two books and continues to imply with the title of his third, *Knowing the Unknowable God*. The issue really comes down to emphasis or perhaps overemphasis of the negative moment, the unknown element in theology. Rightly balanced, the unknown presents a tensive power which can become an invitation to further inquiry and discovery, a stimulus to seek something greater rather than an obstruction leading to resignation. Significantly, Burrell's analogical investigations specify more and more positive content as they proceed.

Where Jüngel's critique has demonstrated the deleterious effects of an excess of apophaticism, evangelical certainty has a quasi-univocal tendency which is prone to an excess of its own. Both extremes, as opposed as they are to one another, can discourage further heuristic effort and judgment. But analogy, when undertaken as the middle way, the golden mean between apophaticism and certainty, can affirm that something has been discovered or revealed and that something yet greater may be discovered or revealed.

THE COMMON SEARCH FOR 'MORE THAN'

Clarke, Burrell, and Jüngel all advocate various types of 'more than' in the search for understanding. Perhaps the most striking of these is

Jüngel's statement that "God is more than necessary." While admitting the logical awkwardness of this notion, he contends:

> If the assertion of the worldly nonnecessity of God is not to lead God into capriciousness, then the affirmation made by the assertion of the nonnecessity of God must mean that God is more than necessary in the world.[2]

God is more than necessary because love is more than necessary, and Jüngel wants us to think through the nonnecessity of the love of God. Likewise, as Clarke and Burrell variously develop *actus*, they too depict love as the more than necessary purpose of creation. The movement of divine love is creative as it goes out from itself into non-being. Divine movement is always meaningful movement; and in the event of its human reception, divine arrival provokes new meaning.

Just as Jüngel attacks *ens necessarium* (necessary being) as a way of thinking of God, so too does Burrell distance himself from its use: "Aquinas nowhere uses 'absolute' of God, nor does he regard *ens necessarium* as a felicitous name."[3] Instead of necessity, Burrell and Clarke have developed the divine/human relation in terms of *intention*, where God may be said to have truly decided to create in a *sui generis* manner, and humans are more properly said to *consent* to the *telos* already provided by divine activity and movement. Putting the relationship in these terms emphasizes human freedom as integral to the purpose of creation. Jüngel's thesis that God is "more than necessary" is actually affirmed by both Clarke and Burrell. Because God has already acted in creation and spoken in history, responsibility to

---

[2]Jüngel, *God as the Mystery of the World*, 24.

[3]Burrell, *Aquinas: God and Action*, 80.

correspond to what God has already done may creatively, but not necessarily, be partnered with freedom.

Similarly, Clarke's argument for the intelligibility of being and its openness to the inquiring mind presupposes that God has already acted and that humans are both free and responsible to respond. Recognizing that humans can and sometimes do deny the intelligibility of existence, Clarke says: "The issue lies beyond the level of rational or logical argument, because it is at the root of all rationality."[4] Denying intelligibility causes a state of lived, not logical contradiction.

So what we see in these three very rational scholars are sundry pursuits of that which surpasses rationality. Each one uses his account to advocate something beyond the category of account. Thus Jüngel promotes the 'event' of direct address which brings speaker, hearer, and world into a differentiated unity *in* the address; Burrell calls for and undertakes a philosophical "performance" requiring the total commitment of the inquirer *in* the inquiry, referring to the process as *manuductio*; and Clarke, in addition to speaking of *manuductio*, calls his own career efforts a journey as he explicates participation *in* the perfections of creation. The common point seems to be that some form of personal engagement is required, one that involves the very existence of the inquirer. The uniqueness of the search for God requires that the very being of the inquirer moves or is moved into the inquiry.

---

[4]Clarke, *Philosophical Approach*, 22.

SELF-COMMUNICATING MOVEMENT:
ACTION AND EVENT

Jüngel's lingual event expresses his doctrine of God. This doctrine is best summed up in the notion of advent--God is the one who comes from the divine self and arrives to the other. God's own self is communicated in the Word; this movement, both within the Trinity and in the movement into non-being outside the Trinity, does not hold anything back. The Word is not an announcement or pointer to some greater reality. The being of God is in the Word and is to be confronted and known directly in that Word. Human speech about God, analogy, is to be a correspondence to this event of arrival, saying yes where God has already said Yes.

Now as Jüngel represents Aquinas' doctrine, God is transcendent, immutable, imperishable, and *supra nos*; Thomistic analogy is then called upon to express the inexpressibility of this God. However, both Clarke and Burrell show that Aquinas' concept of *actus* presents a very different picture of God, humankind, and the universe. Jüngel can represent Aquinas' God as he does only by prescinding 'being' from 'action'. But to do so is already to have done violence to Aquinas' account, for *actus* is the 'more than' aspect of being, the telltale facet which is a transcendental orientation of all being to its original divine source. The last fifty years of neo-Thomist research should have warned Jüngel away from his reading of Aquinas.

As Clarke and Burrell have variously developed Aquinas' category of *actus*, there is no reason that it cannot be combined with Jüngel's development of 'event'. As a broader and more fundamental notion, *actus* can include 'event' within its framework (without the reverse being true).

Clarke has shown that action is the dynamic bond uniting the community of existing things into a universe by turning them toward one another. Anything that exists does so to the degree that it has received its act of being from God, *Ipsum Esse Subsistens*. Understanding God as the pure act of being who has shared being with all that is certainly does not preclude the event of God's speaking. Indeed, Jean Richard has argued that it is simply setting the stage for the *Logos* to arrive among his own. So without discarding Jüngel's theological exposition of advent in the spoken event, *actus* renders an account of the divine outward movement in creation as well as an account of the creature's potential movement toward its Creator. Potential is placed upon the side of the creature, and pure actuality is attributed to the Creator. The Creator experiences movement, joy, suffering and the like within the intentional, relational realm while enjoying plenitude of divine actuality. As Cantor's mathematical work in infinity has demonstrated, adding or subtracting a finite sum from an infinite set does not change the infinity of the set. Thus God can be said to suffer a loss or enjoy a gain without losing or attaining the infinity of the divine act of being. When the Infinite God suffers a loss, infinity is not lost; a finite possibility is lost.

For analogy, '*actus*' surpasses 'event' as a framework because it can be understood as including 'event' in the innate communicability of being. That is, if being is always being in act, and this being in act makes a difference to others through real presence, then we could understand creation as the recurring phenomena of the constant and countless interactions of life as we variously know it. If we could slow the moving picture of the universe down and focus on one of its frames, each interaction could be understood as an *event*. The event of God's speaking to us would be the event of primary significance. It could prophetically overturn, enlighten what is present, or summon us forward to something new. We need place no limits upon divine freedom to say something new or retrieve something old.

From this point of view, what God has done and is doing in creation, and what God has done in the arrival of Christ, portray the same divine character, a character which Jüngel and Clarke have depicted in some very similar ways and language--the language of moving out toward the other. All Jüngel need drop is his polemic against a kind of Thomism which has already been left behind. In fact, if we expand and elaborate Jüngel's event picture and remove any pointilistic connotations, then in the constancy of interactions all the way up and down the scale of being, from the smallest movement of the smallest sub-atomic particle to the relational movements within the Trinity and the creative movement of God into what before had not been, then event and *actus* are nowhere incompatible. Hence neither is *analogia entis* and *analogia fidei*.

Following Aquinas, Burrell and Clarke have asserted that God is *present* to all that has being as the source, sustainer, and true end of all being, and that God's presence is innermost to all that is. From this perspective, the potential for divine meaning hovers over every moment of human life and endeavor (*ST* I.8.1). The divine arrival in Christ is new, but it is no way out of line with what God has been doing in creation all along.

Jüngel's movement toward non-being works quite well in describing God's creative vector; but aside from christological correspondence, human movement is given short shrift. By denying *analogia entis* Jüngel seems to rule out asking about our status other than in the correspondence to the event of Jesus Christ. For given the one "place of light" (*helle Ort*) in Jesus Christ, why would we seek enlightenment elsewhere? Consequently, the anthropology of *God as the Mystery of the World* has an all or nothing texture. Granting Jüngel's claim that events can have a history,[5] there is still an on/off, either/or character in so describing things. Jüngel's analogy, or correspondence, with its character of either/or, right or wrong, seems more suited to univocation, or grasping *essence*, than to the conditioned character of human life with its uncertainties, shifting frameworks, and the responsibility for judgment in the presence of ambiguity.

In contrast, in explicating the *imago dei*, Clarke's notion of negative and positive infinity yields a moving picture which admits of degrees and levels, progressions and perhaps regressions. The identification of God as the infinite plenitude of perfections allows the human, the negative image of infinity, potential to fulfill its created, teleological craving for greater nearness to God: "The nearer things come to God, the more fully they exist" (*ST* I.3.5.2). As Burrell has shown, developing human potential is thus accomplished through "consent." And although consent is developed in terms of creation, there is nothing stopping us from consenting or *corresponding* to the revelatory event (as Jüngel would have us do). 'Consent' essentially represents a 'correspondence' to the patterns of creation, and such consent should only encourage consent to the incarnation of Christ into the history of creation.

---

[5]Jüngel, *God as the Mystery of the World*, 324, n. 22. As Jüngel puts it: "Event is more than a momentary happening. Events can have their history and can make it. The accusation of 'existentialistic punctualism' would simply miss entirely what is being presented here."

God's freedom to reveal the divine self in Christ should not cause us to devalue what God has revealed in creation. And this, I take it, is the point of Neo-Thomist analogy--to express what has been discovered in the gifts of nature as compatible with what has been revealed in the gifts of grace. Clarke insists that "all human knowledge is an interpretation of action."[6] Action (and participation in it) stems from the original and continuing action of the Creator God who is *present* to all that exists (*ST* I.8.1); therefore, allegations of an absent, impassible God *supra nos* are at least misleading. Clarke's explication of action describes an infinite, never-ending series of self-communications. For all their differences, Jüngel and he are both expressing forms of self-communication which go out to another. It is not incidental that Clarke and Jüngel polemicize against Kant and Descartes. The broader framework of action describes the constancy, continuity, and overall unity of a universe of self-communication. We could try to speak of events in a similar manner, but it cannot be easily rid of the on/off association; thus it lacks the "stretch" to express the continuity of human existence and aspiration. But as both Burrell and Clarke have shown, it is precisely that stretch capacity which makes analogy useful in the first place.

ESSENCE vs. EXISTENCE
DEFINING vs. SHOWING
CORRESPONDENCE vs. PARTICIPATION

In following Aquinas, Burrell and Clarke attempt to give expression to existence, which they take to be most fundamental to all, even beyond

---

[6]Clarke, "Action as the Self-Revelation of Being," 64.

form and essence. After all, what value could there be, which was not, at least potentially, an *existing* value? Hence Neo-Thomists generally begin with existence. Focusing on existence, life itself, brings the recognition that some of the most important things cannot be said or strictly defined. However, as Clarke argues, the "systematically vague" character of analogous terms, the fact that they cannot be defined, does not mean that they are empty. A nuanced understanding is in order, and so Burrell says of Aquinas: "He understood when to be silent, yet also seemed to grasp that what could not be said might still be shown."[7] The difficulty involved in defining analogical terms is caused by their incorporation of a living, existential component. By joining concept to existence, more than intellectual understanding is called for: "The presence of analogous terms is itself a sign that something other than describing or accounting is going on."[8] So where Jüngel understood analogous usage in Aquinas as a mode of signification, Burrell's and Clarke's presentations of analogous use demonstrate that something far more involved than a relaxed and distant signification is taking place.

Consistently taking the other side of these issues, Jüngel is concerned with understanding, thinking, and speaking God. In order to do so, Jüngel embraces a kind of essentialism in his stringent definition of God as love. However, his definition portrays the outward movement of love and so avoids any static connotation in his doctrine of God. Actually, Jüngel defines essence in terms of existence in such a way as to approach the position Clarke has taken. A longstanding axiom of Thomism is that God is the only being whose essence is the same as his

---

[7]Burrell, *Analogy and Philosophical Language*, 239.

[8]Ibid., 226.

existence. So when Jüngel defines God's essence in terms of being
moving into non-being, he has not really upset the Thomist cart; but he
has reversed the normal starting point by looking first to the essence.
Jüngel wants theology to claim that it knows something and to say
what it knows. Against the "pious confession of ignorance" witnessed
in the apophatic tradition, he charges responsibility for generating the
aporia of modern theology:

> Must not the thought of God, as a thought which basically is thinking
> something unthinkable, necessarily end with resignation? And has not
> the history of thought about God not arrived at this final
> resignation?[9]

Thus Jüngel understands his own work as a rebuttal against the refusal
to define who God is. Against Aquinas, "who developed the classical
thesis of the unspeakability of God," he charges:

> The problem of the unspeakability of God is ultimately seen to be the
> problem of the possibility of analogous talk about God. Under the
> title of analogy, the whole dispute returns again, in that this is also
> debated: what does it mean to correspond to God?[10]

Yet if the extended analysis of this present work is right, then Jüngel has
attacked a position which the mature Aquinas did not hold; and his
inaccurate understanding of Aquinas has spurred him to an unnecessary
polarization of the issues.

Jüngel has more or less identified himself with Karl Barth on these
issues, who began by criticizing *analogia entis* for claiming too much,
and some years later came to criticize it for not claiming enough, which
is pretty much Jüngel's position. By thinking in all or nothing terms,
either Promethean usurpation of divine prerogatives or hollow

---

[9]Jüngel, *God as the Mystery of the World*, 8-9.

[10]Ibid., 231.

agnosticism, Barth and Jüngel miss the point: Analogy is the path of the middle ground. And the middle ground is the one most fitting to the unique human position between structure and change, contingency and certainty, faith and reason, known and unknown, humanity and divinity. As Burrell commented on Barth:

> "Some knowledge" need not jeopardize the gratuity of faith, whereas rejecting all connection does threaten, if not destroy, the status of faith as an action of the believer.[11]

"Some knowledge" is a two-sided claim. What is known counts; such knowledge matters. However, the existence tension between finite and infinite will not be removed, although there are certainly gracious moments of respite and fulfillment. Yet part of the strange comfort of being a creature, a participant in created reality, is knowing certainty in the presence of uncertainty. That is, it is comforting to know that whatever gains we may achieve, there will be more to discover about the created patterns and the personal relations of God. Once again, saying that we have "some knowledge" is a middle path, a path which supports faith without overwhelming it with either rational or dogmatic certainty.

Increasing faith, trust, is developed as the committed inquiry continues. Over time, successes achieved, and even survivals of failures, demonstrate the soundness of the search for greater intelligibility. Over time, *manuductio* reveals itself as a two-way road; the reality we are seeking is seeking to lead us. Whether we call the meeting *manuductio* or *Entsprechung*, two-way movement is involved. Every correspondence creates the possibilities of new correspondence. Every intensification of participation in the created perfections of God carves out new possibilities of future participation. Incarnation is the

---

[11]Burrell, *Analogy and Philosophical Language*, 126-27.

sure indicator that participation is a meeting ground of human and divine. Incarnation suggests that there is already something important and beautiful in the already created. There is a profitable pull between 'the already' and the 'not yet', a pull which is itself apparently part of the divine plan. Faith trusts that continuing the inquiry is the right thing to do, that the dynamic orientation of our being toward God will result in future actualizations of the 'not yet'. Hence the unknown does not lurk over us as a threat but as a promise. "Some knowledge" is a guarantor of past efforts and a goad to future achievement. We can neither be drawn to the future (*manuductio*) nor provoked to the future (*Entsprechung*), unless we have some standing in the present. As Lonergan put it:

> Every inquiry aims at transforming some unknown into a known.
> Inquiry itself, then, is something between ignorance and knowledge.
> It is less than knowledge, else there would be no need to inquire. It
> is more than sheer ignorance, for it makes ignorance manifest and
> strives to replace it with knowledge.[12]

In both the aspiration which leads to inquiry, and the discovery or revelation which fulfills it, analogy is the appropriate tool for expressing the 'betweenness' of the anthropological condition. Thus analogy is never innocent, but is laden with anthropological and theological presuppositions.

Burrell insists that, in order to culminate the self-involving nature of inquiry, analogy always involves "taking a stand" (*APL*, 244). Clarke sees analogy as expressing the meaningful movements of finite participation in creation. Jüngel sees analogy as humankind's participation in Christ, which is a correspondence to what God has said and will say again in the event of true correspondence to Christ:

---

[12]Lonergan, *Method in Theology*, 22.

> Human talk about God merits being called responsible when its only intention is that God should be permitted to speak. We call that kind of human talk about God . . . "corresponding to God." . . . And it *corresponds* to God in that it *lets him come*. . . . Whether human speech is so used that God can *come* and is able to be *present in the power of the word*--that is the question which must constantly be dealt with in theology as responsible talk about God.[13]

Because of their mutual appreciation and appropriation of Aquinas, Clarke and Burrell at least end up sharing many views. Yet Jüngel's christological analogy is certainly not incompatible with what Clarke and Burrell are advocating. Indeed, both Clarke and Burrell would agree with Jüngel's polemic against analogy being used as the formal expression of an underlying emptiness or radical unknown. As their respective accounts indicate, they would simply disagree that Aquinas did in fact so use analogy. While some of Burrell's earlier apophatic statements might give some credence to Jüngel's claims, Burrell not only moves away from that apophaticism in his last work, he really is doing something else all along: He is *showing* how analogical use, far from hiding an underlying emptiness, is actually the linguistic expression of our most fundamental longings and achievements. Analogy is thus not a signification of a lack of knowledge; it is a living marker that more than knowledge is being expressed.

JUDGMENT: THE ANALOGICAL ACT

The unknown and the uncertain are not to be eliminated from theological talk, for they force us to make the judgments which are undoubtedly part of the creative intention for what it means to be human. Pure, unlimited

---

[13]Jüngel, *God as the Mystery of the World*, 227, Jüngel's emphases.

knowledge would not only remove uncertainty; it would also remove the need for judgment and even for faith. The presence of some uncertainty need not lead to agnosticism. It is merely a necessary condition for the development of judgment and the exercise of faith. By seeking ever greater certainty amid the human conditions of uncertainty, the inquirer receives training in the intangible, existential art form of judgment. The lack of strict logical control is not to be deplored but applauded; for just as in Aristotle's ethics, where action is needed to complete the syllogism, so too can analogical concepts only be completed through the living component of commitment. Otherwise, the existential component is devalued or ignored; and the retreat into essentialism, with its quixotic quest for certainty, is underway.

It is good that argument alone cannot conclusively prove what matters most to us. By enacting truth in our expressed commitments, we perform the analogical act. The analogical act is part of our training in sacred judgment in which we may correspond to the intention of God in creation and the revelation of God in Jesus Christ. In each instance, analogy is not used to establish faith but to express it.

CREATION AND CROSS: *ANALOGIA ENTIS* AND *ANALOGIA FIDEI*

The act of divine creation, the primordial possibility of 'more than', we have extensively discussed in terms of participation metaphysics. The existence of a finite realm represents an "ontological downstepping"[14] by which God has made possible an entirely new level of life and love.

---

[14]Richard, "Analogie et symbolisme chez Saint Thomas," 392.

The freshness of creation is in its limits. The purpose of creation is in the possibility of growth.

Fortunately, participation is bidirectional. The finite terrain of human existence is not foreign ground to divinity; for the incarnation of Christ, from the birth of Jesus to his public ministry, cross, and resurrection, is the ontological upstepping of humankind. Here, in this "place of light," the divine *actus* is given in its sharpest focus. As Jüngel has felicitously put it, God's advent into human language constitutes a *Sprachgewinn* (language gain). Jüngel is quite right that the highest task of theology is to allow this advent to take place. Human talk about God becomes fully responsible as it corresponds to the full range of the incarnation.

However, even though this correspondence is the highest task, it is not the only task. As in Anselm's *fides quaerens intellectum* (faith seeking understanding), the greater achievement is not in isolating faith, but in joining it to other components of human life. Analogy has long been employed to express relation, and it is eminently suited to expressing the relation between creation and cross, wherein "grace upon grace" is received. *Analogia entis* and *analogia fidei* are different, but they are hardly incompatible.

SELECTED BIBLIOGRAPHY

Aristotle. *Nicomachean Ethics.* Translated by Martin Ostwald. Indianapolis, IN: Bobbs-Merrill, 1962.

Balthasar, Hans Urs von. *The Theology of Karl Barth.* Translated by John Drury. New York: Holt, Rinehart and Winston.

Barth, Karl. *Church Dogmatics*: I/1. Translated by Geoffrey Bromiley. Edinburgh: T & T Clark, 1975.

_____. *Letters* 1961-1968. Translated and edited by Geoffrey Bromiley. Grand Rapids: Wm. B. Eerdmands, 1981.

_____. "No!" In *Natural Theology*, 65-128. Translated by Peter Fraenkel with an introduction by John Baillie. London: Geoffrey Bles, The Centenary Press, 1946.

Bobik, Joseph. *On Being and Essence: A Translation and Interpretation.* Notre Dame, IN: University Of Notre Dame Press, 1965.

Bouillard, Henri. *Connaissance de Dieu: Foi chrétienne et théologie naturelle.* Aubier: Montaignes, 1967.

Boyle, Robert R., S.J. "The Nature of Metaphor." *The Modern Schoolman* 31 (May 1954): 257-80.

Brunner, Emil. "Nature and Grace." In *Natural Theology*, 15-63. Translated by Peter Fraenkel with an introduction by John Baillie. London: Geoffry Bles, The Centenary Press, 1946.

Burrell, David, C.S.C. "Aquinas on Naming God." *Theological Studies* 24 (1963): 183-212.

_____. "Beyond a Theory of Analogy." *Proceedings of the American Catholic Philosophical Association* 46 (1972): 114-22.

_____. *Analogy and Philosophical Language.* New Haven and London: Yale University Press, 1973.

_____. *Aquinas: God and Action*. Notre Dame, IN: University of Notre Dame Press, 1979.

_____. "Does Process Theology Rest on a Mistake?" *Theological Studies* 43 (1982): 125-35.

_____. "Argument in Theology: Analogy and Narrative." In *New Dimensions in Philosophical Theology*, ed. Carl A. Raschke, A Thematic Series of the *Journal of the American Academy of Religion* XLIX/1, 37-52.

_____. *Knowing the Unknowable God: Ibn-Sina, Maimonides, Aquinas*. Notre Dame, IN: University of Notre Dame Press, 1986.

_____. "Aquinas' Debt to Maimonides." In *A Straight Path: Studies in Medieval Philosophy and Culture*, 37-48. Edited by Ruth Link-Salinger et al. Washington, D.C.: Catholic University of America Press, 1988.

Cantor, Georg. *Contributions to the Founding of the Theory of Transfinite Numbers*. Translated with an introduction and notes by Philip E. B. Jourdain. New York: Dover Publications, 1915.

Clarke, W. Norris, S.J. *The Philosophical Approach to God: A Contemporary Neo-Thomist Perspective*. Winston-Salem: Wake Forest University Press, 1979.

_____. *The Universe as Journey: Conversations with W. Norris Clarke, S.J.* Edited by Gerald A. McCool, S.J. New York: Fordham University Press, 1988.

_____. "The Limitation of Act by Potency: Aristotelianism or Platonism?" *New Scholasticism* 26 (1952): 167-94.

_____. "The Meaning of Participation in St. Thomas." *Proceedings of the American Catholic Philosophical Association* 26 (1952): 147-57.

_____. "What Is Really Real?" In *Progress and Philosophy*, ed. James A. McWilliams, 61-90. Milwaukee: Bruce, 1955.

_____. "Infinity in Plotinus." *Gregorianum* 40 (1959): 75-98.

_____. "Linguistic Analysis and Natural Theology." *Proceedings of the American Catholic Philosophical Association* 34 (1960): 110-26.

_____. "The Self in Eastern and Western Thought: The Wooster Conference." *International Philosophical Quarterly* 6 (1966): 101-109.

_____. "American Philosophy and Language about God." In *Christian Philosophy and Religious Renewal*, ed. George McLean, O.M.I., 39-73. Washington: Catholic University of America Press, 1966.

_____. "On Facing up to the Truth about Human Truth." *Proceedings of the American Catholic Philosophical Association* 43 (1969): 1-13.

_____. "A Curious Blindspot in the Anglo-American Tradition of Anti-Theistic Argument." *The Monist* 54 (1970): 181-200.

_____. "A New Look at the Immutability of God." In *God Knowable and Unknowable*, ed. Robert J. Roth, S.J., 43-72. New York: Fordham University Press, 1973.

_____. "What Cannot Be Said in St. Thomas' Essence-Existence Doctrine." *The New Scholasticism* 48 (1974): 19-39.

_____. "What Is Most and Least Relevant in St. Thomas' Metaphysics Today?" *International Philosophical Quarterly* 14 (1974): 411-34.

_____. "Interpersonal Dialogue as Key to Realism." In *Person and Community*, ed. Robert J. Roth, S.J., 141-154. New York: Fordham University Press, 1975.

_____. "Analogy and the Meaningfulness of Language about God: A Reply to Kai Neilson." *The Thomist* 40 (1976): 61-95.

_____. "The Philosophical Importance of Doing One's Autobiography." *Proceedings of the American Catholic Philosophical Association* 54 (1980): 17-25.

_____. "Action as the Self-Revelation of Being: A Central Theme in the Thought of St. Thomas." In *History of Philosophy in the Making*, ed. Linus Thro, S.J., 63-80. Washington: University Press of America, 1982.

_____. "To Be Is To Be Self-Communicative: St. Thomas' Vision of Personal Being." *Theology Digest* 33 (1986): 441-54.

Evans, Donald. "Preller's Analogy of Being." In *New Scholasticism* 45:1 (Winter 1971): 1-37.

Fabro, Cornelio. "The Intensive Hermeneutics of Thomistic Philosophy: The Notion of Participation." Translated by B. M. Bonansea, *Review of Metaphysics* 27 (1973-74): 449-90.

_____. *Participation et causalité selon S. Thomas d'Aquin*. Paris: Nauwelaerts, 1961.

Fairweather, A. M. General Introduction to *Nature and Grace: Selections from the Summa Theologica of Thomas Aquinas*. The Library of Christian Classics. Philadelphia: The Westminster Press, 1954.

Farrer, Austin. *Finite and Infinite: A Philosophical Essay*. Westminster: Dacre Press, 1959.

Finance, Joseph de. *Etre et agir*. Paris: Beauchesne, 1945.

Foley, Grover. "The Catholic Critics of Karl Barth: In Outline and Analysis." *Scottish Journal of Theology* 14:2 (1961): 136-55.

Geiger, L.B. O.P. *La Participation dans la philosophie de S. Thomas d'Aquin.* Paris: J. Vrin, 1942.

Gilson, Etienne. *The Christian Philosophy of St. Thomas Aquinas.* New York: Random House, 1956.

Guarino, Thomas. "The Truth Status of Theological Statements: Analogy Revisited." *Irish Theological Quarterly* 54 (1988:2): 140-55.

Henle, R. J. *St. Thomas and Platonism.* The Hague: Martinus Nijhoff, 1956.

Hume, David. *Dialogues Concerning Natural Religion.* Edited with an introduction by Norman Kemp Smith. Indianapolis and New York: Bobbs-Merrill, 1947.

John, Helen James. *The Thomist Spectrum.* New York: Fordham University Press, 1966.

Johnson, Elizabeth, C.S.J. "The Right Way to Speak about God?: Pannenberg on Analogy." *Theological Studies* 43 (December, 1982): 673-92.

Jordan, Mark. "Names of God and the Being of Names." In *Existence and Nature of God*, ed. Alfred J. Freddoso, 161-190. Notre Dame, IN: University of Notre Dame Press, 1983.

Jüngel, Eberhard. *God as the Mystery of the World: On the Foundation of the Theology of the Crucified One in the Dispute between Theism and Atheism.* Translated by Darrell L. Guder. Grand Rapids, Michigan: William B. Eerdmans, 1983.

_____. "God--As a Word in Our Language." In *The Liberating Word*, Translated by Robert Osborn, ed. Fredrick Herzog, 25-41. Nashville: Abingdon Press, 1971.

_____. "Die Möglichkeit theologischer Anthropologie auf dem Grunde der Analogie: Eine Untersuchung zum Analogieverständnis Karl Barths." *Evangelische Theologie* 22 (1962): 535-557.

_____. *The Doctrine of the Trinity: God's Being Is in Becoming.* Translated by Horton Harris. Grand Rapids: William B. Eerdmans, 1976.

_____. *Theological Essays.* Translated with an introduction by J. B. Webster. Edinburgh: T & T Clark, 1989.

Kant, Immanuel. *Critique of Pure Reason.* Translated by Norman Kemp Smith. Unabridged edition. New York: St. Martin's Press, 1965.

_____. *Prolegomena to any Future Metaphysics.* Edited by Lewis White Beck. Indianapolis and New York: Bobbs-Merrill, 1950.

Klubertanz, George, S.J. *St. Thomas Aquinas on Analogy: A Textual Analysis and Systematic Synthesis.* Chicago: Loyola University, 1960.

Kondolean, Theodore J. "The Immutability of God: Some Recent Challenges." *New Scholasticism* 58 (Summer 1984): 293-315.

Lash, Nicholas. "Ideology, Metaphor, and Analogy." In *The Philosophical Frontiers of Christian Theology*, ed. Brian Hebblethwaite and Stewart Sutherland. Cambridge: Cambridge University Press, 1982.

Lindbeck, George. "The A Priori in St. Thomas' Theory of Knowledge." In *The Heritage of Christian Thought: Essays in Honor of Robert Lowry Calhoun*, ed. Robert Earl Cushman, 41-63. New York: Harper and Row, 1965.

Lonergan, Bernard. *Verbum: Word and Idea in Aquinas*. Notre Dame, IN: University of Notre Dame Press, 1957.

_____. *Method in Theology*. New York: Herder and Herder, 1972.

_____. "Religious Knowledge." In *Lonergan Workshop* Vol.1, ed. Fred Lawrence, 309-327. Missoula, Montana: Scholars Press, 1978.

Lyttkens, Hampus. *The Analogy between God and the World: An Investigation of its Background and Interpretation of its Use by Thomas of Aquino*. Translated by Axel Poignant. Uppsala: Almqvist and Wiksells, 1952.

Marc, André. *L'Idée de l'être chez Saint Thomas et dans la scolastique postérieure*. *Archives de Philosophie* 10 (1933).

Milbank, John. "'Between Purgation and Illumination': A Critique of the Theology of Right." In *Christ, Ethics, and Tragedy: Essays in Honour of Donald Mackinnon*, ed. Kenneth Surin, 161-196. Cambridge: Cambridge University Press, 1989.

Miller, Mitch. "Platonic Provocations: Reflections on the Soul and the Good in the *Republic*." In *Platonic Investigations*, ed. Dominic J. O' Meara, Studies in Philosophy and the History of Philosophy, vol. 13. Washington: Catholic University of America Press, 1985.

Montagnes, Bernard, O.P. *La Doctrine de l'analogie de l'être d'après Saint Thomas D'Aquin*. Paris: Nauwelaerts, 1963.

Moore, G. E. "Is Existence a Predicate?" *Aristotelian Society Supplementary* 15 (1936): 175-188.

Nielsen, Niels C. "Analogy as a Principle of Theological Method Historically Considered." In *The Heritage of Christian Thought: Essays in Honor of Robert Lowry Calhoun*, ed. Robert E. Cushman and Egil Grislis, 197-219. New York: Harper and Row, 1965.

Neilson, Kai. "Talk of God and the Doctrine of Analogy." *Thomist* 40 (1976): 32-60.

Niebuhr, H. Richard. *The Meaning of Revelation*. New York: Collier Books, 1941.

Pannenberg, Wolfhart. "Analogy and Doxology." Chap. in *Basic Questions in Theology*, Collected Essays, vol.1, Translated by George H. Kehm, 212-238. Philadelphia: Fortress Press, 1970.

Peters, Ted. Review of *God as the Mystery of the World*. In *Currents in Theology and Mission* 11 (1984): 313.

Pieper, Joseph. *The Silence of St. Thomas*. Translated by John Murray, S.J. and Daniel O' Connor. New York: Pantheon Books, 1957.

Plato. *Collected Dialogues*. Edited by Edith Hamilton and Huntington Cairns with introduction and prefatory notes. Princeton: Princeton University Press, 1961.

Polanyi, Michael. *Personal Knowledge:* Towards a Post-Critical Philosophy. Chicago: University of Chicago Press, 1962.

Preller, Victor. *Divine Science and the Science of God: A Reformulation of Thomas Aquinas*. Princeton, NJ: Princeton University Press, 1967.

Rahner, Karl. *Foundations of Christian Faith: An Introduction to the Idea of Christianity*. Translated by William V. Dych. New York: Crossroad, 1986.

Rémy, Gérard. "L'Analogie selon E. Jüngel. Remarques critiques: L'Enjeu d'un débat." *Revue d'Histoire et de Philosophie Religieuses* 66:2 (1986): 147-177.

Richard, Jean. "Analogie et symbolism chez Saint Thomas." *Laval Théologique et Philosophique*. Commemorative of the Seventh Hundred Anniversary of the Death of St. Thomas Aquinas (October 1974): 379-406.

Richard, Jean. "Théologie évangélique et théologie philosophique à propos d'Eberhard Jüngel." *Science et Esprit* 38:1 (1986): 5-30.

Ryle, Gilbert. *The Concept of Mind*. Harmondsworth: Penguin Books, 1963.

St. Thomas Aquinas. *Expositio in librum Boethii de Hebdomadibus*. Ed. Parmae, reprinted, New York: Musurgia, 1950.

_____. *On the Power of God*. Literally translated by the English Dominican Fathers. Westminster, Maryland: Newman Press, 1952.

_____. *Philosophical Texts*. Selected and Translated with notes and an introduction by Thomas Gilby. London: Oxford University Press, 1951; reprint ed., Durham, NC: Labyrinth Press, 1982.

_____. *Summa Contra Gentiles*, 3 vols. Translated by the Fathers of the English Dominican Province. London: Burns, Oates, and Washbourne, Ltd., 1924.

_____. *Summa Theologiae*, Latin text and English translation. Introduction by Thomas Gilby, O.P., Translated by Herbert McCabe, O.P. London: Eyre and Spottiswoode, 1963.

_____. *Summa Theologica*, Three Parts. Translated by The Fathers of the English Dominican Province. London: Burns, Oates, and Washbourne, 1920.

_____. *Theological Texts*. Selected and Translated with Notes and an introduction by Thomas Gilby. London: Oxford University Press, 1955; reprint ed., Durham, NC: Labyrinth Press, 1983.

_____. *Treatise on Happiness*. Translated by John Oesterle. Notre Dame, IN: University of Notre Dame Press, 1964.

_____. *Treatise on the Virtues*. Translated by John A. Oesterle. Notre Dame, IN: University of Notre Dame Press, 1966.

_____. *The Trinity and the Unicity of the Intellect*. Translated by Sister Rose Emmanuella Brennan, S.H.N. St. Louis: B. Herder, 1946.

_____. *Truth*. Translated by Robert Mulligan, S.J. Chicago: Henry Regnery, 1952.

Scharlemann, Robert. "Fides Quarens Intellectum as Basis of Pluralistic Method." In *The Whirlwind in Culture: In Honor of Langdon Gilkey*, ed. Donald W. Musser and Joseph L. Price, 233-245. Bloomington, IN: Meyer/Stone Books, 1988.

Schweiker, William. "Beyond Imitation: Mimetic Praxis in Gadamer, Ricoeur, and Derrida." *Journal of Religion* 68:1 (January 1988): 21-38.

Sellars, Wilfrid. *Science, Perception, and Reality*. London: Routledge and Kegan Paul, 1963.

Söhngen, Gottlieb. "Wesen und Akt in der scholastischen Lehre von der participatio und analogia entis." *Studium Generale* 11 (December 1955): 649-662.

Surin, Kenneth. "Creation, Revelation, and the Analogy Theory." *Journal of Theological Studies* 32:2 (October 1981): 401-422.

Swinburne, Richard. *The Coherence of Theism*. Oxford: Clarendon Press, 1977.

Tillich, Paul. "Two Types of Philosophy of Religion." In *Theology of Culture*, ed. Robert C. Kimball, 10-29. New York: Oxford University Press, 1959.

Tracy, David. *The Analogical Imagination: Christian Theology and the Culture of Pluralism*. New York: Crossroads, 1986.

Webster, John. "Eberhard Jüngel on the Language of Faith." *Modern Theology* 1:4 (July 1985): 253-276.

Weisheipl, James A., O.P. *Friar Thomas D'Aquino: His Life, Thought, and Works*. Washington: Catholic University Press, 1974.

Weiss, Raymond L. Review of *Knowing the Unknowable God* in *Journal of Religion* 68:2 (1988): 302-5.

Wicker, Brian. *The Story-Shaped World: Fiction and Metaphysics: Some Variations on a Theme.* Notre Dame, IN: University of Notre Dame Press, 1975.

Williams, C. J. F. "The Marriage of Aquinas and Wittgenstein." *Downside Review* 78 (Summer 1960): 203-12.

Wippel, John F. "Thomas Aquinas and Participation." In *Studies in Medieval Philosophy,* ed. John F. Wippel, 117-58. Washington: Catholic University of America Press.

Wittgenstein, Ludwig. *Philosophical Investigations.* Translated by G. E. M. Anscombe. New York: Macmillan, 1953, third ed., 1968.

_____. *Tractatus Logico-Philosophicus.* Translated by D. F. Pears & B. F. McGuinness with an introduction by Bertrand Russell. London: Routledge and Kegan Paul, 1961.

Zeitz, James V. "God's Mystery in Christ: Reflections on Erich Przywara and Eberhard Jüngel." *Communio* 12:2 (Summer 1985): 158-172.

Alexander of Hales, 80

Anselm, 197, 199, 300

Aquinas, St. Thomas, action (*actus*) in, 63-65, 140-151, 246, 289, 291-93; act/potency in 49-53; action and existence in, 26-36; as source, 17; attitude toward, 285-86; complementarity of reason and faith in, 25, 171-72, 265-66; criticism of, 191-93, 200-09, 229-31, 233-34, 239, 295; extrinsic vs. intrinsic predication in, 177-81; the good, development of, 36-39, 137-38; grammar *in divinis* in, 127-51; immutability of God in, 14, 83, 88-94; and the linguistic turn, *see* Part Two, passim, 6, 14, 82, 98, 127, 184; participation metaphysics in, *see* Part One, passim, 5, 41-73, 184-85, 245, 249-50, 280; 'person' in, 5, 8, 88-90; positive affirmations about God in, 61-62, 154, 246-47, 249, 253, 257, 298; also *see* chaps. 2, 3, 6, 7; real relations in, 87, 90-91, 146-51; reinterpretation of, 13-15, 82, 153; relationships in, 164-65; selection of analogous terms, 79-81; synthesis of Aristotelian and Platonic epistemology, 80-81; tautologies, use of, 130-135, 183-84.

Aristotle, 42, 46, 49, 51-53, 83, 102, 104, 110, 120, 158, 162, 165, 203, 205, 207, 246, 278, 299

Aristotelian, 49-51, 53, 58, 80, 87-88, 110, 141, 158, 203, 229, 230, 246, 276

Aristotelianism, 27, 49

Augustine, 32, 231

Avicenna/Ibn-Sina, 98-99, 104, 153, 155, 156-59, 161, 163, 165-66, 181

Balthasar, Hans Urs von, 218, 223

Barth, Karl, 214, 217-20, 222-25, 233, 243, 251, 259, 260, 262-64, 268-69, 282, 295-96

Blondel, Maurice, 17

Bochenski, I. M., 103

Brunner, Emil, 218, 260-66, 285

Brunschvicg, Léon, 51

Buber, Martin, 26

Burrell, David B., C.S.C., *see* Part Two; 6, 7, 15, 56, 196, 201, 206-208, 213, 229, 244, 251, 253, 257, 262, 285-300

Cajetan, 46, 102-03, 207

Cantor, Georg, 92, 290

Clarke, W. Norris, S.J., *see* Part One; 5, 6, 97-99, 102, 106, 112, 118, 119, 123, 125, 134, 137, 138, 143, 146, 149, 150, 157, 158, 167, 175, 183-185, 196, 206, 213, 230, 245, 246, 257, 262, 285-300

Descartes, 31-32, 36, 139, 196, 198-99, 210, 293

Eschmann, Ignatius, 43

Fabro, Cornelio, 26-27, 49, 57-59, 245

Fairweather, A. M., 265

Feinberg, Joel, 129

Feuerbach, Ludwig, 199, 210, 269

Fichte, Johann Gottlieb, 199, 210

Finance, Joseph de, 26, 27

Frege, Gottlieb, 112

Freud, Sigmund, 22, 77

Fuchs, Ernst, 211, 217, 260

Gallie, W. B., 114

Geiger, L. B., 26-27, 57

Gilson, Etienne, 26-27, 43, 111, 163

Hegel, G. W. F., 195, 216, 226

Heidegger, Martin, 34, 36, 257, 276
Henle, Robert J., 46
Henry of Ghent, 104
Hume, David, 280, 281
Ibn-Sina (see Avicenna)
John, Helen James, 17, 24
Johnson, Elizabeth, 103, 282, 283
Jordan, Mark, 154
Jüngel, Eberhard, *see* Part Three; 4,
    6-8, 14, 22, 58, 78, 87, 89, 99,
    117, 121, 150, 157, 182; *see*
    chaps. 10-11, 243-300
Kant, 17, 33-34, 82, 84, 121-22,
    139, 183, 199, 200-08, 228,
    234-35, 244-250, 252, 254,
    259, 280-81, 293
Kierkegaard, Soren, 276
Klubertanz, George, 43-48, 62-63,
    102, 120, 122, 138, 177, 179,
    204, 245
Kondoleon, Theodore J., 14
Locke, John, 35
Lonergan, Bernard, 17-18, 111, 117,
    128, 140, 270, 297
Luther, Martin, 195
Lyttkens, Hampus, 43, 177
Maimonides, 98-99, 122, 138, 153-
    55, 156-57, 161-62, 164, 167,
    168, 181
Marc, André, 24, 26
Marx, Karl, 22
Milbank, John, 180, 185, 250-52,
    258-60, 280, 285
Montagnes, Bernard, 59, 120, 245
Moore, G. E., 139, 158
Nietzsche, Friederich, 22, 196, 199,
    210
Ockham, William of, 67, 102
Pannenberg, Wolfhart, 103, 283
Philo, 51
Pieper, Joseph, 145

Plato, 37, 49-50, 53, 56, 65, 67, 70,
    102, 104, 117-20, 246
Platonic, 46-47, 49-50, 58, 70, 80
Plotinus, 50-51, 55
Polanyi, Michael, 78, 82, 87, 115,
    165
Preller, Victor, 121
Proclus, 51
Przywara, Erich, 269
Pseudo-Dionysius, 30, 51
Raeymaeker, Louis De, 26
Rahner, Karl S. J., 17-18, 153, 221,
    230
Richard, Jean, 222, 247-249, 257-
    258, 263-64, 266, 270-277,
    284, 285, 290, 299
Richards, I. A., 278
Rorty, Richard, 97
Ross, James, 76
Roth, Robert J., 33, 84
Sartre, Jean Paul, 20, 23
Scharlemann, Robert, 209
Scheltens, G., 204
Scotus, John Duns, 64, 102-106, 159
Sellars, Wilfred, 110, 112
Socrates, 37, 60-61, 67, 117-18, 130,
    277
Socratic, 56, 118, 181
Spinoza, Baruch, 57, 208
Tertullian, 196
Tillich, Paul, 42, 122, 274
Webster, John, 244-45, 255-56, 264,
    271, 272, 281-82
Weiss, Raymond L., 166
Wicker, Brian, 278-80, 284, 285,
Wippel, John F., 59, 60, 65,
Wittgenstein, Ludwig, 31, 67, 97-99,
    107, 109, 115-17, 119, 122, 124,
    127-128, 130, 133, 144, 183-87
Wittgensteinian, 15, 66, 103, 127,
    172

act/potency 49-53, 61, 64, 78, 149, 160

action (*actus*) 5, 6, 15-17, 26-39, 61, 63, 70, 84-86, 115, 128, 138, 140-51, 156, 175, 183-84, 187, 229, 246, 255, 287, 289-93, 299-300

activity 31, 89; and judgment, 112-13, 159, 299; as analogy, 169; as philosophy, 116; highest, 163; intentional, 141, 143-44; of God, 26, 146-50, 161, 254, 287; terms, 75, 81;

actus essendi 27, 29, 52, 53, 55, 60, 63, 70, 148, 161, 166, 181, 247, 280

advent 8, 235, 240, 248, 255-56, 263, 265, 271, 281, 283, 289-90, 300

agnosticism 6-7, 33, 45, 104, 120-21, 135, 154, 167-68, 179-80, 191, 247-48, 259, 283, 296, 299

aloof, God as, 134, 145, 207-09, 215; *see* Chapter Eight, 191-216

ambiguity 3, 157, 172, 174, 186, 192, 292

anachronism 183, 247-48

analogia entis (analogy of being) 218-19, 221-23, 225, 231, 233-35, 238, 249, 251, 260-61, 263, 266-67, 271-73, 279, 282-84, 291, 295, 299-300

analogia fidei (analogy of faith) 218-19, 222-23, 225, 231, 233, 236, 243, 251, 271-73, 282-84, 291, 299-300

analogia relationis 220, 224-25

analogical act 8, 169, 298-99

analogous cause, 47; knowledge of God, 3, 45, 60-61, 89, 238, 295; terms, selection of, 75-82, 99,

106-07; terms, use of, 101-03, 105-08, 110-16, 120, 122-25, 136, 142, 162, 173-75, 294; terms, systematically vague nature of, 186, 294

analogy of advent, 235-40; of attribution 3, 203-06, 208, 246; of causal participation, *see* Chapter Two, 41-74; of proportionality, 5, 44, 46, 58, 101-02, 104, 111, 120, 202-04, 206-08, 246, 252; of relationships, 203; theory of, 116, 156; use of, *see* Part Two

analytic 28, 129, 183

anthropology 1, 8, 19, 107, 148, 193, 215, 217, 219, 225, 232-33, 251-52, 292

anthropomorphism 192, 202, 208-09, 226-28, 234, 254

apophatic 56, 99, 120-21, 132, 135, 138, 155, 161, 179, 184, 192, 197-98, 207, 216, 226-27, 229, 246-50, 253, 286, 295, 298

aporia *see* Chapter 8; 7, 195-96, 198-200, 203, 207, 212, 214, 226, 228, 233-35, 250, 270, 275-76, 295

appraisal terms 107, 113, 124

atheism 157, 191-92, 195, 209

balance 279

bidirectionality 80

categories 43, 108-09, 142, 165, 173-74, 201, 283

Catholic 7, 13, 27, 50, 52, 59, 101, 138, 200, 207, 218, 222, 233, 244, 251, 261, 263, 285

causal participation 15, 41-42, 46, 48, 53, 78, 79, 81, 82, 86, 246

cause, causality 3-4, 36-37, 47-48, 58-60, 65, 70, 77-78, 80-81, 89,

122, 138, 144, 147, 149, 157, 160, 178-79, 203-05, 210, 248-51, 280-81, 293

Christ event 254

christological, christology 192, 208-09, 218, 222-23, 228, 260-61; analogy, *see* Chapter Nine; 251-52, 291, 298

circularity 122-23, 143-44

coming 84, 150, 159, 212-14, 230-32, 236, 238, 252, 268, 273; *see* advent

commitment 24, 76, 97, 112, 118, 123, 186, 288, 299

community 3, 27, 31-33, 41, 44, 59, 78-79, 84-85, 110-11, 114-15, 290

compatibility 22-23, 77, 87

complementarity 25, 132, 266, 271

conservatism 172

correspondence 86, 211, 215-16, 218-23, 225, 232, 235-38, 240, 251-52, 255-56, 262-63, 269, 277-78, 289, 291-98, 300

covenant 220, 222-24, 283

creatio ex nihilo 50, 64-65, 166, 214, 215, 232, 280

creation 4, 8, 20, 26, 37, 42, 47, 49, 50, 53, 61, 64, 73, 78-79, 91, 93, 116, 126, 135, 145, 148, 151, 155-57, 161-64, 166-67, 176, 178-80, 213, 215, 222-24, 238, 249-52, 257, 260-67, 272-73, 279, 282-84, 287-88, 290-93, 297, 299-300

death of God 195-96, 209-10, 212, 214-15, 240, 257

dialogue 5, 14, 33, 84-86, 98, 102, 118, 153-54, 266, 268, 271, 284

direct address 211-14

distance 7, 44-45, 101, 127, 138, 208, 211-12, 226, 250, 287

election 224-25

emptiness, empty 7, 27, 36, 58, 76, 79-80, 93, 103-04, 206, 234, 246, 294, 298

epistemology 29-30, 32-33, 35, 38, 80, 84-86, 93, 143

equivocal, equivocation 47, 80, 86, 104-05, 147, 159, 172-176, 180, 256

esse (being) 6, 17, 19-21, 24, 27-29, 31, 35, 49, 53-54, 56, 58, 63-67, 70, 90, 93, 133, 138, 142-43, 145-46, 151, 158-61, 163-67, 175-76, 186, 259, 290

esse commune (being in general) 65-67, 70, 149

essence 19, 27-28, 33-35, 37, 45, 47, 48, 53-58, 61, 62, 64-70, 76, 78, 85, 91, 140, 144, 157-60, 163-64, 166, 175, 178, 196-99, 201, 207-08, 213-14, 219-21, 225-26, 229-32, 234, 239, 244, 246, 249, 252, 255, 259, 292-95

essence/existence 53-58, 61, 64, 66-70, 78, 157-58, 160, 175, 196, 213-14, 255

essentialism 49, 64, 158, 166, 294, 299

eternal world 50, 166

evaluation terms 107, 109-10

event 8, 117-18, 182, 187, 195, 211-13, 217-18, 224, 228, 231-32, 235-39, 254-56, 260, 268-70, 272, 275, 282, 287-92, 297

excess and deficiency 256

extrinsic 45-46, 48, 160, 177-81, 205

faith 6, 18-19, 25-26, 65, 137, 156, 181, 191, 208-10, 213-15, 218-19, 225, 228, 238, 243-44, 248, 251, 255-56, 261, 264-66, 269-72, 296-97, 299-300 finite 5-6, 18-22, 24, 34, 36, 45, 46, 49-54, 58, 60-61, 64-65, 71-73, 80, 89-93, 159, 174, 176, 252, 257-58, 290, 296-97, 299-300

finite and infinite 5-6, 19, 21, 50, 52-53, 296

Five Ways 42

flexibility 42, 76, 106, 116

formal 29, 36, 46, 52, 58, 76, 84-86, 101-04, 110, 112, 115, 128, 130, 133-35, 141, 145-46, 162, 166, 173, 206, 250, 262, 280, 298

freedom 19, 23-24, 26, 81, 101, 114, 147, 163, 247, 273, 287-88, 291, 293

generosity of being 93-94

God, knowability of, 121, 179, 202, 250; speakability of, 203, 209, 211, 284; unspeakability of, 196, 229, 247-48, 253, 295

golden mean 286; *see* middle way or ground

good *see* Chapter One, 17-39; 1-3, 5, 7, 16, 50, 61, 73, 82, 88-89, 91, 102, 106, 111, 116-19, 122-23, 130, 134, 136-40, 143, 148, 172, 176-78, 182, 185, 187, 250, 252, 299

grace 25-26, 94, 218, 222-24, 237, 251-54, 261-62, 265, 293, 300

grammar, grammatical 6, 95, 98-99, 101, 105, 124-25, 127-31, 133-38, 141-43, 146-47, 150-51, 155, 161-62, 171, 180, 183-85

helle Ort see place of light

hermeneutics 49, 59, 228, 260

heuristic 73, 149, 286

hindrance 235

history 4, 15, 26-27, 30, 103, 155, 196, 224, 267, 269-70, 274-75, 287, 292, 295

imago dei 21, 220, 254, 261-63, 265, 268, 292

immutability 14, 83, 87-92

improper 121, 179

incarnation 209, 227-28, 261-62, 264, 269, 282-83, 292, 296-97, 300

ineffability 198

infinite, infinity 5-6, 18-21, 26, 29, 34, 39, 45, 47, 49-54, 58, 61, 64, 71-72, 80-81, 90-94, 158-59, 174, 176, 178, 184-85, 199, 201-02, 246-47, 256-58, 290, 292-93, 296

inquiry 5-7, 15, 23, 25, 95, 98, 101, 113-19, 121, 123-25, 135, 142-44, 149, 153-54, 156, 158, 165, 168, 186-87, 286, 288, 296-97

intelligibility of being 19, 77, 81, 288

intent, intentional, intentionality, intentional 20, 68, 69, 78, 90, 92, 106-07, 110, 115, 141, 143, 147-48, 150-51, 163-66, 173, 290

intrinsic 5, 42, 46, 48, 52, 90, 92, 104, 147, 177-81; *see* predication

Ipsum Esse Subsistens (subsistent existence itself) 6, 20, 21, 29, 53, 64-66, 70, 92, 93, 138, 143, 145-46, 151, 160, 290

judgment 5-6, 8, 22-26, 76, 81-82, 97, 101, 108, 111-16, 123, 125-26, 131, 140, 144, 157-59, 163, 166, 169, 171, 186-87, 202, 286, 292, 298-99

language event 211-13, 217-18, 239

levels of discourse 134, 137

limits 19-20, 26, 35, 47, 54, 58, 64, 71, 85, 102, 113, 118-19, 141, 201, 237-38, 255, 291, 300

limits of language 58, 118-19

lingual event 213, 236, 289

linguistic turn 6, 14, 82, 97, 127, 184
linkage of Kant and Aquinas 121,
    234-35, 244, 245-54, 259; *see*
    Chapter Eight, esp., 200-07
lived use 76, 125
lived contradiction 23
logic 78, 102-03, 112, 118, 123,
    127, 130-31, 135, 140-42, 146,
    148, 168, 180, 208-09
logos 19, 118, 222, 252, 260, 264,
    279, 284, 290
love 39, 70, 72, 75, 81-83, 88, 90-
    94, 147, 151, 197, 221, 229-32,
    236-37, 239-40, 252, 260, 268,
    287, 294, 299
manuductio (leading by the hand) 56,
    98, 119, 121, 123, 128, 154, 165,
    177, 253, 288, 296, 297
Many and One 54, 70-71, 205
mathematics 92, 118
median 67, 104, 105; *see* middle
    ground or way
metaphor 106, 108-10, 116, 128,
    140, 142-43, 168, 171-72, 174,
    177, 181, 224, 262, 277-79
metaphysical tradition 51, 58, 191-
    93, 196-97, 203, 207-09, 236
middle ground or way, analogy as,
    35, 168, 180, 186, 296
mind 15, 19, 20, 22-24, 56-57, 61-
    62, 67, 69, 73, 76-78, 81, 83-84,
    106, 123, 129, 135, 168, 172,
    183, 203, 233, 253, 288
moderate realism 86
modus significandi/res significata 80-
    81, 205
movement of God 291
nature and grace 94, 218, 222-24,
    261-62, 265
necessary 5, 21-22, 76-78, 87, 124-
    25, 150, 197, 198, 201, 205, 210,

219, 229, 248, 268, 271, 276,
    284, 287, 299
necessary being 197, 210, 287
negative theology *see* apophatic
Neo-Thomist 11, 13-14, 17, 23-24,
    33, 38-39, 42, 49, 83-84, 94, 97-
    99, 125, 160, 174, 179, 184, 244-
    45, 289, 293
Neoplatonic 4-5, 27, 37-38, 47, 49,
    51, 88, 138, 184, 246
non-necessity of God 22, 229
ontological downstepping 258, 299
ontological tension 253, 258
ordinary usage 105-06, 109-10, 172-
    73
parable 255-56, 260, 262-64, 268,
    270, 272, 278
participation *see* Chapter Two and
    Chapter Three, 41-94; 5, 6, 11,
    14-17, 26, 27, 29, 41-42, 44, 46,
    48-55, 57-61, 63-73, 75-76, 78-79,
    81-82, 86, 93, 115-16, 125, 138,
    140, 157, 159-61, 166, 168, 184-
    85, 187, 213-14, 220-22, 230,
    236, 245-46, 249-50, 256-60, 267,
    280, 288, 293, 296-97, 299-300
patterns 8, 50, 84, 124, 142, 224,
    252, 265, 273, 279, 282-83, 292,
    296
perfection 5, 27, 29, 38-39, 44, 48,
    50, 52-55, 57, 60, 68-73, 80-82,
    89, 90, 92-94, 137, 139, 160, 178-
    79, 185, 206, 230, 249-50, 252-
    53, 258-59, 284
perfections 42, 47, 54-55, 68, 71-72,
    79, 81, 89, 93, 160, 178-80, 249,
    257-58, 288, 292, 296
performance 15, 77, 117, 128, 139,
    150, 159, 162, 168, 171, 277, 288
person(s) 5, 8, 16, 19, 33, 64, 82-91,
    93, 113, 116, 118, 123-24, 140,

149, 208, 211, 213, 224-25, 227, 231-32, 239, 250, 260-62, 264, 270, 277, 284

personal 1, 31, 39, 70, 78, 82-87, 90-92, 94, 115, 156, 165, 215, 221-22, 225, 230, 283, 288, 296

personality 81, 262

philosophical theology 19, 41, 79, 130, 135, 154-55, 249, 271, 273-75

place of light 219, 221, 223, 238, 240, 252, 292, 300

polemic, polemical 7, 33, 84, 99, 150, 154, 157, 197, 207, 218, 233-35, 246-47, 272, 283, 291, 298

positive analogous terms as, 79-82; attribute of existence, 55, 71; essence, 57; quality (perfection), 5, 79; infinity, 21, 50, 72, 90, 246-47, 257, 292; theological content, 7, 28-29, 62, 99, 121, 154-56, 161-62, 168, 179-81, 187, 197, 200, 286

possibility 2, 15, 18, 20-23, 26, 27, 32, 42, 67, 72, 79, 93, 109, 131, 148, 151, 180, 185, 217, 219, 224, 228-29, 231, 239-40, 247, 249, 258, 260, 262, 263, 273, 282, 284, 290, 295, 299-300

potential 24, 47, 124, 159, 165, 234, 246, 250, 254, 257-58, 266, 290-92

predicamental participation 59-60

predication, intrinsic 177-81; proper and improper, 179

presence 15-16, 28, 31, 33, 75, 110, 113-15, 123, 136, 145-46, 166-67, 172, 182-84, 198, 279, 283, 290-92, 294, 296, 299

presence of God 167

prime analogate 63, 83, 123, 177-78

proofs 42, 73, 216, 226

propaedeutic 129

proportion 2, 20, 44, 201, 204, 262

proportionality *see* analogy

proposition 62, 112, 139, 140, 237

pros hen 3

Protestant 7-8, 200, 218, 233, 235, 244, 251, 261, 285

'real relations' 87, 90, 147, 149-50

reason 5-6, 8, 24-26, 39, 59, 65, 69, 70, 108, 113, 135, 137, 139, 146, 155-56, 168, 197, 201, 205-06, 209, 227-28, 232, 248, 250-51, 253, 265-66, 270-72, 289, 296

res significata 80, 197, 205, 258

responsible talk 200, 233, 235, 298

science 8, 110, 121, 141, 222, 247-48, 266, 270-72, 279

self-communication 29, 31, 34, 36, 61, 63, 68, 84, 94, 226, 229, 231, 237, 240, 293

self-communication of being 61, 63, 84

self-correcting 102, 181

self-indulgence 279

settling down of metaphors 109, 174

signification 195, 197, 210, 212, 227, 236-38, 294, 298

silence 56, 145, 168, 253

silencing 191, 196, 198, 207

simple, simpleness, simplicity 51, 54-55, 61-62, 66, 79, 130-134, 137, 160, 162, 229-30, 250

sin 8, 262-68, 279

speech gain 238-39, 263, 272, 282, 300

spiritual 39, 141, 161, 168, 265

Sprachgewinn see speech gain

stretch-concept 76

synthetic 183

systematically vague 75, 186, 294
tautologies 127, 130, 133-34, 138,
    143, 183
technology 248, 270-71, 284
teleology 251, 280
tensive power 283, 286
theism 103, 191-92, 195, 209
theological anthropology 148, 215,
    217, 225, 232, 251-52
theological context 8, 243, 245
theological failure 195-98
Thomism, Thomist 7, 13-15, 17-19,
    23-26, 30, 33, 38-39, 41-43, 46,
    49, 53-54, 58, 83-84, 87-88, 90-
    91, 94, 97-99, 101, 103, 122, 124-
    25, 143, 153, 157, 160, 167, 174,
    179, 184, 197, 202, 205, 208,
    229-31, 234, 244-45, 249, 251,
    289, 291, 293-95
transcendence 18, 29, 45, 48, 80,
    130, 132-34, 146-47, 154-55, 201,
    247
transcendental 17-19, 26, 59-60, 63,
    72, 81, 106, 124, 136, 139, 155,
    180, 258, 289
Transcendental Thomism 17-26, 124
transcendentals 106-07, 113, 122,
    124
truth as interruption 255
two-way movement 296
unambiguous talk 192
universal intent 115
univocal, univocation, univocity 47,
    58, 60-61, 64, 80, 86, 103-06,
    109-10, 122, 128, 155-56, 159,
    162, 168, 172-76, 180, 186, 283,
    286, 292
unknown 2, 35, 277; and God, 42,
    180, 201-02, 207-08, 234-36, 248,
    253-55, 259, 286; and judgment,

5, 82; and tensive power, 283,
    296-298
via eminentia 4

CPSIA information can be obtained
at www.ICGtesting.com
Printed in the USA
BVHW081326030223
657817BV00002B/166